GANGSTER

GANGSTER

THE INSIDE STORY ON JOHN GILLIGAN,
HIS DRUGS EMPIRE & THE MURDER OF
JOURNALIST VERONICA GUERIN

John Mooney

First published in Great Britain in 2001 by
CUTTING EDGE PRESS
7 Albany Street
Edinburgh EH1 3UG

This edition 2002

ISBN 1 903813 02 6

A catalogue record for this book is available
from the British Library

Typeset in Courier New and Stone Serif
Printed and bound in Great Britain by
Cox and Wyman

ACKNOWLEDGEMENTS

In January 1997, a friend suggested I write a book on John Gilligan and the tragic events surrounding the murder of the journalist Veronica Guerin. I toyed with the idea, making discreet enquiries to see if there was enough material on Gilligan to justify a book or, indeed, if his life was worth writing about at all.

I soon came to the inextricable conclusion there was much more to Gilligan than perhaps anyone thought. The hardest part was deciphering the mountain of lies told to me by his collaborators, his friends and certain elements of the Gardaí. They all had an agenda and nothing they said could be taken at face value, least of all information from those who knew the truth. A select few were honest and to these I am forever indebted.

I would like to thank the following people and organisations: in Britain, Ranald McDonald and Tony Cody of British Customs and Excise, staff at the Regional Crime Squad and National Criminal Intelligence Service. I would also like to thank Pete Walsh for his good advice. In Europe, many thanks go to the Dutch, Belgium and Danish police for their assistance. Assistance from Europol and Interpol was of great importance. In Ireland, help provided by the former staff of Mary Queen of Angels National School in Ballyfermot was invaluable. Some members of An Garda Síochána contributed to the book and their help is forever appreciated. I would also like to sincerely thank the Dublin Brigade of the Provisional IRA, whose secret assistance advanced *Gangster*. Also my thanks go to the anti-drugs movement, most notably Hugh McGeown, his son John Paul, Andre Lydre, Ronald Byrne, Noel

Kirwan and Brian Kenna. George Royal, who passed away recently, also helped a great deal.

On a personal level, support from my trusted and loyal friends Ray Murphy, Chris Finnegan, Leona Evans, Joe Whelan, Cormac Bourke and my parents was inestimable. I also thank the staff at the *Sunday Times*, most notably Fiona McHugh, Maeve Sheehan and John Burns.

A round of applause to Cutting Edge Press for all their help in producing *Gangster*. My thanks also go to Karen Woods and James McGowan, who read the manuscript.

And finally, this book would never have concluded without the help of Jean Harrington, my precious friend who edited the first drafts and checked details with great skill. Jean, thank you so very much.

Someone recently asked to whom I intended dedicating this book. In late 1995, I witnessed many deaths caused by the drug epidemic sweeping through Ireland. The plague prompted hundreds of people drawn from working-class backgrounds to march on the homes of the dealers. These campaigners had no friends; they were vilified by the media and threatened by the pushers. Despite this, many joined the campaign because they had lost precious loved ones to the scourge of heroin. An entire generation of children from the inner city was lost. So I am dedicating this book to them: the men, women and children of the anti-drugs movement, in the hope that their terrible grief will never be forgotten.

J. Mooney
March 2001

CONTENTS

	Prologue	9
1.	The Murder of Veronica Guerin	13
2.	Life Cycles of Violence	23
3.	The Wild West	31
4.	The Bonds	41
5.	Portlaoise	49
6.	A Whirlwind of Crime	59
7.	Easy Money	70
8.	Invisible Criminals	80
9.	Drugs, Guns and Money to Burn	92
10.	Fight Fire with Fire	104
11.	Pineapple	121
12.	A Time to Kill	135
13.	Public Enemy Number One	150
14.	Breaking the Code of Silence	163
15.	The Usual Suspects	183
16.	Fighting Back	198
17.	Retribution	215
	Epilogue	234
	The Judgment	238

PROLOGUE

August 1996

Terminal One, Heathrow Airport, London

He smiled confidently, exchanging courtesies with his fellow travellers as they filtered into the airport's arrivals lounge. Wearing a blue sports jacket, shirt, pressed trousers and standing just over five feet tall, he looked an unlikely criminal.

'You must be the journalist. Pleased to meet you,' he said in a flat Dublin accent whilst shaking my hand.

'How did you know what I looked like?'

'Oh, I just saw you there and you fitted the bill. Come with me, I don't like talking in public places. He pointed to a restaurant which overlooked the airport lobby and signalled to follow. 'This place is good. There's only one way in and out. Let's get something to eat,' he said whilst ushering me towards a table situated in a dimly lit corner, not easily visible from the doorway.

The restaurant was full of businessmen from the four corners of the globe but Arabs were the main clientele, all dining on roast duck, the speciality of the day. A waiter approached with two menus tucked under his arm.

'Would you like to order a drink while you wait, sir?'

'No, two hamburgers with large fries and 7-Up. That okay with you, John?' He eased back into his chair. 'Let me tell you this. Anyone can get anyone killed if they have the money. You don't have to be a criminal. I could have ordered her death but I didn't. I had no hand, act or part in it. That's the truth.'

His words sounded rehearsed, but were considered and spoken with authority.

He leaned forward again, making a point of not breaking eye

9

contact. 'I have been dragged into this because I threatened her before she died. If I was going to kill her I would hardly have advertised it by threatening her. I mean, that's not the way things are done.'

He was interrupted in mid-speech by the sound of my cellular phone ringing. The caller was a republican contact who had helped arrange the meeting.

'Is he with you now?'

'Yes.'

'Are you all right? Is he giving you any trouble?'

'No, he has just arrived.'

'Put him on to me.'

'It's for you.'

He looked across the table with a blank expression on his face, took the phone and held it cautiously to his ear and listened attentively.

'He wants to talk to you now,' he said returning the phone.

'I'm going to ring you on the hour, every hour, to make sure you're okay.'

The line went dead.

'You won't have any problems with me, I've no problem with you. Ask me what you like, I'll answer any question,' he said confidently.

'Did you threaten to kill and kidnap and rape her six-year-old?'

'Yes I did. But it isn't the way you make it out. I knew she didn't fear for herself so I used a tactic, which we used on screws [prison officers] who caused us problems. If a screw's house got turned over, he would get sympathy from his neighbours. They would say look at the poor prison officer, he's only doing his job keeping criminals locked up. So somebody, I don't remember who, came up with the idea that you worked the next door neighbour over, so nobody talked to the screw or his family in case they were next. Instead they blamed the attacks on the screws. It was only a tactic I used, to try to frighten her off, that's all.'

Although I could not have imagined it at the time, I was sitting with the most dangerous criminal ever to emerge from the Irish underworld. In the hours of conversation that followed, he spoke about drug dealing, hijackings, gunrunning and racketeering, his background and his separation from his wife. Crime, he proclaimed with a degree of smugness, had earned him close to £15 million.

But it was the public's reaction to the cold-blooded murder of a crime reporter on the streets of Dublin six weeks earlier that preoccupied him. He kept returning to the subject of the shooting, saying he wasn't responsible, that the media was unfairly targeting him by labelling him chief suspect. The assignment of blame and guilt was passed to others.

'I'm not as black as they portray me although I am a criminal. This is hype by journalists. That's all,' he proclaimed.

When the interview concluded hours later, I asked if he had any objections to his photograph being taken. He looked nervous. 'Can you get one off another newspaper?' he asked.

'No, it's better that I take one now.'

After much persuasion, he agreed and I pointed the camera in his direction. As I focused the lens, I noticed he was staring at the ground.

'Could you look directly at the camera?'

'No, I'm fine like this,' he said, looking uncomfortable and agitated.

I took two photographs before he stood up and said, 'That's enough.'

The camera annoyed him and he found this difficult to hide.

'You don't like your picture being taken?'

'No, it doesn't bother me too much. Did you see the pictures of me in the papers last week, the one with me wearing the sunglasses?' he enquired, smiling once again.

'Yes. Yes I did.'

'What did you think of them?'

'What do you mean?'

'Do you think I looked good? Everyone said I looked cool. Some of the fellas from home even rang. They thought I looked cool, like a guy from the Mafia, a real gangster.'

CHAPTER 1

The Murder of Veronica Guerin

'We know who killed her – and he's untouchable.'
HEADLINE FROM THE *IRISH INDEPENDENT*

The assassin held the .357 Magnum with both hands and fired six shots at point-blank range through the side window of the car. He shot once, then twice, before discharging another three shots into his terrified victim. The sound of the gunfire reverberated in the hearts of those watching the nightmare unfold. The victim had seen her killer stride towards her car, but had no time to escape. Overcome by fear, she raised her right arm to shield off the bullets, which ripped through her arms, torso and upper body, killing her within a matter of seconds. It was 12.54 p.m. on Wednesday, 26 June 1996.

The victim was Veronica Guerin, crime reporter for the *Sunday Independent* newspaper. She was 37 years of age, a wife and mother. The scene of her slaying was the traffic intersection which adjoins the Boot Road to the Naas Road in Clondalkin, a suburb that lies south-west of Dublin City. The main road is known as the N7.

She was travelling to her office in the city centre from the town of Naas in County Kildare, where she had appeared earlier in court on a minor speeding charge. A red light temporarily halted her journey. When she stopped, a powerful motorcycle carrying two men pulled up alongside her red Opel Calibra sports car. The rider and the pillion passenger both wore dark clothes and full-size helmets which concealed their identities. Neither she nor the other drivers stopped in the traffic or took much notice of them. That was until the pillion passenger dismounted.

It wasn't until the last moment that she noticed her killer. Veronica Guerin was forever on the phone and when her killer struck, she was leaving a message on a friend's answering machine. The call was to say she had not been banned from driving and the answering machine recorded her last words. 'I did very well. Aah, fined a maximum of £150.'

Her voice was interrupted in mid-sentence by the sound of a crack, followed by the sound of a mobile phone key being pressed, and then a second crack, the sound of gunfire. Many people witnessed her death.

Michael Kirby was giving a driving lesson from the passenger seat of a lorry parked in the traffic. 'I heard what sounded like a crack, followed by a few more. The driver's window was open. I looked out and saw what was taking place. This guy was shooting somebody in the car. I saw the gun. It was like something you would see on TV,' he remembered.

Brian McNamara and his wife were also present; sitting parked in the traffic, he heard what he thought was a car backfire. When he looked to his right, he saw a gunman shooting into a red car, Veronica's car. McNamara later recalled how the gunman 'seemed to lean over with the gun for the last few shots' before stuffing the gun into his jacket, jumping back on the motorcycle and speeding off. McNamara ran to Veronica's car to see what had happened. When he looked in, he saw a woman lying slumped over the passenger seat. She was covered in fragments of smashed glass and blood. McNamara ran back to his wife and told her someone had been shot.

When the traffic lights turned green, Brenda Grogan stepped out of her car to see what was causing the delay. Grogan was on her way to a nearby hospital where she worked as a nurse. As she approached Veronica's car, she saw a woman slumped over the passenger seat and went to administer first aid. 'I felt for a pulse on her neck. We were joined by another nurse. We moved her to try clear her airway. We put her upright in the driver's seat,' she said.

The other nurse was Michelle Wall from the Rotunda Hospital's maternity unit. She too gave Veronica first aid. As Wall felt for a pulse, she noticed a small, black hole at the back of the victim's shoulder and another hole in her blouse. She moved the car seat down to alleviate the pain, but it was too late.

Veronica was dead.

A combination of shock and haemorrhage caused by multiple bullet wounds, which lacerated her lungs and the artery supplying blood to her right arm, caused her death. A 999 call was made to the emergency services, which in turn relayed the call to Garda headquarters. It was a matter of minutes before armed Gardaí arrived on the scene and Clondalkin was swamped with patrol cars, but there was no sign of the assassins. They had long gone, vanishing into the afternoon traffic. All that was left was bullet-shattered glass, blood and Veronica's body.

Passers-by screamed, some went into a state of shock and panic. Witnesses pointed arriving Gardaí in the direction of Tallaght, saying the assassins had headed towards the sprawling housing scheme that lies at the foothills of the Dublin Mountains. Police detectives arrived and took details and descriptions of the killers from anaesthetised by-standers. The descriptions of the killers were sketchy but left no doubt that the shooting was a professional hit. The crime scene was sealed off immediately and forensic experts wearing white jump suits arrived and began an inch-by-inch examination of the scene. They painstakingly searched for the usual clues: blood, hair, spent bullet cases, torn fabric – anything. They erected a steel frame around the journalist's car, which contained her body, covered only by a crimson blanket. People gathered and stared in disbelief at the macabre sight.

Pat Byrne, a deputy Garda commissioner, arrived at the scene. He knew the victim well. 'I spoke to the detectives. I was in shock, I couldn't believe what had happened. And I couldn't look at the body,' he said. 'I was too afraid.'

From his office window in Scoil Mhuire National School, Father Heber McMahon saw the commotion and wondered what it was about. He walked over to the carnage and was told the news. Years earlier, in 1985, the priest had officiated at Veronica's wedding. 'It says an awful lot about freedom of speech, doesn't it? I just feel so awful for her family.'

Stricken by a deep sense of sadness, he told reporters at the scene that he had received a Christmas card from Veronica. He had written back to her, berating her for writing articles about Bishop Casey's passionate love affair. 'I said if she was looking for a third clerical candidate, she should come out here to Clondalkin.'

News of the murder soon reached the news-desks of Irish television and radio stations. Journalists in the *Sunday Independent* broke down in tears mourning the loss of their colleague. An unofficial news

GANGSTER

blackout on the killing was put in place. Ending that day's lunchtime news programme on RTE, presenter Sean O'Rourke announced that a woman had been shot but could not disclose the identity of the victim.

And with good reason: Veronica's husband, Graham Turley, her six-year-old son Cathal and the couple's family were unaware of her murder.

The first family member to learn about the killing was Graham. He was visiting a construction site in Malahide on Dublin's northside when his wife was gunned down. The Gardaí had called his office and were told of his whereabouts. Detective Inspector Cathal Cryan of Coolock Garda station raced to the site. He knew the couple personally and made the initial approach to Graham in the most humane way possible. Speaking on the Irish chat show, *The Late Late Show*, Graham later recalled what happened.

'I was in Malahide, and a guard, a friend of ours came into the site and said to me, I sort of said, "How are you doing, Cathal?" And he said, "Not good." And I said, "What's wrong, sure it was only £150."' Graham was referring to the fine imposed on his wife for speeding. '"Oh no, it's a lot worse, there's after being another shooting." And I said, "I don't believe you," and he said, "It's not good, it's not good at all. I think we should go to Coolock Garda station." So I got into my car. I wouldn't go with him because I wanted to go and see her, to see that she was all right. And I drove to Coolock Garda station. And I was there for about ten or fifteen minutes and then they came in and told me Veronica was dead.'

Nora Owen, the Minister for Justice, was on the far side of the Atlantic when Veronica was gunned down. She was in New York attending a United Nations conference on international drug trafficking. She was standing in the lobby of Fitzpatrick's Hotel when her private secretary John O'Dwyer pulled her aside. He said, 'I need to speak to you privately, very quickly.' She knew there was something wrong.

The two stepped into a lift and O'Dwyer pressed the button for the sixth floor. The doors closed and he told her what happened. Dumbstruck, because the two women had been friends, Owen stood out of the lift and walked to her room. 'To be honest I went into the room on my own and just cried, I was absolutely in bits about it and

I then rang home, I was told that she'd been shot at traffic lights. I knew immediately I had to go back.' She called Graham. 'He was absolutely devastated, and he was only hearing the details of it. I just felt the blood, and every bit of my life, draining out of me with the horror of what had happened.'

O'Dwyer arranged for Owen to fly home immediately but before she could leave she had to deliver a speech on organised crime to the United Nations as President of the Council of Ministers of Europe. She arrived at the United Nations building two hours later and delivered a highly charged address. Her voice trembling, she went off script and spoke about Veronica. 'I said I had just received information that a young woman journalist had been shot dead by a criminal gang. I brought it right home. Afterwards I was surrounded by ministers from dozens of countries. I was in a terrible state of shock, what they were saying was going in one ear and out the other.'

Veronica's body was still in her car at the time because the State Pathologist, Doctor John F. Harbison, was attending an inquest. It could not be moved until he arrived and carried out an examination. This happened at 5.30 p.m. Veronica's remains were removed to James Connolly Memorial Hospital, Blanchardstown at 6 p.m. Accompanied by his friend, Father Declan Doyle, Graham travelled to his wife's parental home where he sat with Bernadette Guerin, Veronica's mother, and her family. They consoled each other before Graham left for Blanchardstown to formally identify his wife's remains later that evening. Father Doyle and a brother-in-law went with him.

'Until ten o'clock that night, in the morgue in Blanchardstown hospital, when I saw Veronica, or I had to identify her for the first time, it was the first time that it started sinking in. That it was Veronica there. I was hoping that somebody had taken her car, or something different. Because you can't kill Veronica. That was my policy, she was too hard to kill. And she never will be dead as far as I'm concerned.'

He travelled to his own mother's home where his son was staying. The child was asleep, so he was left to rest for the night and was told the next morning as he played with Lego. Father Doyle was present when Graham broke the news to his son. Graham recounted later the story to Sean O'Rourke on RTE radio.

'I sat down on the chair and said, "How are things?" and he said, "Grand, Dad." He had been kept away from the television and the papers and nobody had said anything to him. So I said, "Cathal, do you remember the last time Mum was shot? Well it's happened again."

'And he said, "Yeah? Where was she shot this time?"

'And I said, "Shot in the heart." And he came over and sat on my knee and he comforted me. And Declan said to him, "Cathal, can you make a courthouse?" And Cathal said, "Yeah." And we made the courthouse in Naas, and we made two cars and a motorbike, and then he asked, "Who was on the motorbike?" And I said, "Well, there were two men on the motorbike, and they seem to have been wearing black helmets. And they pulled up, alongside Mum, and they shot into the car and hit Mum."

'"Where did they hit Mum?"

'And I said, "They hit Mum three times around the heart, and they hit her in the neck."

'"Is Mum coming home?"

'And I said, "No, she's not coming home, but she's going to be here minding us, because remember we talked about this before."

'"Oh I got it," he says. "She's with God now, and she'll be looking down on me and everything I do from now on."

'And it's been like that ever since, that everything we discuss, Mum has always been there and always will be. And we left there, my mother's house, and we went to Staffords funeral home, and Veronica was there, and we had a chat a cuddle and a laugh, like we always did, the three of us together. And we talked, and Cathal was saying, "Mum, you're very cold" and things like this. And then we left.'

The assassination was formally announced at a packed press conference in Lucan Garda Station on the outskirts of the capital at 4.30 p.m. at which Superintendent Brian O'Higgins of the Garda Press Office said he knew Veronica extremely well and this made it all the more difficult. He described her assassination as 'cold, callous and planned'.

News of the murder prompted a wave of revulsion and public outrage. Among the many atrocities that had convulsed Ireland, Veronica's murder stood out as by far the most despicable and cruel.

Ireland was in the grip of organised crime that manifested itself in the cold-blooded murder of a journalist. The idea that gangland killings were never solved prospered in the underworld and the notion that the drug barons were untouchable was injected into the national consciousness.

In the Dáil, the Taoiseach, John Bruton, described the killing as sinister to the extreme. 'Someone, somewhere decided to take her life and almost certainly did so to prevent information coming into the public arena.' He went on to describe Veronica as a 'particularly gifted and professional investigative journalist' who had written about the unacceptable face of life. 'She did so with care and with compassion. In doing so, she made an important contribution to the public life of this country. Without the work, which she did much of the recent public debate on crime would not have been as informed as it was.'

The Tánaiste and leader of the Labour Party, Dick Spring, stood up and told the hushed Dáil chambers that her murder was linked to her work. 'That she should be shot down in this fashion is an attack on all of us and on the values that democracy and democratic politics are based on. It is an outrageous attack on the freedom of the press and the invaluable work that journalists do.'

The leader of Fianna Fáil, Bertie Ahern, expressed his shock, saying he hoped no effort would be spared to find her killers. But it was Mary Harney of the Progressive Democrats Party who made the most poignant tribute: 'The greatest liberty we have is the liberty of free expression and the greatest guarantee we have of that liberty is a free press. Veronica Guerin died because she fearlessly pursued the truth. She was no ordinary journalist. She was a woman apart. Today the criminal underworld decided that in order that they could continue with their activities, she had to be murdered. In a matter of seconds, that enormous talent was taken away, and she had no chance.'

In the following days, papers devoted pages upon pages to the life and precious work of Veronica Guerin. The *Irish Independent*, a sister newspaper of the *Sunday Independent*, carried the headline 'OUR DARKEST DAY'. In a front-page comment piece, the paper's leader writer proclaimed: 'Veronica Guerin knew no fear. She was attacked and threatened, but she carried on bravely in the noblest traditions of her craft with her work of investigating and exposing the crime barons. Now the barons have silenced her by depriving her of her right to life, the most fundamental right of all. They have shown themselves as much a threat to free speech as any totalitarian regime or terrorist organisation.'

There was an outpouring of grief by the public, the likes of which had never been witnessed in Ireland. Ordinary people queued outside the offices of Independent Newspapers in Abbey Street to sign a book of condolences. Many voiced their anger over the airwaves, demanding that action be taken to jail the drug barons. Ordinary people arrived outside Government buildings with floral wreaths and children's toys and laid them at the gates along with letters written to the murdered journalist. 'May Our TD's show a fraction of your courage, Veronica. Rest in Peace . . . God comfort your family,' read one letter attached to the stem of a single red rose.

The National Union of Journalists described the murder as a barbarous act designed to intimidate the media. 'Veronica Guerin paid the ultimate price for her pursuit of the truth,' the NUJ statement read. Editions of both Irish and British newspapers the next morning vowed never to give in to intimidation and resolved to implement a set of guidelines, aptly called the Guerin Principles. Dedicated to her memory, the principles stated that a fair, free and independent media was essential to democracy.

'The State must ensure that a constitutional and legislative environment exists to facilitate freedom of expression and a free media,' the principles urged. And in a final acknowledgement to the courage of the murdered journalist, the principles stated: 'Media workers resolve to resist any attempts at intimidation in whatever form and from whatever quarter.'

Veronica's body was removed from Staffords funeral home to the Church of Our Lady Queen of Heaven on the Malahide Road, beside Dublin Airport, two days later, on the following Friday. The funeral cortège left at 6 p.m. and arrived 30 minutes later to a packed church.

Three weeks earlier, Veronica and her husband had attended the funeral of Detective Garda Jerry McCabe who was shot dead by the Provisional IRA in Limerick during a botched hijacking. While attending the mass, Veronica had told her husband that if she were ever killed, she would like the hymn 'Be Not Afraid' sung at her funeral. In accordance with her wish, the congregation sang the hymn while her coffin was brought quietly into the sombre church and received by her friend Father Doyle and more than a dozen priests. As the coffin reached the altar, Cathal and his father slowly reached out and touched the casket. It was a deeply moving sight.

An air of calm descended on the church and as Father Doyle commenced the ceremony, Cathal left his seat and went alone to the Church sacristy. He returned a short time later and handed his sorrowing father a glass of water. Father Doyle summed up the mood as a 'very sad and lonely day for all of us'. 'Veronica's death is one of those events when a nation stops, when time stands still, when we look at ourselves as a society and ask: Where are we going? This time of questioning is a special moment in history. The frame is frozen. It is a time of change in Irish society, a time of decision and debate and thought. Where is Irish society headed? What forces are vying for power? What is the future of our country? And all of this prompted by the death of Veronica.'

She was buried the next morning in Dardistown Cemetery, a sacred ground adjacent to Dublin Airport. There was a short sermon in the church and Graham addressed those gathered in a moving tribute to his beloved wife. 'The best day I ever had was 21 September 1985, the year myself and Veronica promised to love, cherish and honour each other "'til death do us part".' He spoke a few more words and walked to his seat. As he did so, the entire congregation stood and applauded.

Placed on her coffin were items which marked out Veronica Guerin's life. A football, a pair of Manchester United gloves and a programme from the FA Cup semi-final were there. Her cherished photograph of Eric Cantona, the Manchester United soccer star, standing alongside her was there too. The picture showed a youthful and vibrant Veronica looking more like a schoolgirl posing alongside her favourite pop star. There were her national and international media awards and, of course, her wedding photograph. Before her casket was removed, her sister Claire read from the Book of Wisdom and recited the words: 'Over wisdom, evil can never triumph.'

Graham, carrying his son in his arms, followed the coffin out of the church. Cathal carried a spray of lilies with a red rose in the centre. On the way out, the child wrapped his arms around President Mary Robinson, hugging her like a friend. 'He was very good,' the immensely proud father told the President whilst clutching his son's tiny hand.

The two men in Veronica's life stood at the side of her grave and kissed her coffin before she was finally laid to rest. Cathal stood on the side of the grave and knelt down to say a Hail Mary. His father crouched down beside him holding his waist and fighting back the tears. When the child finished saying his prayer, he blew his murdered mother a kiss. 'Goodbye Mummy.'

There was a sense of foreboding in Dardistown that day as the crowd departed from the cemetery; anger and rage filled the air. Nora Owen like many others felt it within. 'I was vicious about these bastards who had done this, and you know my sense of effrontery, how dare they attack somebody like this, and really attack one of the organs of our democracy which was a free press. You kind of felt you wanted to get them by the throat and throttle them. They were not feelings I wanted to have. I knew I had the responsibility to make sure this never happened again.'

Who was responsible? Who had left a young man widowed and a young child motherless? What sort of person would do such a thing?

One man's name was on everyone's mind. John Gilligan.

CHAPTER 2

Life Cycles of Violence

'John had an awful, terrible childhood.'
GERALDINE GILLIGAN

The planets of war and conflict were clashing and colliding when John Joseph Gilligan entered the world. The orbital paths of Saturn and Neptune had crossed to the north-east of the skies leaving Venus, Jupiter and Mercury in ascent, which in celestial terms destined anyone born on that day to a fiery and violent future.

Gilligan was born in Dublin on 29 March 1952 under the star sign of Aries, the masculine fire sign. It is said that Aries characters have many positive traits, of which passion and enthusiasm are two. But their negative tendencies are anarchistic, a quickness of temper and selfishness that makes them want to succeed, regardless of the consequences; another unique Aries trait is the deep distrust of authority.

The symbol of the Ram used to express the characteristics of Aries is one of the New Age traditions. The symbol used in the Chinese lunar calendar is far more appropriate; Gilligan was born in the year of the Dragon. Persons of this sign tend to intimidate those who cross them, and, although colourful, are irrational by nature.

The story of John Gilligan began years before in the Dublin of the early 1940s. Today the city is truly cosmopolitan and vibrant with people on the move. The economy is a powerhouse of activity with the highest rate of industrial and business growth in Europe. Apartment blocks occupied by young professionals sit alongside the terraced houses that traditionally housed the working class. Above all there are jobs, far more than there were in the 1940s when young men and women moved between menial occupations to put bread on the table. Nowhere was this more evident than in Dublin's inner city. The people there are a proud but friendly bunch who look out for their neighbours, marry locally and take pride in their community. They speak plain Dublin, a dialect of English that involves the pronounced use of vowels and syllables. 'How are you' is pronounced 'howaaryah' and so on. Regardless of the way they talk they are warm and friendly, just as they were back in the post-war 1940s where this story begins.

John Gilligan's father was a miscreant youth from Dublin's north inner city who had a fondness for drink, gambling and getting into trouble with the law. 'Johnno', like his father before him, who worked as an engineering smith on the Dublin docks and by night plied the trade of a petty criminal, found theft and crime more attractive than hard labour. Not that he was a professional criminal; he just stole when opportunity came his way, which was fairly frequently. Easy money could be made by robbing and he subscribed to the belief that living life as a law-abiding citizen was a waste of time – in other words, crime paid.

Occasionally he did manage to earn an honest living by legitimate means. In 1944, at the age of 21, he started working as a bailer attendant at a factory in Dublin. As far as anyone knows romance had not featured in his life until this time when a chance encounter brought him into contact with a girl called Sarah Teresa Howard. She was the pretty 20-year-old daughter of Henry Howard, a local CIE signalman. Like most young women of her generation, she loved dancing to the music of the day – jive and swing. On Friday nights, after work in the laundry, she and her friends would head for the Macushla Hall to dance the night away, watched eagerly by the young men. Johnno was not a great dancer, but with a few drinks in him he would jive his heart out.

The two fell in love instantly and were by all accounts distracted by each other's presence. She had a passionate nature and sincere longing to get married and have children – a trait she inherited from her mother. Years later when her children started their own families, her love of children was inspiring. She loved deeply her numerous grand and great grandchildren who fondly called her 'Nana'.

What made Johnno attractive to her was his manner. He was young and had wild ways about him; he did as he pleased and winked at so many girls that they believed him to have wealth far beyond him. Sarah's blissful innocence and looks overwhelmed

Johnno. She was in the bloom of youth and would fall in love at the drop of a hat. The young couple started courting, much to the consternation of Henry Howard who could see the inevitable life which lay ahead of his daughter should Johnno propose and she accept.

Sarah, however, did not think this way and agreed to marry her beau when he mustered up the courage to ask. There was nothing Henry could do or say to dissuade his daughter. The Rev. Donald Quinnlivan married the couple on 5 August 1945 in the Church of Our Lady of Good Counsel on the Mourne Road in Drimnagh, Dublin. The ceremony was a small and dignified affair attended by friends and neighbours; Johnno's brother, Thomas, was groomsman while one of Sarah's childhood friends, Veronica Sweeney, was bridesmaid. Johnno spoke with affection to his young bride but Henry Howard did not need a fortune-teller to realise his daughter had made a mistake. He was in time proved right.

The newly-weds moved into a house on Galtymore Road and for a time Johnno went straight, which seemed a miracle to anyone who knew him. But Johnno Gilligan was not a man who could go without a drink for long and in the space of a few months, he had virtually destroyed his marriage through alcohol, gambling and squandering what little cash he had on failed racehorses.

Even when Sarah got pregnant it didn't put a stop to her husband's random visits to the bookmakers and local hostelries. He became even more intolerable, beating his wife and taking out his aggression on those around him. If he had no money, he would break into his neighbours' homes or nearby shops where he would help himself to whatever he could sell in the local pubs. In this whirlwind of drunken violence, Sarah somehow managed to keep her life on track. In contrast to her husband, she found consolation and warmth in her submissiveness.

The prosperity of the post-Second World War years caused a labour boom in Dublin, particularly around the docklands where cargo ships laden with coal and oil created a demand for cheap labour. In part to be nearer this potentially lucrative source of employment and partly because of the constant trouble Johnno was causing around Ballyfermot, the couple moved north across the Liffey to 15 Prussia Street. It was here on the night of Tuesday, 29 March 1952, that Sarah gave birth to John Joseph, whom she named after his father.

In her lifetime, she would give birth to nine children – five girls and four boys. In those days, women traditionally gave up their jobs when they married; therefore Sarah was reliant on her husband's income, which in turn was reliant on crime. She was trapped in a vicious circle, deploring the source of Johnno's income whilst urging him to provide more for her young children.

The marriage entered into further difficulties which threw Sarah into bouts of depression. At night Johnno would arrive home drunk, pass out in the kitchen and snore all night. His wife would leave him in his drunken stupor and be careful not to disturb him. Such were the problems in the Gilligan household that she did not even register John Gilligan's birth until the following August – some five months later.

In the throes of such hostilities, Sarah mustered up the courage to escape from the inner city and return to Ballyfermot. Prussia Street was a rat-infested slum where neighbours shared a single toilet – hygiene and sanitation were luxuries the residents could simply not afford.

Dublin Corporation at the time were trying to clean out the city and had embarked on an ambitious project to build 10,000 houses in Ballyfermot where the people of the slums could live. Sarah needed no encouragement from her husband and applied for one of the new homes under construction. Johnno took no interest in her plans, nor in his young family for that matter, so Sarah signed all the tenancy paperwork herself, much to the bemusement of the corporation clerks. Sarah and her eight-month old baby John moved into 5 Lough Conn Road, Ballyfermot, on 6 December 1952.

Johnno was missing, so the neighbours helped her move what few belongings she had to Ballyfermot. If her marriage was in difficulties before she took control, from this point onwards it got decidedly bleak, with Johnno spending more and more time away from home. His gambling problem continued to intensify as he moved between jobs.

The turbulence in the Gilligan household had an immense effect on the young John Gilligan, although it did not manifest itself until early adulthood. He would later feel cheated of his youth and become obsessively protective of his own children.

Inside 5 Lough Conn Road, life was miserable and as John Gilligan grew up he did so at the mercy of his father's whims. Johnno would often arrive home and send him to the local bookmaker's to place bets on horses doomed to lose. When the young Gilligan would return home with the inevitable bad news, he would be beaten black and blue. As was his mother. Despite Sarah's best efforts, the family often went without dinner – though Johnno rarely went without a drink. In a home martyred by violence, the young John Gilligan found the calm and security he needed in school.

When the Gilligans first moved to Ballyfermot there wasn't even a school so the young Gilligan was shunted for lessons between the Louise Convent on the Drumfin Road which was run by the Sisters of Charity and Johnstown House run by the Christian Brothers. In 1960, Mary Queen of Angels National School opened, taking in Lough Conn Road to its catchment area. The school was run by the Catholic Church who appointed Canon Troy, a brash cleric from Listowel in County Kerry, as manager whilst Joe Doherty, a young teacher from Clontarf was appointed principal.

Gilligan's home life did not affect his education to the degree that one might imagine. Gilligan, although not highly intelligent, was not slow to learn either. He was an average child who interacted well with his fellow classmates and teachers and avoided trouble. Driven perhaps by the sheer turmoil of home life, Gilligan liked the time he spent in Mary Queen of Angels where he received a good all-round education in Maths, English and Irish. Daily life in Mary Queen of Angels was good for Gilligan. Barrack Yard Drill (BYD) was one part of his education that he applied himself to with zeal. BYD was run by Mick O'Neill, a retired soldier who used to visit the school every week and put the children through their paces in the school playground, lining the students up and instructing them in a military-like way to touch their toes, stretch and stand to attention. O'Neill had a great rapport with the young Gilligan and his classmates who rewarded him by throwing pennies into his hat.

Mary Queen of Angels gave Gilligan confidence. It was a place where he could develop as a child while at home he was given jobs and subjected to violence. In school he could do as the other children did, play marbles in the spring, relivio in the summer and conkers in the autumn when the chestnuts would fall. Friends of his from the time say he excelled at spinning tops, a game where the children pitched coins at a wall and whoever landed the closest got the money. Gilligan's interest in gambling commenced early on in his life.

The young Gilligans went without comics and luxury items like toys because of their father's fondness for alcohol; all they could do was dream about action men and toy soldiers while music was something they occasionally heard on the radio. Television was a novelty sometimes seen in the homes of privileged neighbours.

By the time John Gilligan was 12 years old his father had become a burglar well known to members of An Garda Síochána; but it was in the north inner city that Johnno was most notorious. There he recruited youngsters slightly older than his own children to steal from local shops.

'Old Johnno had this knack of hitting his backside off the door to break the lock,' remembered one youth from his gang. 'He was such a small man, that we used to wonder how he did it. He would rob anything, sweets, money, anything. A big thing with him was Gillette razor blades. He would sell them around the docks.'

In life, Johnno's brothers had faired much better than he had. His brother Thomas had joined the British Army while Frank had become an important figure in the Seaman's Union of Ireland; a position he used to secure Johnno menial work on the Britain & Irish ferry line. Sarah Gilligan did not want her sons turning out like their father so when John Gilligan left Mary Queen of Angels without any qualifications at 14 years of age, she sent him to Uncle Frank who got him a job with the B&I.

Frank was fond of his nephew and started him off working as a cabin boy in the hope that he would join the merchant navy and get a decent career. He worked on the ferries that crossed between Holyhead and Liverpool; he is remembered as being a 'good little worker who gave no cheek'.

Gilligan kept in touch with the staff of Mary Queen of Angels and often returned to the school to look for advice and to say hello. For this he is still remembered. A year after he left school, John Gilligan had his first brush with the law. He was not yet 15 when he appeared in Rathfarnham District Court on 3 March 1967 charged with larceny. He was given probation and warned not to get into trouble again by the judge.

But John Gilligan was destined to a life of crime. He also lived in the shadow of his father's reputation; nothing seemed to work for him. No matter how hard he tried, he could not shake off his father's reputation for being a drunkard although he himself rarely consumed alcohol. He spent the next few years at sea moving between various jobs on ferries and merchant ships that travelled between Ireland and England.

He joined the merchant navy and travelled the world, making 36 trips to far-flung destinations. He worked on the now defunct Canadian Pacific line that travelled between Montreal and Liverpool. His seaman's record book, numbered E10214, describes his conduct as 'very good'. He was formally discharged as a seaman on 31 July 1980.

Like most of the youngsters he grew up with, Gilligan never moved out of home and left his possessions at Lough Conn Road. When on shore leave, he would head towards Ballyfermot to see his family and catch up with friends and talk at length about rock 'n' roll, his travels at sea and of course girls, one of whom he was developing a keen interest in. Matilda Geraldine Dunne was the 'besotted girl next door' who developed a crush on John Gilligan when she was just 14 years of age. She remembered: 'I think I was skipping or playing with my friends and I saw him. I thought he was great – just gorgeous – and fell for him. He was just a happy-go-lucky sort of fella. He was a nice fella and that's why I liked him.'

What she saw in him, no one knows. Gilligan was certainly more mature than his admirer. The two also came from diametrically opposed backgrounds. Geraldine's parents were a resolutely respectable family who lived on Kylemore Drive; her father Martin and mother Martha, née Lynch, were highly regarded by their peers and neighbours. Martin Dunne held a steady job working as a boilerman for CIE. Geraldine was the black sheep of his brood, leaving school at 12 to work as a trainee dressmaker in a shop called Abbots Belts, Buckles and Buttons. Her next job was in Suede's of Ireland.

The Gilligans were an altogether different family. But love works in strange ways and work it did. Gilligan took more than a passing interest in Geraldine. The two started courting and soon fell in love. Everything else in the world was of no consequence to them. They longed to be together and get married. All that was stopping them was Geraldine's young age. Her parents were panic-stricken at their wayward daughter's passion but there was nothing they could do, least of all because John Gilligan was in full-time employment and could afford to fund her 'romance'. Then Geraldine started working as a chef on the ferries, accompanying Gilligan on voyages. Martin Dunne had serious doubts about his future son-in-law's suitability but was powerless to do anything. If he said no to the romance, Geraldine would have taken flight and he feared she would not return.

Her parents pressed the young couple to get married in the Catholic Church. Two days before John Gilligan's 22nd birthday, on 27 March 1974, Father John Wall married them in Ballyfermot Church. Six months later, on 11 September Geraldine gave birth to a daughter, Tracy. The couple also produced a son, born on 13 September 1975. Geraldine decided against calling Darren after his father on the advice of Uncle Frank. 'Frank told me not to call him John because he would have felt he had to live up to his father. I think there were four generations of John Gilligans and Frank said it was time to break the chain. All the Johns had ended up as criminals. That's why Darren wasn't called John after his dad,' Geraldine once recounted.

Geraldine's in-laws liked her. They saw her as a stabilising influence on Gilligan who was fast developing a deep interest in crime and robbery. The newly weds couldn't afford their own home and so moved into the already overcrowded 5 Lough Conn Road with Sarah Gilligan and her growing brood. Their presence added to the sheer turmoil of the house. They wanted their own privacy but couldn't get it in a house filled to capacity with people. Geraldine pushed her husband to get a house or flat; anything away from the sprawling housing estates of Ballyfermot.

Eventually Gilligan found a flat on Charleville Avenue in Dublin's North Strand. It was small and cluttered but at least the newly weds had privacy and could come and go as they pleased. The couple lived between houses until 1977, when they moved into a council house at 13 Corduff Avenue in Blanchardstown in west Dublin.

But John Gilligan followed the life path already determined for him by the stars. He stopped working on the ferry line and turned to crime like his father before him. Gilligan, though, changed his world to accomplish what old Johnno could only dream of, the notoriety of being a multimillionaire gangster and the most dangerous man in the underworld.

CHAPTER 3

The Wild West

'Those were the best days of my life.'
JOHN GILLIGAN

From 1896 to 1901, Robert Leroy Parker and his sidekick Harry Longbaugh, forever known as Butch Cassidy and the Sundance Kid, roamed the desolate plains of Wyoming, Utah and Colorado with a gang of ten or so misfits robbing whenever the opportunity arose. They were collectively known as the Hole in the Wall gang and, under the tutelage of Parker, pioneered the art of robbing banks, mail vans and stagecoaches using means other than armed confrontation. Instead, the outlaws would blast their way into bank vaults using dynamite stolen from the Union Pacific Railroad and help themselves to whatever they could get away with. Almost a century later, history repeated itself when a similar bunch of misfits came together.

They too called themselves the Hole in the Wall gang. Only this time, they roamed the industrial estates of West Dublin in stolen vans and trucks, breaking into warehouses, hijacking mail vans and freight containers laden with goods destined for supermarket shelves. They too entered premises by making a hole in a wall, only their technique involved brute force: smashing down bricks and mortar with sledgehammers. These men also looked up to a leader – a young man, meticulous in his approach to crime and as devious and cunning. Like all gangster figures, he was given his own nickname by the press – they called him Warehouse John. The police called him John Gilligan.

He had given up working at sea. 'If you want to get rich, why work when you can rob? Why get up at eight in the morning when you can go out at eight at night and get anything you like?' were words he repeated to friends. This became his philosophy. From 1980 to 1990, Gilligan's Hole in the Wall gang wreaked havoc plundering the industrial estates lying scattered off the motorways that take travellers from Dublin to the cities of Cork and Limerick. They would steal anything they could lay their hands on: trucks, cars, refrigerators, animal health promoters, computer games, vacuum cleaners, sweets, chocolates, power tools – anything that could be sold. He orchestrated hundreds of robberies that netted him hundreds of thousands, most of which he squandered gambling. He knew every square foot of his stomping ground: every road; every warehouse; every fire escape; every side entrance; the waste grounds; and so he knew where to strike, when to strike and how to escape.

'They were the good old days,' he once remarked. 'I used to tell people that I lived in the "hereafter land" because when I arrived in the industrial estates I would say, "This is what I'm here after" and the Garda Síochána would say, "We're here after Gilligan." They were great days. There was loads of times when we'd get chased, sometimes we'd get something, other times we'd get nothing. I got a great buzz in those days. Nine times out of ten the owners wouldn't have known we'd been in. In some cases, the owners were happy because they got insurance on devalued goods. I wasn't into bank robberies because that involved firearms and I could get shot. When we'd go down for a stretch we'd write to the other lads, messing, pretending to sell the rights to steal from other industrial estates. It was great fun because we knew the prison officials saw the letters. We were like the Mafia.'

Although his flat Dublin accent and shabby dress code bore no similarity to the suave gangsters of the Cosa Nostra he watched in films, his criminal operation was as sophisticated. The truth was that in the space of a few years, by the time he was 30 years old, Gilligan had become a major figure in organised crime. By day he would act out the part of the family man, the hard-working loyal husband and father. This persona lived in Corduff and travelled into Dublin city centre where he ran a second-hand car salesroom. Here he would sell second-hand Ford Capris and other cheap models to anyone unfortunate enough to venture on to his forecourt. Unfortunate because if the car broke down, Gilligan simply wouldn't entertain them.

It was at night that the true criminal in John Gilligan emerged.

Whilst the city slept, he would emerge with his band of thieves and set about plundering warehouses. Accompanied by one or two of his lieutenants, he would drive south across the city to his turf, the Robinhood or Cookstown industrial estates. Like a cat burglar, he would reconnoitre his surroundings, looking for ways to break and enter; he would search for an entrance in the perimeter fencing and ways to bypass security systems. 'We would sit there all night, waiting for the security guard to arrive, time how long it took the guard to check the locks, what doors he checked, how thorough his checks were and see which way he approached,' remembered one member of the gang.

Gilligan would then scout around looking for rubbish. 'Get me some pallets, we need to light a bit of a fire,' he would say. He would build a bonfire against the side of the warehouse and set it alight before retreating back into the undergrowth. The raiders would return the next night. 'Right, lads, we know what we're here to do. Everyone into position.'

They would act with military-like co-ordination. Two men would run towards the industrial estate entrance, walkie-talkies in hand at the ready, should a passing Garda patrol stumble upon the heist. With professional skill, another two men would approach the warehouse and skirt around the wall until they found the section scorched by the fire Gilligan had set ablaze the previous night. 'Come on, lads, faster, faster,' he would shout.

With resolute body co-ordination, they would attack the wall with sledgehammers. The heat from the fire would have dried out the mortar and the brickwork, so it would just crumble away, leaving a gaping hole for the thieves to enter.

Thump . . . thump . . . thump . . .

'We're through, boss.'

Gilligan would inspect the demolition work. 'Well, what are you waiting for?'

Security systems in those days were humble devices designed to act as deterrents. Alarms were mostly battery operated, so Gilligan would simply knock them off the walls and take out the batteries. Once the 'security system' was disabled, he would set about the warehouse, stock-taking, compiling a mental inventory of the goods on offer. Once this was done, he would order one of the gang to prepare for the trucks. Walkie-talkie in hand, he would give the call sign and they would arrive in minutes, entering the warehouse via the goods entrance.

'Remember, lads, what's my favourite saying?'

'Why leave anything, boss?'

'Get to work,' he would shout.

Entire warehouses and factories would be cleared. Nothing of any value was left. 'We would spend hours just loading up our own trucks and making sure we left no fingerprints or evidence. He would take everything, paint brushes, boxes of nails, he even robbed the spare tyres off lorries and the tools. If it was worth anything, he would take it. I never saw anyone like him. Ropes, hammers, nails, car batteries – everything would be taken,' recalled one of the robbers.

The Hole in the Wall gang's stomping ground lay between the industrial expanses that surround Tallaght, Clondalkin and Ballyfermot. Businesses located in the Robinhood and Cookstown industrial estates were particularly affected because of Gilligan's familiarity with the area. He believed that even if the Gardaí should catch him robbing a factory here, he could escape.

At that time, the Garda Síochána concentrated all its efforts and resources into combating the Provisional IRA and the other paramilitary organisations. Organised crime was considered something ephemeral in Garda headquarters; men like John Gilligan didn't rate in the general scheme of things. The Government and the Department of Justice were categorically told there was no organised crime problem in Ireland. This belief filtered its way through all sections of Irish society and was quoted verbatim by the media at large, with the exception of some individual journalists. There were of course, some Gardaí who could see what was happening. Gilligan's small stature, devil-may-care attitude and churlishness towards authority didn't fool them. They were watching a petty thief turn into a master criminal before their eyes. There was no stopping his gang.

Gilligan expanded his operation to rural areas. By 1985 he felt confident using weapons and extreme violence. Warehouse robberies were no longer his speciality – he targeted mail vans and payroll deliveries. Violence was something the Hole in the Wall gang had no problem dispensing.

The Garda found it was near to impossible to combat his criminal operation. Gilligan had so much regard for the Gardaí and the lengths they would go to charge him with a serious offence that he never took the same route twice, discussed crime on a phone or left anything that could link him to any crime. He made all the arrangements for the gang so that no one could betray him. If he had to meet someone, he went to them. Under no circumstances did they arrive at his front door. He never held any stolen property at his home in Corduff, and so the Garda knew there was no point in raiding it.

His extensive connections in the business world were more than willing to allow him to store stolen goods in their warehouses. And because he sold his loot at knockdown prices to 'reputable businessmen', he slept assured that his products were laundered into the system fast, making it almost impossible to trace them.

Even when the Garda did manage to catch him redhanded, he always seemed to find a loophole to beat the charges, as happened in the Nilfisk case.

There wasn't a star in the sky when Niall McClory closed the door behind him and locked up. Grey clouds, the type that seem to float in suspended animation over Dublin's skyline, blotted out the moonlight. Cookstown Industrial Estate was lifeless; the familiar sound of forklifts and delivery trucks that normally deafened those working there was absent. It was 2 January 1986. The managers and factory workers were still on holiday, recuperating from the Christmas and New Year celebrations. It was McClory's first day back at Nilfisk. He had to return early to take delivery of 850 new vacuum cleaners that had arrived from Germany. What better way to start off the year than with a new delivery, he thought to himself as he walked to his car parked outside the warehouse. He had just got in when he saw a masked man wielding a baton approach.

'Get out of the car,' he yelled.

More appeared to drag him out. 'Open the door. Open the door.'

McClory was overcome by fear. His assailants had come from nowhere; he had no way of escaping in any case, so he opened the door.

'Get down on the floor. If you don't co-operate we'll shoot you. Do you understand?'

He could not see a weapon, but fearing they had a gun and would shoot him dead, he obeyed the command. One of the gang handcuffed his hands behind his back and the factory's security man was forced to lie in a similar position. They were made to look down. The next few hours seemed eternal and the atmosphere was tense as the two hostages wondered if they would be freed. Wearing a balaclava, Gilligan stood with a two-way radio clenched in one hand shouting instructions to the rest. 'Send in the truck.'

From his position, McClory could hear a truck arriving and the sound of the factory's forklift starting up, then reversing and moving to and fro. Gilligan and the Hole in the Wall gang were cleaning out Nilfisk, stealing the vacuum cleaners that had just arrived. When every one of the boxed vacuums was loaded, the gang left, vanishing as fast as they arrived. The alarm was raised almost immediately afterwards when McClory managed to press a panic button in the office.

Gardaí arriving on the scene set about making inquiries but they had only one suspect in mind: John Gilligan.

It was inconceivable for Gilligan to travel far with such a massive cargo of stolen goods. The Gardaí would be mounting checkpoints looking for the stolen vacuums, so he arranged to store the vacuums in a warehouse located nearby, at Unit 22, Weatherwell Industrial Estate in Clondalkin. From here, the vacuum cleaners would be sold off in small lots by the gang, one of whom was a young criminal and new addition to the gang, 23-year-old David Weafer.

The Nilfisk heist was to work as follows. The loot would be divided into seven cuts; Gilligan and two others would take the lion's share while the rest, like Weafer, would receive a smaller amount of vacuums to sell themselves. Gilligan correctly envisaged that he would not be able to fence the load all at once because Nilfisk would issue a general warning or possibly offer a reward for the return of the goods. Therefore, whenever one of the gang wanted access to their share of the vacuums, they would ring Gilligan and arrange to meet at Weatherwell. Gilligan held the keys because it was his hiding place and he would ensure that everyone got their fair share.

Gilligan's prediction that Nilfisk and the Garda Press Office would highlight the robbery proved correct. Two days later, the *Irish Independent* carried an article warning housewives to beware of door-to-door salesmen selling cheap vacuum cleaners. Nilfisk's managing director Pat Murphy told the *Independent* that the vacuums would not be sold through established outlets.

'It would be very difficult to get them into electrical shops. The only alternative would be door to door. Somebody somewhere should be able to give us a clue. I am as intrigued as you are as to how the gang is going to get rid of these machines. I would love to know what they are going to do with them,' he said.

The vacuum cleaners were being sold door to door but faster than the Gardaí could have imagined. Weafer in particular was selling more than the others, more than his allocation, unknown to Gilligan who had given him the keys of Unit 22 to help himself. Fearing that he would 'vanish' should Gilligan find out about his 'sales drive', he leaked information about where the stolen vacuums were being kept to the Gardaí. If they raided Unit 22 and found the vacuums, Gilligan would never find out about his double-crossing. But the Gardaí wanted Gilligan, and so placed Unit 22 under surveillance with the intention of arresting him redhanded with the stolen property.

Weafer co-operated and arranged to meet Gilligan at Unit 22 a week later on 9 January. Gilligan didn't want to go near the stash – the Gardaí were running a major operation looking for the vacuums and would be no doubt monitoring his movements. But Weafer insisted, saying he needed to get more vacuums to sell, he needed the cash. The two met at Weatherwell Industrial Estate which, unknown to Gilligan, was surrounded by armed detectives. Gilligan approached the warehouse door and became suspicious. Years of avoiding the Gardaí had taught him to take various precautions. In this case, he had affixed to the side of the entrance door a small wooden stick which would snap should anyone but he enter. The stick had snapped, thereby indicating someone had been inside.

He turned to Weafer and asked if he had been near the vacuums, taking more than his fair share. Weafer denied this and said he was in a hurry to return home. Gilligan took a small key from his pocket and opened the lock that secured the door and the two went inside. The detectives could not believe their luck – here was John Gilligan handling stolen goods. Once Gilligan was inside, the Gardaí moved in just as the two unloaded boxes of vacuums from the truck used in the heist.

'Armed Garda. Don't move,' shouted one officer. The two criminals put their hands up in the air before being handcuffed and driven away to be charged with offences including the robbery of the vacuums, unlawfully detaining the men in the factory and the theft of the trucks found in the warehouse. The vehicles alone were valued at £45,000 whilst the vacuum cleaner consignment found in Unit 22 was worth £54,000, making the charges extremely serious. Gilligan and Weafer were charged before the Dublin District Court.

The case came up for hearing over two years later in March 1988 in the Circuit Criminal Court before Judge Gerard Buchanan. Gilligan's future looked bleak. He would certainly be convicted and sentenced. In his opening address to the jury, prosecuting counsel Erwin Mill Arden, BL, said the evidence before the court would link all the items with the accused and the vacuum cleaners. The accused, he said, was not charged with the theft of any of the items but with receiving them knowing them to have been stolen.

The court heard evidence of how Gilligan's fingerprints had been found on a can of paint that had been used in one of the stolen vehicles found in Unit 22. Detective Inspector John Anders of Tallaght Garda station also gave evidence of finding Gilligan and Weafer unloading cartons containing the stolen vacuums from a lorry. Gilligan, he said, had thrown away a key before he was arrested under the Offences Against the State Act. The key fitted the padlock on the unit's small door, which Gilligan had been seen opening. The inspector went on to say a search order had been obtained under the Offences Against the State Act because it was suspected that a firearm or firearms used in the raid in which the vacuum cleaners were stolen might be found. The prosecution's case appeared to be going according to plan until day two when the receiving charge was withdrawn after legal issues were raised about ownership of the vacuums. The delivery docket for the vacuum cleaners apparently hadn't been signed, hence ownership of the vacuums couldn't be established.

Gilligan couldn't believe his luck; this was too good to be true. But he still faced charges of receiving three vehicles and a hydraulic tailgate found in Unit 22. Then these charges were eventually withdrawn, as were all the charges connected with the case.

But the Gardaí had kept up the pressure.

Immediately after his arrest on the Nilfisk charges, Gilligan and the Hole in the Wall gang had gone back to business, stealing and robbing. The fear of prison however had made him all the more impromptu, believing himself to be destined for jail in any case; he developed a lax attitude to security, which proved to be his downfall. It was not long before he slipped up. Gilligan temporarily stopped carrying out raids down the country, for if he were to be arrested while on bail for the Nilfisk heist he would certainly be held on remand. But his familiarity with the factories of Robinhood Industrial Estate eased him into a false sense of safety. Having spent hundreds of hours prowling around the industrial estates in the midnight hours, he had managed to convince himself he was untouchable once he stayed in Dublin. He deluded himself into believing the Gardaí could never catch him, that he was too clever, that he could outwit them mentally. He believed they had got lucky with Weafer but that the rest of his team was solid and trustworthy. The Gardaí would never get that close again, or so he believed.

It was approaching Easter, April 1987, when Gilligan decided to rob the Rose Confectionery premises at 23A Robinhood Industrial Estate. He assembled two of his most trusted lieutenants and they broke into the factory on Good Friday, 17 April. It was meant to be an easy job – break in, steal sweets and chocolates and sell them off. He would have no problem selling such items, not with Easter approaching. The gang assembled at the usual rendezvous point outside the industrial estate and made their way to the sweet factory. Once inside, Gilligan started helping himself to jelly babies, toffees and chocolates of all flavours. 'Check and make sure everything is okay outside,' he ordered one of the gang whilst stuffing his mouth full.

'Yes, boss.'

While Gilligan continued to wolf down the sweets, the raider walked over to the office window and opened the blind, only to see a security guard staring back at him. Not knowing whether the guard had realised that he was a thief, the raider shouted and alerted Gilligan to what had happened.

'Did he look back at you?' Gilligan inquired.

'I don't know, he just looked at me and kept going,' the raider responded.

'You're probably just on edge. It will be all right. No one would notice us in here,' Gilligan responded.

The security guard had indeed seen the thief but rather than tackle him on his own, drove on and radioed for help and the Gardaí. Gilligan had made a fatal mistake – he didn't remember his golden rule of taking no chances – and within a matter of minutes Rose Confectionery was surrounded by Gardaí, some of whom, knowing his ways of old, suspected Gilligan might be inside. The Gardaí approached the warehouse and shouted at whoever was inside to come out. By this stage, the gang was in a state of panic. Gilligan, however, reassured them, saying they had stolen nothing and would only be charged with breaking and entering. He wasn't too concerned, even if he was convicted; he would be going to prison anyway because of the Nilfisk charge. The two sentences would run concurrently. One of the gang tried to hide but couldn't find a suitable place. Gilligan thought this was funny and asked if he jumped in with the jelly babies, would the others put the lid back on the jar. He knew he was caught red-handed.

Although he had rehearsed various escape routes out of Robinhood hundreds of times in his mind, he couldn't escape. He gave himself up, walking out the door with his hands placed on his head to the astonishment of the Gardaí. Never expecting to beat the Nilfisk charges, he pleaded guilty and was released on bail. His case came up for hearing the following May in the Circuit Criminal Court when he appeared before Judge Frank Roe. Detective Inspector John McLoughlin gave evidence of having known Gilligan for 15 years and told the court he was the leader of gangs which robbed warehouses all over the country. John Gilligan, he said, was one of Ireland's biggest players in organised crime and his only source of income was from crime. Details of Gilligan's extensive criminal record were read out to the court. Burglary, attempted larceny, stealing and receiving, the list went on and on. Gilligan was physically sick – he had hoped he would get a suspended sentence or a 'bender' as he called it. Two months previous, he had walked away from the Nilfisk heist a free man, now he was going to jail for stealing sweets.

Judge Roe sentenced him to 18 months in Mountjoy jail despite hearing evidence of Gilligan's good character from the director of a riding centre where he stabled three ponies. This woman described him as a kind, generous and considerate person who placed his ponies at the disposal of disadvantaged children. Although things hadn't gone his way, he felt reassured going into prison that he would have plenty of cash when freed. The gangster had made thousands stealing from warehouses; thievery had proved to be a lucrative occupation for him. Little did he know he would get to play a pivotal role in the biggest robbery in the world.

CHAPTER 4

The Bonds

'He was a little Hitler.'
IRA MEMBER TALKING ABOUT GILLIGAN

Gilligan opened his eyes and wondered if his captors were going to murder him – shoot him through the side of his head to make sure he died. He sat with an expressionless look on his face – it seemed unthinkable that the Provisional IRA would kill him now. He probably contemplated an escape. He could run, maybe overpower one or two of his abductors and head off into the night. He figured there were about four of them and possibly two more outside keeping watch. What if he made a run for it? He probably pictured the escape route in his mind and thought about how long it would take him to get to a safe house. But he knew they would catch up with him; if not on that night, it would be some other when he least expected it. That was the way the IRA worked. There was no escaping them; they would catch him eventually. Gilligan likened them to birds of prey. They moved silently above, occasionally plunging on unsuspecting prey. If they didn't kill, they would make demands that had to be met. No criminal ever stood up to them because they had strength in numbers and if you took on one, you took on them all. When people working the streets talked about the army, they talked about the IRA.

Gilligan could never deal with the 'politicos' as he called them. The IRA did what they did out of belief, his only belief was in financial rewards. He had no interest in their war and hated the way they threw their weight around. He considered his predicament.

Although he was not the enemy as in some British soldier or Special Branch detective, he knew he was in danger, having overstepped the mark. His kidnappers had repeated to him what they wanted over and over again but he refused to give in, declaring they would have to kill him because they were not getting what they wanted. Now his captors were thinking about doing just that. Shooting him dead for £77 million worth of stolen bearer bonds.

Gilligan was resolute; the bonds were worth dying for. He was about to find out whether the IRA felt the same. For a criminal protagonist like Gilligan, republicanism meant nothing; the IRA was merely another organisation he and his ilk had to deal with occasionally. Years before, he had tried to ingratiate himself with the leaders of the Provisionals' Dublin Brigade by allowing an old garage he owned in the Crumlin area of Dublin to be used for storing stolen vehicles, weapons and explosives.

Inside Gilligan's garage, the cars stolen by the IRA would be prepared for use in a bombing, robbery or assassination. The vehicles would have false registration plates fitted along with industrial shock absorbers to conceal the weight of the explosives or mortars hidden in their boots. The arrangement worked well until Gilligan started to tell anyone who crossed his path that he was an IRA sympathiser, whose garage was being used for the cause. He had good reason to let this be known publicly. His adversaries would be far less likely to cross him if he had strong IRA connections. But the IRA had other ideas – once they heard about his loose talk, they were gone. What past favours he had done for the Provisionals were irrelevant now. They wanted the bonds.

On 2 May 1990 at 9.30 a.m., John Goddard, a 58-year-old messenger with the financial brokerage Sheppards, was taking his usual route along King William Street in London's financial district. He had travelled the route many times previously with no security problems, delivering certificates of deposits and treasury bills to the financial houses.

On that particular morning, Goddard was carrying 301 bearer bonds worth £292 million in his satchel. These were in bearer form and as good as cash to anyone with possession of them. There was nothing unusual in Goddard's satchel. Every day London's financial houses borrowed and loaned money using certificates of deposits, or CDs and treasury bills used by the Government – bearer bonds. He suspected nothing when he saw a young black youth approach him on the street, until he produced a knife and demanded he hand over his satchel. He hesitated, but fearing for his life, the courier handed over the pouch.

By 11.20 a.m. that morning, investors, banks and stock traders across the world were made aware of what had happened. Goddard's assailant had escaped with 301 bills, many of which were made out for £1 million each. Immediately after the mugging took place, the Bank of England notified financial institutions across the world, warning them not to accept the bonds in business transactions. The serial numbers of the bonds were circulated. The Bank of England purposely released inaccurate information through spokesmen who announced the bonds couldn't be cashed and were useless – statements that couldn't have been further from the truth. The bonds were valuable.

Such was the fear among the international financial community that Sheppards felt compelled to take out an insurance policy with Lloyds should the thief try to cash the bonds. The premium cost the courier company £750,000. The detective squad at Bishopsgate in London was given the unenviable task of locating the stolen goods. They hoped against hope the theft was just the work of a mugger and the bonds would be found thrown away. Within the space of a few days, they realised this was not the case and Operation Starling was born.

Some ten days later, they got their first break when a faxed copy of a stolen bond arrived from a source in Northern Ireland. Then one of the bonds was lodged in a branch of the NatWest bank in Glasgow. The person who lodged it was judged an innocent pawn.

The Operation Starling team followed the source of the bond back to a small syndicate of criminals who had come together for the theft and had planned to launder the stolen bearer bonds in Liechtenstein. But the thieves decided against this plan for various reasons. Operation Starling was making inroads into their organisation, and investigators hired by Lloyds were also searching for the bonds whilst the Bank of England was using its influence to have the bonds returned. Those behind the theft resorted to plan B; this involved Gilligan. Details of his involvement in the conspiracy remain a well-guarded secret to this day.

Gilligan's involvement in the biggest robbery in the world happened through his association with Thomas Coyle, a mastermind criminal who lived in Drogheda in County Louth. Coyle was a fence, someone

Gilligan used to sell stolen goods. He was reliable, managed to avoid the Gardaí and ran a smooth criminal organisation although no one has ever been sure how. He mixed with loyalist paramilitaries in the Ulster Defence Association (UDA) north of the border whilst managing to maintain contacts with the Irish National Liberation Army (INLA) and to a lesser extent the Provisional IRA.

Anyone else would have been murdered for mixing in rival circles, but not Coyle. No one in the Irish underworld expected anything else of him. He had connections everywhere and was regarded as being good at his job. Therefore, it came as no surprise that he acquired 80 of the bonds to fence within weeks of the theft. Coyle was shrewd enough to know that he wasn't capable of laundering the bonds single-handedly, so he enlisted Gilligan.

'They didn't really understand what they had. The whole thing was a non-starter. But Gilligan had what he believed was stolen gear worth £80 million, and he went around trying to get anyone to buy one of the bonds,' explained an IRA source.

Laundering such valuable documents into the international banking system was a crime Gilligan simply didn't have the intelligence to carry out. Instead, he tried to sell them to fellow criminals, fraudsters and the like. 'He came to me with a photocopy of one of the bonds. That was proof that he had them. He wanted £10,000 cash for each one, then ten per cent of whatever they fetched when they were fenced. These things were for a million. No one could fence something like that, so no one did the business with him,' recalled one fraudster who was offered the bonds outside the Four Courts building.

Gilligan then turned to Jim Beirne, a businessman with international criminal connections. Beirne was known as The Danger and came from County Roscommon. He specialised in fraud but would later enter into the world of international drug trafficking.

Beirne had the connections in the United States to launder the bonds. His connection came through John Francis Conlon. Born in Westport, County Mayo, Conlon was somewhat of an international figure in the intelligence community, having worked for the Israeli intelligence agency Mossad and the Central Intelligence Agency as well as British Intelligence and US Customs and Excise. He moved between Norfolk, England, and Miami, America. He was an associate of Monzer Al-Kassar, the world's biggest illegal arms dealer, who sold weapons to terrorists. He also sold arms to Colonel Oliver North, a deal that would later spark off the Arms-to-Iran crisis. Conlon was effectively a double agent. He came to prominence in the intelligence community during the Middle-Eastern conflict.

He set up an arms deal for T-62 tanks to be sold to two Israelis in a flat in Amsterdam on behalf of the Syrians. This was to draw the Israelis into a trap. The Syrians were planning on killing the Israelis when they arrived. Al-Kassar didn't know that Conlon was also working for Israeli intelligence and had given details of the raid to his Mossad controller. The Israelis alerted the police and the flat was raided. In 1989 Al-Kassar put a contract of £20,000 on Conlon's head and later raised it to £100,000.

Among the three men, a conspiracy emerged to smuggle the bonds to the United States, where Conlon felt his Mafia connections could launder anything. Gilligan and Coyle trusted Beirne's credentials and left everything to him. All they would have to do was go along with his instructions. Fuelled by a lust to make it big, however, all the participants in the conspiracy let their guards down. With the exception of Conlon and Beirne, all were dabbling in unfamiliar territory and didn't see the warning signs of informers in their ranks.

Arrangements were made to have the bonds smuggled to Miami on 29 May, the day Operation Starling scored its first blow. The official version of what happened is that customs officers accidentally intercepted a suitcase full of bonds as a result of a random search and later arrested three men. The arrested men were Thomas Coyle, his brother-in-law Anthony Rooney and Edward Dunne, who had departed from Dublin Airport earlier that morning. Coyle had hidden the bonds in one of the group's suitcases, which were all tagged to Dunne. Neither Dunne nor Rooney knew the bonds were concealed in the luggage. They were completely innocent.

Dunne's flight went ahead as scheduled whilst Coyle's and Rooney's was delayed. All three were due to fly to Heathrow where they would catch a connecting flight to Miami, for the purpose of buying a racehorse. But on his arrival Dunne was stopped by customs and taken into custody. Coyle and Rooney arrived shortly afterwards and were stopped. An examination of Rooney's baggage discovered 80 bonds. Rooney and Coyle said they had never seen the bonds, did not know what was in Dunne's suitcase and told investigating police this was all a mistake.

The newspaper headlines the next morning announced that three men were due in court charged with attempting to handle the stolen bearer bonds worth £77.3 million. The names of the three were released and they were charged that on or before 29 May 1990 they attempted within the jurisdiction of the Old Bailey to handle stolen property, namely Treasury Bills and Certificates of Deposit, which if misused could have caused the owners loss worth £77.3 million. The charges were made under Section 11 of the 1977 Criminal Law Act. Coyle and Rooney were charged separately from Dunne.

Their case went to trial in February 1991 before Knightsbridge Crown Court but collapsed on a legal technicality. The prosecution had claimed the bonds were part of the stolen £291 million haul from the mugging. Coyle and Rooney maintained their defence, claiming they didn't know what was inside the case. Rooney certainly didn't. But after hearing several days of evidence, both Rooney and Coyle were freed when their trial judge instructed the jury to acquit them because they hadn't handled the bonds in a British jurisdiction. Coyle couldn't believe his luck. The Crown Prosecution then offered no evidence on a conspiracy charge. The prosecution case against Edward Dunne fell apart after it emerged that he had not signed the docket, which accompanied his baggage. He was legally required to do this. He was freed. Speaking to the *Sunday World* after the acquittal, Coyle said the cockroaches in his cell were as big as mice. 'I feel very hurt that at this stage in our lives we had to spend months inside for something that we knew nothing about. For fellas like us, who had never been in prison before, you can imagine what it was like to be thrown in with murderers, child molesters and peeping toms.'

Rooney described his ordeal. 'I made the tea for all the officers and Thomas was the head cleaner. We had to do something to get out of that cell, otherwise we would have been behind bars for 23 hours a day.'

Coyle concluded the interview, saying: 'Our biggest fear was that we would be arrested again. We just couldn't trust the British system and the feeling when we touched down in Ireland was just unbelievable. At last we knew we were home safe and sound.' Years later, Coyle would boast of his escape. He even purchased a racehorse which he named 77mill.

The police assigned to Operation Starling went on to intercept more bonds. In Cyprus, 80 bonds were retrieved whilst the FBI in Miami intercepted more. But it was the manner in which these were intercepted, or the story behind them, that proved dangerous for the criminals involved. Those responsible for the delivery of the bonds to Miami said they were working with the Provisional IRA and were filmed saying this by the FBI.

Acting on intelligence, US customs agents intercepted the 71 British bonds worth $18 million dollars inside a package being sent on an outbound Air Peru flight destined for Lima. The bonds were concealed inside two hollowed-out phone books.

The sheer scale of the theft had naturally aroused the interest of the British media and it wasn't long before allegations of IRA involvement made it into the press. What caused the upset was the linking of the Provisional IRA to loyalist paramilitaries, from whom earlier consignments of bonds had been seized. Television programmes proclaiming the IRA were involved with the UDA were broadcast whilst newspapers in Britain started saying the IRA and UDA were co-operating to launder the bonds. The IRA launched an inquiry that went straight to Gilligan. One of his interrogators wanted to shoot Gilligan, but was overruled by his superior who ordered that Gilligan be released. 'I think our own people realised it was all a non-starter. Here were a group of Dublin criminals trying to launder £80 million, which was way out of their league. When it emerged that they had been telling people that they were working with the IRA, then that was different. At one point it got way out of hand, the British press were running wild with stories about our involvement with the bonds. The truth was that we had never gotten them.'

Like everything in Gilligan's criminal career, he was not brought to court for his role in this serious crime but instead went down for receiving stolen tools worth a mere £3,000.

The goods had been stolen from Bolger's Hardware and Builders Providers in Kilcannon, Enniscorthy, County Wexford, months earlier. The Warehouse gang had been busy and had cleared out the family business. The goods were recovered days later by Gardaí following a surveillance operation that resulted in Gilligan's arrest.

Gilligan was charged before the Special Criminal Court where Judge Robert Barr described him as being 'involved in serious crime for many years'. Gilligan, whose address was given as Corduff

Avenue, Blanchardstown, Dublin, was found guilty of receiving assorted hardware items worth £3,000 between 26 and 28 January but was cleared of the theft of £15,000 worth of stolen goods. The court was told that Gilligan had been arrested after Gardaí had staked out a lorry parked on the Ballymount Road in Dublin. The lorry contained the proceeds of the Wexford robbery and Gilligan and three others were seen removing the goods from it in two vans.

When Gilligan was convicted, Detective Sergeant Felix McKenna told the court that Gilligan had 12 previous convictions and was the leader of the gang. Barr sentenced Gilligan to four years. Although the conviction was a huge success, it would have unforeseen consequences. No one standing in the courtroom that day could have predicted that Gilligan was about to undergo a metamorphosis, transforming himself from a streetwise thief into a career criminal. This transformation occurred in the maximum-security wing of Portlaoise Prison over the next three years, with unimagined consequences for the system that put him there.

CHAPTER 5

Portlaoise

'He was a natural born networker.'
BRIAN KENNA, FORMER OFFICER COMMANDING OF THE PROVISIONAL IRA
PRISONERS HELD IN PORTLAOISE PRISON, TALKING ABOUT GILLIGAN

The video footage shows a small man smiling at the camera, shaking hands with some of Ireland's most infamous gangsters. He is cordial and is greeted with respect; the type shown by sons to their fathers. He looks nervous in front of the camera; ill at ease about being filmed, but manages to continue smiling as if he has not a care in the world. John Gilligan is networking. He shouts at Dessie O'Hare. The INLA gunman, forever known as the Border Fox, is walking through the frame looking solemn. 'Dessie . . . Dessie . . . Dessie . . . come here.'

O'Hare ignores him, staring straight ahead and walks away. Gilligan runs towards him and embraces him whilst cajoling him into smiling at the camera. Then he's off, shaking hands with other prisoners, patting them on the back, congratulating some on playing well whilst commiserating with others. He is everyone's friend.

The inmates of Portlaoise Prison had just organised an inter-prison soccer tournament, the final of which had been filmed on video for posterity. Below the barbed wire and watchtowers, soccer teams drawn from the prison population waged war against each other to secure a place in the cup final. Because he was not a good footballer, Gilligan was nominated to provide a running commentary of the qualifying matches as they were filmed. That his vocabulary was limited and his words were spoken in guttural tones that seemed to melt into one another didn't dissuade his appointment. Some of his commentary when later played was impossible to decipher. Oddly, at times when O'Hare was playing he spoke with clarity – although he repeated himself constantly. 'The Border Fox has the ball. Good kick by Dessie O'Hare, the Fox to Hippo Ward . . . Nice pass to Larry Dunne . . . Larry Dunne. Good man, Larry.'

It was late in the summer of 1991 and Gilligan was a relative newcomer to Portlaoise, yet he was the centre of attention – greeted like a patriarchal figure. In the grey confines of the prison, Gilligan had the power without the throne. He slept in the same type of cell as the other prisoners, ate the same food, wakened at the same time and was told when to go to bed. The only thing that marked him apart was his ability to network. And network in prison he did, creating a coterie of trusted sidekicks who would later give him the muscle to become a major player in the world of crime. Far from rehabilitating himself for society, Gilligan metamorphosed from a thief into a gangster.

John Gilligan arrived in Portlaoise Prison courtesy of the Special Criminal Court on 7 November 1990. The prison itself was built in 1850 and lies in the centre of Portlaoise town in County Laois. The jail is divided into two wings – D Block and E Block, each wing four storeys in height. D Block holds delinquents jailed for car theft and other such misdemeanours. E Block is a prison within a prison and is partly reserved for those the system deems a serious threat to the security of the state.

The ground floor of E Block is called E1 and is home to a select group of criminals the Department of Justice regards as being involved in organised crime. The second floor is called E2. The Irish National Liberation Army (INLA) shares this floor with the Provisional IRA volunteers whose ranks also account for the cells on E3 and E4. Gilligan lived on E1 and it was here that he evolved in criminal terms.

Gilligan could always make people feel comfortable. He might smile at them, give them space when required, talk to them as if they were his best friend but, most important of all, listen without interrupting. He possessed a genius capability for paying attention; he had a knack of listening to monotonous conversations without appearing bored. It was this talent he used to full effect in Portlaoise, making friends with criminals that would be of use to him on his release. His secret was giving off the impression that he was just another criminal. No one who encountered him during this period considered him anything but a thief. He was a small man who smiled continuously, knew a few tricky businessmen and relied on his wife's visits. Gambling was his only character flaw.

He gambled on everything. Whether he was on the prison landings or in the exercise yard, he would produce a deck of cards to passers-by. He would bet on two flies crawling up a wall. 'Pick a card, buy a Crunchie,' he would say, holding out a shuffled deck. Two cards would be drawn. Whoever chose the lowest would be obliged to buy a Crunchie in the prison tuck shop. But this was a front, a persona he created for life behind bars.

With perfect cunning, Gilligan managed to become a central figure on E1, effectively representing the prisoners to the authorities but at all times staying in the background. He nominated others to approach the Governor on issues relating to their living conditions.

Brian Kenna was the then Officer Commanding of the Provisional IRA volunteers gaoled in Portlaoise at the time. 'Gilligan became like a spokesman for the prisoners down in E1. In a lot of cases others would go and argue with the Governor but it was under the direction of John Gilligan. The others didn't seem to be bothered one way or the other. They didn't seem to care who represented them or whether they were represented at all. If they had a problem, they would go see the Governor themselves. Gilligan seemed to be the main mover,' he said.

In other words, Gilligan directed manoeuvres from a discreet distance. These were inklings of Gilligan's organisational skills. 'You could see him getting organised; he was also clever enough to keep a distance between himself and the Governor so that he wasn't seen to be rocking the boat,' said Kenna.

By fighting for better conditions in the prison, Gilligan ingratiated himself with his fellow inmates, though his small-minded attitude annoyed the most amicable of Portlaoise's resident population. Hence jail provided him with opportunities to ingratiate himself with the hardest of the hard. Because he was a natural born networker, he devoted his energies to getting to know everyone inside. If this was part of some grand plan to build a coterie of accomplices around him, it is only known to him. But this is exactly what happened.

Prison prepared him for a life of organised crime and drug trafficking. Housing violent criminals in Portlaoise alongside the likes of Gilligan was, Kenna says, a recipe for disaster. 'Men like

Gilligan were the nearest thing Ireland had seen to organised crime – they had the gangs, contacts in the Gardaí, prison system, social welfare, the courts, basically extensive networks on the outside. Or, in some cases, they had the ability to develop networks. They were career criminals.

'Gilligan was introduced to strong or hard men in Portlaoise, men he was able to manipulate. A lot of these were in awe of Gilligan. It was easy for him to manipulate these people, who frankly mightn't have had an awful lot between their ears. They were just fellas who got involved in crime but would never have made much money. But when these were introduced to people like Gilligan, who could scheme long term, the prison system effectively gave him foot soldiers,' he added.

While Gilligan resisted joining an established criminal gang, he certainly learned from them, particularly the concepts of how to run paramilitary organisations. He watched the INLA and how they operated, and listened to Dessie O'Hare's ramblings about revolutionary and guerrilla warfare. Although most of what he heard was defunct nonsense, Gilligan did gain insight into how groups like the INLA hand-picked men to perform certain tasks and how they worked in cells.

'The top criminal brains were housed on the one landing and so they compared notes. That's where Gilligan came into his own. He sat back and identified people in any particular area, whether it be someone with a van, someone with a yard, someone who could get registration numbers checked. He met them in Portlaoise and recruited them,' explained Kenna.

It is easy to conjecture how this happened. Kenna saw Gilligan as having a remarkable ability to learn from others. 'He could pick everybody's brains, even without having to talk to them, by just sitting there and listening to them. He used everyone's skills. He was like a personnel manager for want of a better word. He was good at managing people on a one-to-one basis for a bigger picture. And he obviously did that very effectively.'

High-profile prisoners serving sentences usually avoid each other in prison to lessen confrontations. Portlaoise, however, forced some of the State's most hardened adversaries to talk.

'You had 40 top-profile prisoners confined in a small space that couldn't break out, control, subvert or bully anyone. You had the most unruly criminals in the State and republicans keeping them in line. Did they run amuck?' Kenna asked rhetorically.

True to form, most of the criminals of E1 did keep to themselves. Some of the younger, more impressionable, ones looked up to Gilligan. He would talk to them as if he were their father, defend them when necessary and help them out. They would eat breakfast, lunch and tea in his company and follow him around the exercise yard.

Paul Ward, a miscreant youth who grew up in Windmill Park in Crumlin, was one. Hippo, as he was called, would listen in silence to Gilligan's pronunciations on crime and prison life with intensity. The fact he was in prison for armed robbery and had 25 convictions, the first of which he received at a young age in the Children's Criminal Court, gave him impeccable credentials.

Brian Meehan was a protégé of Martin Cahill, the gangland criminal known as The General. Cahill had recruited Meehan as a youth and turned him into a highly skilled getaway driver. Meehan had a number of dysfunctional character flaws and no sense of family values. He was reared by his grandmother in the run-down drug-infested Fatima Mansions complex, but later lived with his parents, Kevin and Frances, on Stanaway Road in Crumlin. With 15 convictions under his belt, he was serving time in Portlaoise for his role in an armed raid on the Allied Irish Bank in Grafton Street. He and Ward would discuss crime with Gilligan in his cell, sometimes for hours.

Gilligan never said much, recalled George Royal, one former inmate. 'They would all be sitting in the cell. Meehan would be the loudmouth, going on about how one fella he knew was making thousands selling drugs. They'd be all looking at each other saying, "How can he be making that much from selling dope?" They would say, "Sure he's a fucking eejit. If he can do it, so can we. Think how much we could make, with the backup we have."

'This was all talk with Meehan and Ward but Gilligan would sit there and listen. He never said a word, he just listened, but was taking everything in. Make no doubt about it, that's where it all started,' said Royal.

Not everything about prison life proved positive for Gilligan. Contrary to what he would have everyone believe, he was deeply insecure with regards to his personal life. Fear of losing Geraldine perturbed him greatly: he lamented that he was not with his wife and at home to see his two children through the turbulent teenage years. He felt ill at ease about his marriage, often convincing himself that she would leave him for another or simply seek a separation or marriage annulment, although this seemed only a potential reality to him. It fuelled an irrational hatred of prison and this festered in his psyche. It played on his mind, annoyed him and thwarted whatever sense of logic he possessed. A desire for release absorbed his energies and consumed his mind.

By the summer of 1992 this craving for freedom began to eat away at him. He missed Geraldine intensely. He would write long letters to her, exposing his innermost secrets in the full knowledge that the prison authorities would see his softer side. One of the letters showed the tender side of their relationship.

> Portlaoise Prison
> Dublin Road
> Portlaoise
> Co. Laois
> 10 August 92
>
> Dear Geraldine,
> Just a line or two to say I love you so very, very much and that you looked so beautiful today, your lovely. I'm so proud to be your husband and best friend so I am. Ger I really had a nice day. I hope it was half as good for you. I will find out tomorrow when I am going up to Dublin and then let you know on the phone this week or the weekend ok. Geraldine tell Darren I said thanks for been so good, so good for you, he is a good son thank God.
>
> Well honey I can't wait to get Christmas over with its less than 20 weeks away and as soon as its over with we will be only counting the months that I have left (agree) ok but for now lets take it at a week at a time agree.
>
> Geraldine I know I ask you to do a lot for me but as you know I would do the same for you. Geraldine I think this letter is after going from a love one to a do this or do that (agree) I'm sorry love its just I want things to go right for you as you could do with the money They all owe me ok love.

Geraldine do you still love me I know I know its hard. I'm just lovesick. Sure head I would die for you, I love you that much. Geraldine I will say good night and god bless you, you're my dream come, true so you my love are.
From your loving tea maker HA. HA.
All my love your
Husband and best Friend, I love You Billions
Love John
xxxxx

Out of his dreams and private thoughts, inside the prison environs he was an altogether different man. He made unreasonable demands on the prison service. He became hard to deal with; in essence a problematic prisoner. This irrational behaviour continued unabated and culminated in him attacking Tom Dormer, the Chief Prison Officer in charge of E1, on 22 October 1992. Gilligan had requested that the prison authorities supply him with copies of confidential records he wanted to give to Geraldine. He knew he was not entitled to prison files but had made the request anyway. At 4 p.m. Dormer approached him on the prison landing to tell him his request had been denied. When he turned his back on Gilligan, the prisoner lashed out, punching him from behind. The blow loosened Dormer's teeth and left his jaw bruised. Notwithstanding the apparent ease at which Gilligan had struck Dormer, the prison authorities transferred Gilligan to Cork Prison immediately. He was held there in solitary confinement for the next two months without privileges.

The Gardaí were called in to investigate the attack and took a statement from Dormer and another warden who witnessed the attack. Gilligan declined to make any comment to the police.

Solitary confinement affected him deeply. Solitude broke him and he became dispirited, unhygienic, dirty and lacking in any self-respect. Realising that he was slipping into a depression, Geraldine travelled to him. She urged him to do something about his situation, take redress through the courts.

Her endeavours prompted him to take an appeal to the High Court seeking his return to Portlaoise. It was here that Gilligan first met Donal Ó Siodhacháin and Pat Herron from Paralegal and Technical Services (PATS). Ó Siodhacháin was a former member of the Sinn Féin Ard Chomhairle and the Provisional IRA. He met Herron, whom he describes as a fiery redhead, whilst seeking help for a complex legal case and the two went on to set up PATS in 1985. Neither are solicitors but both have a good understanding of the courts system and judicial process. 'We'd prepare briefing documents for solicitors and help people fight cases against the Garda, ESB, corporation, and the like.' The meeting with Gilligan was purely accidental. 'He was in the High Court and had just made an application to the judge but he wasn't able to get across what he wanted. He was in very bad shape physically. He was being held in Cork in solitary confinement. He looked shell-shocked, he wasn't wearing any stockings in his shoes,' remembers Ó Siodhacháin.

The judge delayed hearing Gilligan's application and so he took a seat at the back of the courtroom where Ó Siodhacháin was sitting. 'He was anything but the figure he was made out to be later. The prisoner officer handcuffed to him dozed off to sleep, and I passed a card under his nose. I'd written on the back of it, "Apply for a two-week adjournment, ask for legal aid under the Attorney Generals Act and do you want our help?"'

Gilligan nodded to all three and Ó Siodhacháin pointed to his red-haired companion, Herron, who visited him the following day. Ó Siodhacháin was dubious about Gilligan, having no idea about his background and his story. Because of these fears, which he kept to himself, he arranged to meet Geraldine. 'We asked about their income. They were living in Blanchardstown and she produced photographs of the land in Kildare with a few buildings on it. This was long before they built Jessbrook. She had photos of it and it looked run-down and grotty. In fact, it was so bad at that stage that when she tried get some grant to upgrade the stable, it was condemned as being not fit to keep horses in it.'

Unknown to them, they were dealing with a serious criminal. They put a briefing document together for Gilligan to approach a solicitor. 'We had no idea he was such a heavyweight criminal.'

By this stage, Gilligan had been charged with Common Assault in Portlaoise District Court on 5 February 1993 and was convicted. He was sentenced to six months in jail, which was subsumed into his sentence. But he was still being held in Cork Prison.

Ó Siodhacháin soon realised that his best intentions were being lost on Gilligan. Having succeeded in getting taken out of solitary confinement, Gilligan pulled a stunt.

'We prepared the legal papers for him and he got a further adjournment. Our mistake was to include a judicial review. When he saw how it was done, he photocopied the papers and started passing them around to other cronies and they all went applying for judicial reviews and he was put back in solitary confinement.'

In typical fashion, Geraldine approached them again begging for help, prompting Ó Siodhacháin to take action again. 'On the information she gave me, I went before a judge in the High Court and was granted a Habeas Corpus application. I gave notice to the Governor of Cork Prison to bring him before a court within 24 hours.'

In spite of his efforts, Gilligan would not listen to their advice – in short Ó Siodhacháin believed he was a liar and would cut a deal behind their backs, or anyone else's for that matter. 'In our experience of dealing with criminals they would sell out their own mother, so I asked Geraldine out straight, would he deal straight and would she deal straight? She said she would, but that he would cut a deal. So once I knew he would do this I pulled away.'

Ó Siodhacháin would later get the occasional call from Geraldine to say thanks. 'My recollection of Geraldine at that time and afterwards was that she was fed up with criminality and the situation. This was going to be the last time she stood by him and that she was going out on her own. They were separating, that was it,' he recounted. 'That's what she said from day one to me. That she wanted to get on with her life and develop this place in Kildare to do a bit of a riding school, bring people out from the city. I think she believed she could make a go of it financially. I had no reason to disbelieve her. She displayed none of the trappings of wealth. We were doing this on a voluntary basis, we had no reason to disbelieve them.'

Gilligan was eventually returned to Portlaoise Prison. He had lodged an appeal against the assault conviction by sending a letter written in his own illegible handwriting but later withdrew it. He settled back in prison life, even managing to get temporary release in the run up to his release date. He was released from Portlaoise Prison on 15 November 1993, having served just three years of a four-year sentence.

He emerged a professional criminal with a master plan and the determination to carry it out. Whatever crimes he had committed in the past were about to pale into insignificance. He learned a great deal in Portlaoise. He learned much from his fellow inmates. He learned the essentials of crime: how to run an efficient criminal organisation using a cell-structured system, how to intimidate – and most importantly of all he had the bones of a new gang, a young and improved version of the Warehouse gang. Its members adored him, regarded him as a father figure and could be trusted. But most importantly of all, most staggeringly, they looked upon him as the boss. He didn't have to soften his tone around them; they were willing to follow his instructions without question.

In criminal terms, Gilligan was now light years ahead of his contemporaries and was about to show society just how far he'd travelled. Perhaps the best indication of this could be seen on the video made of the soccer tournament played in 1991 that featured Gilligan's narration. It later became somewhat of a tradition for inmates to receive a duplicate video on their release as a keepsake. The prisoners who edited it could have been successful in many occupations but not as video editors. They overdubbed the soccer matches with music and in naming the players gave them nicknames like Dessie 'The Fox' – unsuitable names for undesirable characters. Only one was appropriate because of its foreboding nature. They called Gilligan Mr Big.

CHAPTER 6

A Whirlwind of Crime

'No one even knew it was happening.'
DETECTIVE SPEAKING ABOUT THE METEORIC RISE OF GILLIGAN'S GANG

Having spent over three years in jail, Gilligan wasted no time getting back into crime, creating the illusion that he was still someone to be reckoned with. The truth, however, was far removed from what he had people believe. He was cash starved. He no longer had surplus funds, hidden stashes of hard cash or stolen property to sell. Not since his childhood had he been so vulnerable. With no money and a lengthy criminal record under his belt, his future looked bleak. He was poor, his family was poor and they had no future.

The Warehouse gang was now a defunct gang of ex-convicts, incapable of carrying out the spectacular heists of previous years. The fearsome reputation afforded to Gilligan in the '80s was all but a distant memory. Crime had changed. Companies took security seriously. They installed systems that were not easily bypassed. Drugs, contraband, computer chips and arms, not stolen washing machines and tools, were the new currencies of the black market. A new generation of hoodlum had arrived and they did not yield to the threat of violence, they readily embraced it. Armed confrontation was their first resort.

Nevertheless Gilligan was clear-sighted about his situation. He wanted back into crime. He knew drug trafficking was the gateway to certain riches and he wanted his slice of the burgeoning market. Listening to Hippo and Meehan and their tales of wealth that narcotics could provide had convinced him of that. But he had two obstacles: lack of cash and muscle, and a partner.

John Traynor was one of Dublin's most celebrated criminals. Gilligan had known Traynor since his youth when the latter worked for Irish Shipping, later getting involved in the Seaman's Union whilst Gilligan was at sea. Traynor, in Gilligan's view, was a militant criminal and had the trophies to prove it. For a start he was wealthy. He was also a man who could be relied upon because of his impeccable criminal credentials. The Coach, as he was sometimes called, had been in trouble with the law all his life. He was first charged for housebreaking at nine years of age and he went on to amass over a dozen convictions ranging from housebreaking to possession of firearms and ammunition in the following years. He was a portly looking, big man who had many mistresses on the go whilst maintaining a wife and family. He could mix with anyone from the petty thief to the banking executive. With his middle-class accent, large frame and casual appearance, he could carry off elaborate deceptions. Duplicity was an art form at which he excelled.

His most glorious moment as far as Gilligan was concerned had come years before when he relieved the Revenue Commissions of close to £1 million. Traynor recruited an insider who stole confidential lists containing the names and addresses of people due to receive tax rebates. His magic trick was to simply change the address of the payee to the address of his laundry on Aungier Street. No sooner would the cheque arrive than it would be endorsed and cashed at another location – a pub, shop or bank. When the Gardaí finally caught up with him he responded by issuing threats.

Detective Garda Dominic Hearns, who investigated the crime, named him as being the brains behind the scam in a subsequent court case. 'Traynor is a major fraud criminal known to travel the world and is away at present,' he said. That he was named in court was bad enough but when his name appeared in the following morning's newspapers, Traynor's impulsive nature prompted him to call Hearns directly and issue threats. He was in hospital at the time and made the call from his bed, specifying that he would kill the policeman if he should ever mention his name again.

Gilligan approved of such recourse. He saw in Traynor viciousness coupled with respectability. Of course, what Gilligan could not see was his dual personae – that of the informer, a criminal willing to negotiate his way out of anything. This was the secret side to Traynor. In 1992, he was asked by Scotland Yard and the Gardaí to 'assist' with their inquiries into the theft of art from Russborough House in Wicklow. Martin Cahill, the criminal forever known as The General, had stolen the paintings.

The Coach was just two years into a seven-year sentence imposed for handling when he was mysteriously granted a weekend pass from prison. Once released, he quickly made his way to Dublin. The Gardaí soon started locating the stolen paintings. Traynor was also instrumental in securing the safe return of some 145 files stolen from the offices of the Director of Public Prosecutions, files of a highly sensitive nature that Cahill had also stolen. These were 'found' in a disused launderette in Arbour Hill in Dublin.

All this was lost on Gilligan, although he was certainly aware of Traynor's more than unusual sexual habits. The Coach engaged in several relationships with prostitutes behind his wife's back. The affairs were not simply of a sexual nature; they were perverse. His girlfriends worked brothels where they offered a variety of sexual services to clients, whom Traynor secretly filmed. He told friends the films were for blackmail purposes, but anyone familiar with his private life knew they were for his own gratification. 'He always had prostitutes around him. I don't think he was gay, but I think he got blowjobs from fellas in prison,' Gilligan would later remark.

Traynor could always be relied upon to seize an opportunity and embraced Gilligan's idea with open arms. With Traynor in position, the gangster's next move was to ingratiate himself with Dublin's criminal hierarchy, some of whom were unaware that he was a free man. He was also looking for work, any means of raising cash.

His first port of call was to The General, the undisputed No. 1 gangster in Ireland. The two men knew each other of old, having taken part together in several robberies. They were first introduced by George Royal about three months after Cahill heisted the O'Connor's jewellery factory in Harold's Cross in July 1983, a crime that netted him £2 million. Cahill and Gilligan, helped by one of the latter's Ballyfermot neighbours, George Mitchell, hijacked the ADC cigarette factory in Johnstown, County Kildare. They got away with £100,000 worth of cigarettes, which Gilligan fenced.

'Cahill didn't trust Gilligan because he was always shouting his mouth off, giving orders, telling people what to do. He was an arrogant little bastard. But Cahill knew he had the contacts to sell anything and that's why he worked with him,' said Royal, who participated in the ADC heist.

Gilligan had watched from his cell in Portlaoise Cahill's reputation reach staggering heights; Cahill fascinated the press and public. Newspapers devoted pages upon pages to the elusive criminal declaring him unstoppable, a cunning genius who not only outwitted the law but taunted it. The General was the ultimate anti-hero.

The truth, which Gilligan and everyone else who worked with Cahill knew, was far different. Cahill was a fat, balding diabetic. He had been caught carrying out an armed robbery early in his career but escaped incarceration through a legal technicality. The truth was that he should have been in jail when he committed the catalogue of crimes he later became famous for. Yet he was a dangerous adversary. Anyone who got in the way was shot or threatened. Dr Jim Donovan, the head of the Government's Forensic Laboratory, was the subject of two assassination attempts. His first escape happened in December 1981 when a bomb planted under his car failed to detonate. Weeks later, in January 1982, he wasn't so lucky. His left leg was completely blown off when his car fireballed, blown up by a booby trap. 'He did it to impress other criminals,' believes Donovan. 'It would have been like another feather in his cap. It's only when misfortune, pain and suffering come to your door that you know his reality.'

Always mindful of a bullet with his name written on it, Cahill told Gilligan he was planning on an early retirement. He still had in his possession parts of the Beit art collection and asked whether Gilligan would like to fence the paintings. With his scruffy dress code, hard accent and small stature, Gilligan made an unlikely art dealer. The General himself had failed on numerous occasions to sell the collection and in his endeavours to get a monetary return from the theft he was nearly arrested in undercover police operations mounted by the Gardaí in conjunction with Scotland Yard. Before his incarceration, Gilligan had shown himself to be able to sell anything, so why not paintings? Gilligan accepted the offer.

But Cahill also had hard cash at his disposal and offered to loan Gilligan any amount to set himself up in the drugs distribution business. The General accepted Traynor as a guarantor. Gilligan asked for £600,000. Cahill said he'd be in touch.

A stroke of good fortune then came his way when one of Traynor's contacts acquired hundreds of stolen bank drafts and cheques, worth hard cash to anyone who could launder them. Just weeks out of prison, Gilligan was strapped for cash and offered to rub the drafts through a friend from Tallaght, John Bolger. Bolger was a fool of a man. He was greedy, asinine and incapable of bettering himself; in short, he wanted to get rich quick through crime. He was 31 years old and married with three children. He had not accomplished much else. He had several convictions, mainly for petty crime, but saw himself as a serious player in the underworld. He knew Cahill and this was his only claim to fame.

When Gilligan asked him to launder or sell the consignment of stolen bank drafts, he could smell the money. Gilligan knew Bolger of old and made him an irresistible offer. The bank drafts made an ideal commodity for fraud. All you have to do is either lodge them in an account or cash them. Gilligan wanted Bolger to find a buyer for the drafts or to set up a deal whereby another firm would get the drafts cashed. They would then return a percentage of the proceeds to Bolger who would pass it on to Gilligan. The trick was to convince people with legitimate bank accounts to lodge the drafts. Bolger accepted the deal and approached the Provisional IRA leadership in Tallaght offering the blank drafts.

'He arrived up to the house with copies of these drafts offering them to us. He wanted us to either buy them for a fee or launder them and give him a cut of the money,' recalled one IRA figure. 'I was looking at the drafts, then Bolger mentioned Gilligan's name. We told him to fuck off. There were suspicions that Gilligan was an informer. We weren't getting involved.'

Drafts in hand, Bolger went to the Irish National Liberation Army (INLA). He approached the organisation's commander in Dublin. This man knew as much about left-wing politics as Gilligan did. He was a bully and under his control, the INLA became nothing more than a criminal outfit available for hire. It was a perfect match. Bolger and the INLA cut a deal whereby all three parties would get a third of the profits.

All the paramilitaries had to do was recruit locals to lodge the drafts in their bank accounts and withdraw the cash. The deal was sweet for everybody concerned. Gilligan took a back seat, content to allow Bolger to front the operation. Because bank drafts are effectively cash, once they were lodged the account owner could draw money from his credited account without having to wait for the draft to be cleared. Bouncing or kiting drafts was all about sleight of hand. The immersion stage where the draft is passed over is vital. If the person passing the draft looks penniless or nervous, the conspiracy comes unstuck.

The fraudsters also had to convince those lodging the drafts that they would inevitably be arrested because their identities would be exposed. Gilligan prepared for this, telling Bolger to instruct the people lodging the drafts to have a cover story when cautioned by the police. Under no circumstances was his name to be mentioned; he was paranoid about being implicated for fear of ending up in Portlaoise. Then again, the INLA felt confident that no one would betray them for fear of reprisal. And they were right – no one did.

The drafts were put through a cycle of transactions to obscure where they came from. No sooner would one of Gilligan's stolen drafts be lodged than it would be endorsed and cashed at another location. By the time the bank discovered the draft was fraudulent, the identity of the people who lodged it was obscured or they would have prepared a cover story for investigating police officers.

The scam got under way with Gilligan, Bolger and the INLA earning thousands between them. It was the perfect crime. There were no victims – just the banking institutions. Everyone was happy. Everyone was making money. In the following weeks, Gilligan and Traynor got to know the INLA staff. The two criminals were firmly apolitical; they knew nothing of left-wing politics, republicanism or the vicious internal feuds within the Official IRA that had caused the birth of the INLA. Nor were they interested, for that matter.

Gilligan, though, was at least able to converse with the paramilitaries on their own level. He had served his sentence alongside influential republicans, one of whom was Dominic McGlinchey, a man with an unequalled reputation for extreme violence. In his dealings with the INLA, Gilligan also came to understand the concept of a cell-structured organisation and the importance of staying three steps removed from the scene of a crime. All this was irrelevant, though. Only one thing was important as far as Gilligan and Traynor were concerned. It was brutally simple: the INLA were a force to be reckoned with, they would do business and they could be manipulated. This prevailing wisdom would, in time, bring about an unholy alliance with

Gilligan and Traynor becoming de facto commanders of the INLA in Dublin.

The scam brought Bolger prosperity he could only have dreamed of. The INLA were, in theory, involved in an effort to generate cash for their armed struggle north of the border. 'It became the biggest joke. I'd say a fifth of what they made was redirected to Belfast,' remarked one of the team. 'If they got £10,000, they would send a message to GHQ in Belfast and someone would be sent to collect the cash in Drogheda. But Dublin [Brigade] were just spending it on themselves. There were about six of them involved and they were all living it up. They were buying clothes, watches and drugs with the cash. I remember one occasion, where they turned up with a couple of hundred left out of £10,000. There was no discipline in the organisation because McGlinchey had just been shot and no one was in charge. It was a free-for-all. And Gilligan capitalised on it.'

Gilligan trusted Bolger to the degree that he allowed him a free rein. Once he wasn't costing him money or inviting attention from the Gardaí, the boss, as Bolger named him, was blithe. He had more pressing business interests preoccupying his mind – drugs.

There is no doubt that Gilligan thought long and hard before taking his first step into the lucrative world of drug trafficking. Perhaps, for the first time in his life, he was scared of the consequences, particularly fearful of the IRA and the odium that dealing attracts. He had seen people overdose from heroin and children turn themselves into addicts, selling their bodies for their next fix. For all his immorality, Gilligan's mind told him to say no, but his greed urged him to say yes. The lure of easy money for Gilligan was more addictive than heroin. Cahill, as promised, had produced the £600,000 loan allowing Gilligan to enter the big league.

Traynor was at the time already importing small consignments of heroin from Liverpool, later sold through a network of dealers protected by the Tallaght Brigade of the INLA. Gilligan, with an intense craving for power, saw this as small time. If nothing else his instinct told him it would end in failure. The threat of the Gardaí didn't perturb him much; it was the IRA. Should his name be associated with heroin, of all drugs, he would be a target. Traynor, ever the fool, could not see his partner's logic.

Gilligan had other plans. He believed it would be better to change the product from heroin to cannabis or cocaine and start supplying the suppliers. The distinction was important as far as he was concerned. First, the Gardaí rarely went after international traffickers, instead concentrating on jailing local dealers. His second reason was more practical; if Traynor kept importing heroin, he would inevitably cross swords with the IRA. Gilligan stood firm on this point and Traynor conceded. Anyway they had Cahill's money to deal with the serious players.

In this whirlwind of crime, Gilligan went to the young criminals whom he had taken under his wing in Portlaoise. They were now free men. They too found the capital a transformed city, bustling with business, money and new-found prosperity. Youth culture had undergone a transformation; dance culture was no longer an underground trend but the mainstream choice. The idea of a DJ playing to a frenzied crowd of clubbers dancing to the repetitive rhythm of hard house music under a canopy of strobe lights and flashing colours was the celebrated image. The music, which had a tempo slightly faster than the human heartbeat, was the driving force behind this new fashionable trend.

House music had first established itself in the gay clubs of New York where it became synonymous with a new drug called ecstasy. Methylene Dioxy Methamphetamine (MDMA), to give it its proper title, was originally invented for use as slimming pills in 1910 by two German scientists. In the late '70s, pharmaceutical companies started selling it as a slimming tablet. Few used it to lose weight though. Instead, people out partying swallowed it because it made them want to dance. MDMA soon became an essential ingredient for the enjoyment of dance music, in much the same way that LSD became an intrinsic part of the '60s hippie culture. The narcotic swept through Ireland, crossing the social divides, introducing teenagers to the notion of recreational drug use.

It was into this environment that Meehan and Hippo were released. They flung themselves into the subculture, partying five nights a week to make up for lost time. Meehan, more than the others, was enamoured of the scene. For the first few months of his release he lived the high life. Clubbing and cocaine became his routine. Like the ecstasy pills he swallowed, he crossed the social divide and mixed, mingled with and bedded socialites. He supplied cheap cocaine to impressionable young women who, impressed by this new breed of gangster chic, were only too happy to return the favour between the sheets. 'We're talking about dozens of women here,' one of his friends later remarked.

During his early nocturnal outings, Meeham met Peter Mitchell, a clumsy, overweight pusher from Summer Hill, who was capitalising on the burgeoning dance economy. Ecstasy was earning him serious cash, far more business than he could handle. In the false belief that he could open a distribution ring in Crumlin through Meehan, he got him involved in the dealing, asking his advice and taking him into his confidence. Meehan, however, soon took control. Within months, he was flagged by Garda intelligence as one of the biggest dealers in the city.

Gilligan realised the drugs business operated through the people involved; the most prolific dealers, he realised, were the ones who always showed themselves adept at finding people they needed. When he met Meehan, he outlined his future plan and enquired if he would be willing to sell hashish. He trusted Meehan. First, he had proved himself, having served time in Portlaoise. That he was already dealing was an unexpected bonus. Gilligan could place himself at arm's length from the product while reaping the rewards. Meehan readily agreed. All that was left for him to do was find a supplier.

Gilligan turned to Amsterdam. The city has a long history of broad-minded liberalism and toleration. Coffee shops serve cannabis, although many do not even sell alcohol. Prostitution is legal. But Holland's liberalism has been worn thin by violation. The city of Amsterdam has through time become a Mecca for organised crime, a city where illicitness flourishes. Its location makes it a strategic point for smuggling to any part of Europe. That Rotterdam is the largest entrepôt in Europe with thousands of freight containers arriving each day makes trafficking narcotics easier than in most ports.

In his life, Gilligan showed himself prone to proverbial good fortune. And it was a stroke of good luck that paved his way to the suppliers in the Dam. While he was endeavouring to get an introduction to a supplier, one of his associates in Dublin was arrested with a small consignment of hashish. Once he was charged, the associate thought it prudent to disengage from the drugs business, at least for the time being. But he offered to introduce Gilligan to his supplier.

His name was Simon Rahman. He was born in the Paramaribo

district to Moroccan immigrants and therefore spoke English with a slightly Arabic accent. Trafficking in arms and hashish had provided him with a lifestyle that allowed him to climb the social ladder, buying an expensive house in the district of Meedervoot in The Hague. Though Gilligan didn't know it at the time, Rahman represented the interests of a pan-European organisation that smuggled cannabis and guns from suppliers in Morocco and Tunisia via an assortment of routes into Europe. Several criminals, who like Gilligan bore the status of wealthy businessman, controlled the organisation, which had representatives in Denmark, Belgium, Spain, Holland and England.

A 32-year old Dane who lived on Palmones Algeciras, a fashionable road in Madrid, held authority over the others. He dealt in cannabis by the tonnage. Naturally he was a wealthy man whose lifestyle was opulent. He owned all the toys – a BMW convertible and a yacht and, of course, was married to a beautiful Spanish woman. The cartel had a man in Copenhagen. Another man, a robust 44-year old from the tax haven island of Curacao, was the link in Belgium. He lived between two addresses to avoid surveillance. If he suspected the Belgium police were watching him, he left his home in a small town on the Dutch–Belgium border and drove across the border into the Netherlands where he owned a modest apartment in the Heerlen district.

The Dane, though, was the boss. He sourced hashish from wherever he could. He bought from North Africans living on the Costa del Sol and if they could not meet the demand, he would fly to Agadir in Morocco and buy directly from producers who farmed cannabis plants in remote villages in the mountains. If he could not bribe a trawler captain to smuggle the load across the Mediterranean, he would send it to the Gambia, where it would be concealed inside shipments of rice and smuggled directly to Rotterdam or Antwerp. The associate arranged a meeting. Gilligan flew at once to Amsterdam. Rahman was more than willing to supply and the two struck a deal that would see Gilligan buying up to 100 kilos of cannabis every second week at £1,200 a kilo. Rahman could package the cannabis whatever way he liked. He could also provide whatever documentation and invoices were required, but passage to Ireland was his client's problem.

After he returned to Dublin, Gilligan set about finding a

competent way of smuggling drugs into Dublin. Transporting hashish in articulated lorry containers, he believed, was a precarious method of smuggling. The chances of shipments being intercepted was high, given that any truck en route to Ireland would have to pass through Britain or France before clearing the Irish port authorities, thus doubling the risk.

Around the same time, he was given a chance introduction to a transport manager living in Cork. John Dunne was a 38-year-old married father of three from Middleton in County Cork. Dunne worked for a reputable freight company called Sea Bridge. He first crossed paths with Gilligan in the Silver Granite Pub in Palmerstown. Dunne was drinking with Denis 'Danny' Meredith when Gilligan walked in.

The stocky little man made an impression on Dunne. They chatted and had a drink. Before he left, Gilligan asked for his telephone number. A few weeks later, in early November, Dunne was working in the Sea Bridge offices when his mobile telephone rang. It was Gilligan. He asked if he they could meet. Dunne, out of politeness, agreed and asked him when and where. 'I'm sitting outside your office,' said Gilligan.

Dunne looked out the office window. There he saw Gilligan sitting with a portly man in a green Nissan Primera. It was Traynor. Dunne walked out and sat in the car. Gilligan wasted no time and came straight to the point. 'He asked about importing goods from the UK and Holland. Sea Bridge did not ship goods ourselves from Amsterdam, so I gave him the name of three agents in Holland,' he later recalled.

The gangster, speaking with authority, put the following proposal to him. If he agreed to transport boxes of 'cigarettes' from Holland and deliver them to Dublin, he would be paid handsomely – £1,000 hard cash for each consignment. Dunne readily agreed and explained that he would have to pay groupage fees of £300–£400 out of the cash but was more than happy. He would make £600 profit on the consignment.

CHAPTER 7

Easy Money

'You think I'm big, he's fucking huge.'
JOHN TRAYNOR TALKING TO VERONICA GUERIN ABOUT GILLIGAN

The first shipment of cannabis arrived in April 1994. It was 75 kilos of top-grade cannabis resin. Rahman had carefully packed the drugs into two wooden boxes, which he delivered to one of the freight companies Dunne had advised the gangsters to deal with. Gilligan relayed the time of arrival to Dunne who drove down to the docks in his Hiace van and collected the crates. From here he drove straight to the Ambassador Hotel in Kildare town. When he was 30 minutes away from the rendezvous point, he called Gilligan. 'I never gave it a thought, it was pure greed,' Dunne would later say.

When he arrived, Gilligan and Traynor were waiting, parked on a slip road. Another car was parked nearby; Charlie Bowden, one of Mitchell's runners, drove it. Meehan had ordered him to collect the drugs. Gilligan and Traynor had no intentions of handling the load themselves. Gilligan drove into the hotel car park and as his car passed Dunne's van, he rolled down the window and said Bowden would make the collection. Gilligan's car, which was chauffeured by one of his runners, drove out as Bowden drove in. 'John Dunne is up there waiting for you.' He said nothing else. Bowden pulled up alongside Dunne's van and helped him unload the crates.

The conspiracy ran smoothly without any hitch. Bowden drove back to Dublin in less than an hour. He wasn't stopped by any Garda. Meehan had taken the necessary precautions to make sure he didn't arouse any suspicions. 'They bought a car for me. I registered it in a bogus name because I was banned for drunken driving,' he said.

Even if his car had been seen by a police patrol it would have meant nothing. Bowden delivered the drugs to a warehouse at

Emmett Road in Inchicore, which he rented out in a bogus name. The two boxes were made out of plywood and were rectangular in shape with metal stripping around the edges. 'Inside there would be strips of styrofoam around the sides and on top. The cannabis was packed in 9oz bars sealed in plastic wrapping,' said Bowden. Rahman sprayed the bottom of the crates with hardening foam, which prevented the valuable contents from being damaged. The foam also concealed the smell should the crates be checked by sniffer dogs. There were about 20 bars of hash in all.

And so Gilligan's career as a drug trafficker *par excellence* began. For the first time since his release from prison, he was operating in the premier league working between the INLA, Traynor and Meehan's gang. It was an unholy alliance held together by the lure of cash. It was the perfect crime. He bought the cannabis at a reasonable price – £1,200 a kilo. He sold it for £2,000. Meehan in turn sold it for £2,300 to £2,400. At no time was Gilligan at risk of arrest because he never even saw the drugs.

In the meantime, the bank draft scam was running – but not as planned. Bolger had got involved with the INLA way out of his league. He was telling people that he was a tough guy, he felt capable of taking anyone on. He couldn't see the INLA gang were mere criminals masquerading as militant republicans.

Gilligan was acutely aware of this danger but Bolger seemed oblivious to the threat. If he handed out business cards they would have read John Bolger, financial consultant to the INLA. He invited INLA fugitives to stay in his home, drank beer in pubs with them and socialised with them as if he'd known them for years. 'Bolger thought he was running the INLA. He was telling us what to do, who was boss. He was a fucking eejit. Gilligan kept out of it. All he wanted was the money, he was happy to allow Bolger to do the dirty work,' said one of the INLA gang.

Whether he knew it or not, Bolger was dealing with highly dangerous men. While Gilligan had an uncanny talent for knowing how far he could push people, Bolger did not possess such skills. His biggest mistake was his failure to realise that he was not an essential player in the fraud. Gilligan was the source of the drafts, the INLA laundered them; Bolger was just a middleman. He was disposable.

Perhaps he should have taken a leaf out of Gilligan's book – he didn't. But Bolger actually came to rely on the INLA for protection, albeit because he was trying to protect a young girl. The girl, a 14-year-old, had been raped by her own father, one of Martin Cahill's right-hand men. Bolger had offered to protect her after she agreed to testify against her father, much to the protestations of Cahill. Bolger came under serious pressure from Cahill for allowing what The General described as a 'tout' to live under his protection.

Cahill's refusal to stop threatening the rape victim resulted in a stand-off between Cahill and Bolger, with the latter calling on the INLA to provide protection. Gilligan took Bolger's side.

The atmosphere caused by the dispute raised the temperature around Bolger considerably. This rubbed off on Gilligan who believed the INLA would fight his battles. He too came to threaten adversaries without thinking twice. He knew that if anyone was to take him on, he had the manpower and weapons to have his enemy dispatched. In this respect, power went straight to Gilligan's head. He became a megalomaniac, threatening people who crossed him for the slightest reasons. Bolger developed a similar attitude. 'They were running the INLA in Dublin. It was unreal. Here were Gilligan and Bolger telling us what to do. And [names INLA officer commanding] was telling us to do what they said,' recalled a source.

Besides taking the INLA for granted, Gilligan correctly saw his conspirators as being less clever than him, but what he failed to realise was their volatility. The INLA chief's continuing support for Gilligan, who was putting thousands of pounds his way, provoked jealousy. Characteristically for the maverick republicans, one side said enough was enough and Bolger lost his life.

At 2 a.m. on 22 July 1994, Bolger was shot at point-blank range with a military assault rifle outside the Glimmerman pub on Dublin's Clanbrassil Street. Bolger had tried to swindle two INLA activists out of cash earned from the fraud. The police believe the INLA set out to rough Bolger up but went too far and shot him dead. The row had been brewing for some time. Bolger's widow, Jean, later recalled: 'Before his death, John was receiving death threats and warnings from people whom he met on the street. There were so many threats made against John that we both started to take them for granted. In some ways they didn't frighten us because we got used to them.'

Detectives from Kevin Street Garda Station arrested four men after the murder. They were interrogated at length but all were released without charge. The man who pulled the trigger vanished without trace. Gilligan was enraged at Bolger's murder. Geraldine and Bolger's widow were close friends and he felt responsible. He went straight to the INLA demanding action. Three young children had been left without a father.

Bobby Tohill was one of the INLA team present when Bolger was shot. In compliance with Gilligan's demand, the INLA chief set up a kangaroo court and decided that Tohill should be disciplined for using INLA weapons without permission. Tohill was born in England but grew up in Belfast where he was a member of the Provisional IRA, INLA and the Irish People's Liberation Army. He had been convicted for terrorist offences in the Diplock court system but these were overturned. He moved to Crumlin on his release from prison where he resumed involvement in the INLA. The INLA command in Dublin sent word to Tohill that he was going to be court-martialled.

The car park of the Kiltalwn shopping centre in Jobstown, Tallaght, would be the venue for punishment: 12.30 a.m. on 16 August the time and date. Tohill went for a drink with his cohorts who told him he wouldn't be too seriously injured. He then left the pub and sat on a wall outside a nearby Chinese takeaway where he was approached by two men, one of whom shot him, once above the left knee and twice below the right. He survived the attack. Satisfied justice had been done, Gilligan put Bolger's death to the back of his mind.

By this stage, the deliveries of cannabis were arriving on average three times weekly, in wooden crates marked as machinery parts. Mindful of how useful the INLA could be, Gilligan had also started importing military weapons. It wasn't sawn-off shotguns or small hand pistols he was dealing with, but Ingram sub-machine guns, assault rifles and an arsenal of military firearms. Some of these were donated to the paramilitary group. This served a number of purposes.

North of the border the INLA was well equipped, but in Dublin, where its membership was fluid and consisted of criminals, such weapons were seen as a godsend. That the INLA's Dublin Brigade could acquire military weapons for free and without risking jail or running the gauntlet of British intelligence, which carefully monitored the sale and supply of arms in Europe, bolstered the unit's standing in the organisation. Gilligan was a dream come true for the INLA renegades, a valuable asset that had to be pleased at all costs. Although he had been released from Portlaoise for just seven months, he had put together a fraternity that worked along the same lines as a criminal cartel.

Cleverly, he coerced the INLA into a position where they worked for him, not with him. As for Meehan and Mitchell, they too pledged their support to Gilligan. Pulling these two potent forces together, Gilligan decided to see just how far he could go.

When Martin Cahill threatened Bolger for his decision to protect the incest victim, it enraged Gilligan. In threatening Bolger, Cahill, with malice aforethought, sent out a clear warning to Gilligan's firm. Gilligan would later comment: 'He was a criminal who attacked an incest victim, a girl who was raped by her father. That's all there is to him. Enough said. He was just a scumbag.' Pure jealousy was also a cause of animosity. Soon after Bolger's death, Gilligan let it be known through the appropriate channels that he did not like Cahill. In response, Cahill said he wanted his £600,000 back.

Traynor decided not to get involved, instead opting to stand on the sidelines. He knew what Cahill was capable of and was sure he wouldn't accept Gilligan's defiance, believing it was only a matter of time before The General retaliated. The truth was that Gilligan was earning such vast amounts of cash that it went straight to his head. He became intolerant of anyone who didn't agree with him – in other words, anyone who told him the truth. He was a man who couldn't read or write properly but suddenly found himself with money beyond his dreams. His ego inflated in tandem with a festering hatred of Cahill until he decided to eliminate The General, a plan which fitted in perfectly with those of the INLA, who were also in a running dispute with Cahill.

The General had crossed swords with a member of the Dublin Brigade of the INLA over the tenancy agreement of a flat in the south inner city. A relative of Cahill's had squatted in the flat for a year when Dublin Corporation served an eviction notice through the Sheriff. Cahill petrol-bombed the flat to stop another tenant moving in. He didn't know the new tenant had links to the INLA. Corrupt to the core, the commanding INLA officer of Dublin sanctioned Cahill's killing. And so Gilligan and maverick republicans entered into a bloody deal to see The General dead. There is some evidence that

Gilligan paid a gunman £25,000 to assassinate Cahill but if he did, it was money squandered because the IRA beat them to it.

The IRA command in Dublin was literally gunning for Cahill. The General had made the fatal mistake of doing business with the Ulster Volunteer Force (UVF), albeit through Gilligan. But what brought the matter to a head was the UVF attack on the Widow Scallon's pub in Dublin's Pearse Street, where on the night of Saturday, 21 May 1994, Sinn Féin were holding a fund-raising event.

Martin Doherty, known to his friends as Docho, was standing guard on the door watching the unmarked Garda patrol cars driving by. The 35-year-old father of two from Ballymun was an experienced IRA man, having been involved in weapons smuggling and intelligence gathering for many years. Shortly before 11 p.m., as the function was drawing to a close, two men approached him at the door. They were loyalists from the UVF. One was armed with a handgun, the other was carrying an 18lb bomb in a sports bag. Doherty didn't know them and refused to let them in. One of the bombers produced his gun and shot Doherty at point-blank range, killing him dead. There were 300 people attending the fund-raiser.

Another doorman, who was not a member of Sinn Féin, seeing the events unfold, pulled the door shut and was shot through the door. The bombers panicked and threw the bomb into the hallway, causing it to be made safe. It would have blown up the entire building if it had gone off. Their getaway car was found burned out 15 minutes later in the North Strand, which is an IRA stronghold.

The UVF attack threw the Dublin Brigade of the IRA into disarray. 'The loyalists had not attacked Dublin in over 20 years. It terrified the Provos that the UVF felt comfortable enough to travel to Dublin. It was no secret that the UVF and UDA were doing business with criminals in Dublin, but no one thought this would ever happen,' said one IRA source. IRA intelligence officers were dispatched across the city to make inquiries into what members of Dublin's underworld were doing business with loyalists. One man's name kept popping up. He stood accused of assisting the loyalists, helping them dispose of their getaway car. His name was Martin Cahill. When approached by the IRA Cahill told them politely to fuck off.

'We grabbed one of his gang, who told us Cahill drank in a loyalist pub near Portadown. He was actually called a Fenian bastard in the pub by someone drinking there. We sent in the reports and the order to kill him came back,' recalled one of the IRA squad charged with overseeing his execution. 'Cahill had brought loyalists down to dogfights in Dublin. That's when they first started to reconnoitre Dublin for a bombing.'

Cahill was shot dead by the IRA at 3.20 p.m. on the afternoon of 18 August 1994. Cahill most likely knew he was about to die when he saw the .357 Magnum. His assassin was standing yards away, preparing to fire the revolver at point-blank range. If any thoughts wandered through Cahill's mind in the last few seconds of his life, they were probably of surprise. He would not have expected death to visit him in such a fashion.

His assassin had made several attempts on his life in the previous weeks. He had followed Cahill everywhere, logged his every move, but The General proved an elusive quarry. He was saved from certain death several times when chance encounters with Gardaí forced his killers to shy away. They would later remark: 'It was as if God was watching over him, as if there was a shield around him.'

An IRA squad comprising five people carried out the hit. 'You have no idea how many times we tried to kill him. We must have went for him about six times but something always happened. I remember a Garda appeared out of nowhere as he was about to be executed. I don't like using the word murdered,' said one.

His 'executioner' struck as he pulled up to a traffic intersection that lies between the Oxford and Charlestown Road in the leafy suburb of Ranelagh. It was far from a meticulously planned assassination – the IRA were desperate to murder The General.

His killers were acutely aware that he would be untouchable in two weeks' time when the leadership would declare its first cease-fire. The month of August was their last window of opportunity. On the day of the actual killing, the hitman dressed as a Dublin Corporation worker pretending to count cars as they drove by. Another member of the unit assigned to carry out the shooting drove a motorcycle. Yet another was perched nearby scanning the Garda frequencies with a hand-held scanner whilst another two IRA men waited nearby to drive the killers to safety and dispose of the motorcycle.

The bike rider dressed as a courier and was charged with keeping Cahill's Corporation home on Swan Grove under surveillance. At 3.10 p.m. Cahill emerged from the front doorway of his house and sat in his Black Renault 5. He was heading to a nearby video store to return a copy of the film, *A Bronx Tale*. He paid no attention to the courier who sped off when he stepped outside his door.

When Cahill pulled up, the Corporation worker stopped counting traffic, walked towards his car and fired directly through the front windscreen. The bullets hit their target in the head and shoulder. The first shot knocked The General unconscious, causing him to lose control of his car, which throttled across the road. The gunman was under orders to kill. So having spent weeks following The General, he spent a few more minutes making sure Cahill did not survive. 'That would have been a public relations disaster for the IRA. Even if he had have been left in a wheelchair we would have had to go after him again. Once the order was given,' said one of his killers, 'he had to die.'

The gunman calmly followed Cahill's car as it chugged across the road crashing into a garden wall and fired another three shots into The General. He even put his head in the car window to make sure Cahill was dead before jumping on a getaway motorcycle. The IRA had carried out another professional hit.

That is what police investigating his murder assumed, the radio reports announced over the airwaves and journalists wrote in the morning papers. John Gilligan thought otherwise. In his own mind, he believed his associates had scalped The General, that a paid INLA gunman had shot him dead. In the hours following Cahill's slaying, the INLA, using a recognised code-word, claimed in a telephone call to the 98FM radio station that it had carried out the shooting. Two and a half hours later the IRA, also using a recognised code-word, said one of its volunteers had carried out the shooting using a .357 magnum. The IRA statement said Cahill's activities had included extortion, intimidation, robbery and drug dealing. 'However it was his involvement with and assistance to pro-British death squads which forced us to act. Through their association with the UVF, Cahill's gang have endangered the lives of many more Dublin people. The IRA reserve the right to execute those who finance or otherwise assist loyalist killer gangs.' Then came a third statement to the radio station, this time from the INLA, denying all involvement in the killing and threatening those who had made the first call.

The Garda investigation into The General's slaying went nowhere. The detectives assigned to trace his killers were met with a wall of silence. No one knew anything. The IRA leadership who organised the 'execution' took all the necessary precautions to cover their tracks. They instructed an IRA member from Dun Laoghaire to let it be known that he had assassinated Cahill to throw the police off the scent. This information, as planned, filtered back to Garda headquarters who attributed the crime to the republican in their intelligence files. However, this man had nothing to do with the shooting. He wasn't even in Dublin on the day.

Cahill had proverbially lived by the sword and died by it. At the time of his death, most of his friends were in Portlaoise. When news of his death reached E1, it sent shock waves through the prison. Cahill's brother John was serving a sentence in the prison. Fearful of a reprisal by the inmates, the INLA prisoners asked the IRA for protection. The request was rescinded minutes after the IRA claimed responsibility. John Cahill himself then went to the IRA leadership in the prison. He accused the IRA of doing the State's dirty work. After being told in no uncertain terms that The General's days of bullying and intimidation were over, he left. Later the same day, he sent a message to Brian Kenna to say the prison Mass on Sunday morning would be dedicated to his brother. Few of the criminals went to Mass, so Kenna voiced no objection, telling him that was his own business.

But the proverb that nothing is more wonderful than faith proved true in Portlaoise Prison that week. Before the Mass began, every prisoner from E1 walked into the small church and one by one kneeled down and prayed for the soul of Martin Cahill. The mood was both sombre and tense inside the oratory, the prayers were said not so much out of religious belief, but more in an act of defiance to the IRA.

Gilligan to this day believes his associates killed Cahill. The IRA abducted all but one of Dublin's leading crime figures after they shot The General. Many, like Martin Foley, a trusted lieutenant of Cahill's, were dragged from their homes as they pleaded for mercy. They all confessed. Traynor did, George Mitchell did. 'The rest were beating a path to Sinn Féin headquarters in Parnell Street. There was a queue of them around the corner, promising this, that and the other,' joked one IRA officer.

But the Provisionals missed one key player – Gilligan escaped the round-up. The IRA had arranged to collect him from a house in Crumlin for interrogation purposes. Gilligan had volunteered to go. But on the night in question, fuelled by the belief that he had the INLA standing behind him, he made a number of demands. He told the IRA intelligence officer charged with overseeing his 'arrest' that he wanted assurances he would not be harmed. He also wanted to know when he would be released. He would not consent to a blindfold either.

His demands were phoned through to the Chief of Staff. Gilligan, he said, was to be left alone. They would deal with him later. The next day, Gilligan sent a message to the IRA apologising for his insubordination. 'We were supposed to go back and shoot him. But we didn't, not for any particular reason, but because we were in the middle of peace negotiations and Gilligan was way down the list of priorities. It was as simple as that,' said one of the IRA unit.

Regardless, the series of events as they unfolded left Gilligan in a very powerful position. Cahill was dead and his gang were now running scared from the IRA. Gilligan believed his gang had killed the most notorious gangster to have emerged from the Irish underworld and he'd told the IRA to harass someone else and got away with it. Traynor, an influential figure in the underworld was by his side. He was also rich.

This gave him confidence. Two years after the killing, whilst on the run for Guerin's murder, he remarked that if the IRA stood up in a witness box and said they murdered Cahill, he still wouldn't believe them: 'I know who murdered The General and it wasn't the IRA.'

CHAPTER 8

Invisible Criminals

'He was a fella who suffered from mood swings.'
TONY CODY, CUSTOMS & EXCISE, MANCHESTER, TALKING ABOUT GILLIGAN

Dublin's north inner was Brian Meehan's and Peter Mitchell's stomping ground. It is a hard area, where unemployment is high, heroin addiction among the youth spirals and AIDS is a common ailment. Thousands of people live in dilapidated flat complexes ignored by Ireland's political parties, who turn a blind eye to the social injustices inflicted on the people who live there. For the most part, heroin is the root of its misery. Walk 200 metres in any direction from Buckingham Street, a road that runs through the area, and you will pass a house bought with the proceeds of drug trafficking. Therefore, it is one of the most heavily policed communities in Ireland; not that this ever stopped the pushers. Nevertheless the police stationed there are more conscious of stopping and searching criminals on sight. So when Garda Dave Cherry and his colleague Vincent Marky stumbled upon Meehan driving a green Mitsubishi Colt with Mitchell sitting in the passenger seat on Dorset Street, on the evening of 24 August 1994, six days after Cahill's death, they stopped the car and asked them to step out.

Cherry asked Meehan where he was going, then through the corner of his eye noticed a plastic bag lying on the floor. He asked what was in the bag. Mitchell, a normally confrontational criminal, looked nervous as Meehan said the bag was his, sounding as if he knew how evasive his answer was. Cherry opened the bag. Inside was hard cash – what looked like thousands of pounds wrapped in small bundles. Cherry told Meehan he was seizing the cash under a police property act. Meehan argued he had no right to take the cash and was arrested. He was taken to Fitzgibbon Street station for questioning.

GANGSTER

The Gardaí counted the cash, which came to £46,175 in Irish punts and £120 sterling. In typical fashion, Meehan refused to say anything. Later that evening he was released without charge. Hours later, he returned, only this time accompanied by Gilligan who stood outside the station while Meehan went inside and asked for Cherry. The Garda stepped outside where Gilligan introduced himself as a professional gambler. Meehan, he said, was minding the cash for him, the profits of a day's gambling. As the Garda stood there, Gilligan produced betting dockets to support his story. He haggled with Cherry who believed none of it. He said he would let the courts decide the matter. Gilligan didn't give a damn. This was a temporary setback and there was no cause for anxiety – he would get the money back.

The greatest trick John Gilligan ever played was convincing society he didn't exist. By becoming obsessively secretive, he ensured few outside Dublin's criminal fraternity and the police knew anything of him. Of those who did, most only knew his name. The force's criminal intelligence section knew little about him. Few of Dublin's young gangsters knew what he looked like, where he lived or how he conducted his business. He likened himself to the clandestine gangland figures of old. People knew only what he wanted them to know. His name was spoken in hushed voices by criminals; he was known as a man with no clear sense of what was rational, a man capable of striking out without thinking; a psychopath. Under this cloak of anonymity, he had immersed himself in the drugs trade, importing cannabis in bulk.

The business was good to him, earning him hundreds of thousands of pounds. It was also good to Meehan and Mitchell who sold his product with the competency of shrewd businessmen. Slowly they started supplying the suppliers, effectively becoming wholesalers to the dealers. Other criminal organisations couldn't match their prices or reliability. There was never a shortage of product, none was ever seized and Gilligan reaped the rewards. The link between money and crime was absolute for Gilligan though. His life changed beyond his wildest dreams. For a start, he began combing his hair and changed his dress code. Gone were the tracksuits and jeans. He left behind his scruffy appearance and started dressing the part – suits, shirts and sports jackets. That he pretended to be a professional gambler had to be one of his most arrogant oversights.

If there were matters in life that John Gilligan didn't know about, money laundering wasn't one. He understood it was the lifeblood of organised crime. He earned so much cash that he spent money to launder it. Money laundering derives its name from the practice of putting cash earned from crime through a cycle of transactions that obscure its origin. The most important thing is to make sure the owner of the cash remains anonymous. In this case, Gilligan paid a team of young couriers to launder his cash and to keep his name out of the picture. The scam was simple. He would place £100,000 in bets on every horse running in a race. Because one was sure to win, depending on the betting odds, he would make a return of around £80,000. The winnings would be paid out in cheques and could be lodged in an account without the bank feeling obliged to report the lodgement as a suspicious transaction. He wrote off the £20,000 he lost as a business expense. The 'cleaned cash' could then be used to purchase whatever he wished. This was foolproof. 'Sheer genius,' he would say. He targeted reputable bookmaker chains – the Power Leisure Group, Coral Racing, Ladbrokes and Boyles. None of the bookmakers had any idea that Gilligan was using them to launder drugs cash.

The Power Leisure Group was the first chain to be targeted when on 18 June 1994 he sent his minions into the chain's shops. Between this date and 11 April 1995, people working under his instruction placed bets totalling a whopping £1,052,282 inclusive of tax. He won £880,301, showing a loss of £171, 981. This money represented the tip of the iceberg.

Within weeks of Cahill's murder, he started investing in a derelict house on five acres he had purchased in his own name for £7,000 in 1987, although he later joined Geraldine's name to the title. The property was located in Mucklon in County Kildare, miles away from Dublin. He decided to pump as much cash as possible into the cottage. It underwent a complete overhaul. As soon as it became habitable, the Gilligans moved from their Dublin Corporation home in Corduff.

Geraldine had great ambitions. She saw wealth she could only dream off. She lost her flat Dublin accent and started speaking differently, with a defined gravelly voice. She held parties at Jessbrook attended by horse breeders, dealers and society figures from all walks of life. She decorated the family home but with gaudy furniture and items. She installed a minibar in the backroom, similar to the type seen in the BBC sitcom *Only Fools and Horses*. She devoted herself to opening up a riding school on land adjoining the site. This she called the Jessbrook Equestrian Centre, named after a pony the couple owned, Jessie. 'Brook' was added to round off the riding school's name.

Throughout their life together Geraldine had always pushed John to better himself. She now had serious aspirations of climbing the social ladder and ingratiated herself with the hunting fraternity. With ample cash coming in Gilligan started buying up as much land as possible next to the house. In August 1994, he bought 30 acres for £50,000. Geraldine was registered as the owner but she did not register the title in her name.

The couple then purchased 15 more acres, paying £28,000 for a parcel of fields located between Mucklon and the townslands of Mulgeeth. Another eight acres were acquired costing £16,000. He couldn't buy enough land. Anything that came on the market was purchased. He bought a further four acres for £28,000 and finally 21 more acres for £40,000. In all, he would spend £169,000 buying land to graze Geraldine's beloved horses.

He couldn't spend enough cash. When there was no more land left to purchase, he decided to finance the construction of a showjumping centre built to international specifications – the jewel in his crown. Professional architects, designers and building contractors were hired – all oblivious to the true source of his wealth. He would over the next two years spend £1,516,553 on this part of the development. Architectural plans for the house and arena cost £10,000. The renovation of the cottage cost £57,000. Constructing the showjumping centre cost £300,000 for the building alone. Building it cost £107,311. Geraldine wanted Jessbrook designed to international standards so the structure incorporated steelwork that cost £407,000. The arena was also fitted with purpose-made seats. These cost £300,050. Building stables to livery horses cost £66,900. There were other expenses paid with cash from drugs. The windows cost £106,522, dry fitting £25,000, dry filling £20,000, Fiber Sand £21,870, polytrack £30,250 and £18,000 was spent fencing off the land. When Jessbrook was finally completed, the Gilligans bought the freehold address at 13 Corduff Avenue in an up-yours gesture to the State.

John Gilligan was affected in an entirely different way. Riches changed him into a psychopath. He thought he could do anything. He saw himself as an awesome gangster in the underworld, a man to be reckoned with. He surrounded himself with people he believed he could trust and, most importantly, who believed in him.

John Traynor fulfilled this role, telling Gilligan what he wanted to hear. Traynor was of a distinctly different character. He was a hopeless bluffer, a man deeply insecure about himself, his personal life and his criminal career. 'He didn't know whether he was a gangster or a businessman,' said one detective of him. 'He didn't know his place. That's what made him dangerous.'

Traynor was Gilligan's confidant, a man he trusted implicitly. Few criminals could tolerate Gilligan's irrational mood swings and arrogance, but Traynor could. He would listen and agree with everything Gilligan said. He liked the fact that Gilligan confided in him. What Gilligan didn't know, or failed to realise, was that his confidant told his secrets to just about anyone willing to listen and Veronica Guerin was a good listener.

Like all great journalists, Veronica had an insatiable appetite for news. This passion brought her public recognition and shaped the lives of those around her. She was born on 5 July 1958, the second youngest of five children – three girls and two boys. She grew up on Brookwood Avenue in Artane, a solidly middle-class suburb in Dublin where the children spoke with polite accents and left school with the necessary qualifications. Her father, Christopher, was an accountant who ran a practice from a small office on Gardiner Place in Dublin City. She was unlike the other girls, loving football and Manchester United. She loved sports, playing basketball for the local team, the Killester Kittens, and was skilled enough to play women's soccer for the Irish team. Because she grew up in a highly political household, it came as a surprise to no one when she joined Fianna Fáil.

Politics and Charles Haughey were her passions in life. She canvassed for Haughey, knocking on doors, encouraging voters to 'do the right thing' and vote for Charlie. Haughey saw in her a loyal supporter and in 1982 he rewarded her by appointing her to the board of the NIHE College in North Dublin. Two years later, she became the Fianna Fáil secretary of the New Ireland Forum. This was a highly prestigious posting by any standards. She married Graham

Turley, a man she met through the party, a year later in a ceremony attended by political dignitaries from across the political spectrum.

Her entry into journalism was accidental. When she left school, after finishing the Leaving Certificate in 1976, she worked as a secretary in a Credit Union office in Meath Street. She then worked in her father's practice for about a year. At one point, she attempted to make a living running a small catering company but this enterprise failed miserably. Evergreen, a small vegetable shop she opened with Graham in the village of Malahide, was her next foray into business. It shut down three months after opening. Veronica worked in a travel agent's for a while, then suddenly decided to become a journalist in the autumn of 1990.

The *Sunday Business Post* was a relatively young publication at the time and so Veronica decided it should be her first port of call. She literally walked into the office off the street where she was introduced to Aileen O'Toole, the newspaper's deputy editor. 'She had never written an article for a newspaper before but wanted to give journalism a shot. At the time, she was doing research on the aviation sector and filled our heads with facts, figures and concerns about the unstoppable growth of GPA,' O'Toole later wrote.

Veronica was not a particularly skilled writer but was more than capable of getting information that no one wanted disclosed. She started penning articles, at first business articles about the aviation industry, moving on to politics. She contributed to the paper for the next three years, also working with RTE.

Her next employer was the *Sunday Tribune*. It was here that she became, in journalistic terms, a force to be reckoned with. She delved into controversy, seeking out stories that raised eyebrows. She rejoiced in getting the impossible interviews, like that with Jim Livingstone, the head of the Revenue Commissioners Special Investigation Branch, whose wife Grace had been murdered.

She wrote about The General, how he had stolen the Beit art collection, and incisive political stories. But it was her interview with Bishop Eamonn Casey that made her famous, trebling her newspaper's sales. Casey had fathered a child with an American divorcee, Annie Murphy, and fled to Ecuador when his clandestine love affair became public. Veronica, on her own initiative, flew to Ecuador where she found Casey living in a clerical friend's house outside Quito.

'I established more or less the general area where he was. I arrived in Ecuador at six in the morning, and by four that afternoon I had found the house where he was staying. A priest answered the door and I knew immediately that Casey was staying with him. I said, "Look, I don't want to hassle him, I don't want to create any difficulties. If he doesn't want to talk to me, that's fine."

'At half nine that night I was in bed in my hotel and I was knackered, and the priest rang from the lobby and said, "We're downstairs." I walked down and there was Casey. It was incredible. We spoke for five hours but I didn't publish a word. About six weeks later he called me and said he'd give me an interview.'

It ran for three weeks, catapulting Veronica into the public eye. Ireland's biggest selling newspaper, the *Sunday Independent*, headhunted her weeks later. These were to be the happiest days of her life. It was here that she drifted into crime journalism and Dublin's murky underworld, seeking out informants with hard information, the stuff exclusives are made of.

John Gilligan had never attained the anti-hero status that his old adversary Cahill did. Cahill flirted with the media and enjoyed the chase, posing for photographers outside the courts and granting interviews to a select few. His extraordinary sexual activity, taking two sisters as lovers, whetted Veronica's appetite and, in the wake of his murder, she dedicated her energies towards uncovering The General's love life. It was in making these enquiries that she came across Traynor.

At the time, he owned two garages – Church Motors in Rathmines, Dublin, and Naas Auto Stop in Naas, County Kildare. She called him at his Dublin office, presumably after being directed there by a Garda contact. Traynor was interested. Here was one of Ireland's most famous reporters seeking his help. He arranged to meet her in a coffee shop in Montague Lane, between Camden Street and Harcourt Street.

He later recalled that Guerin astonished him by telling him details of a social outing – described by her as an 'escapade' – he had had with a friend of his, who just happened to be a Garda. He told all. He felt important whilst Veronica got her exclusive, three in total – the first appearing in the last week in August and the last two in September in the newspaper's Living and Leisure section.

But one caused more interest than the others. It was called 'The

General's Two Women' and revealed the most intimate and salacious details of Cahill's sex life. Her mistake was to write that she was getting information from someone close to the Cahill family. Traynor became the main suspect. To cover his own tracks, he let it be known among the criminal fraternity that he would have Veronica Guerin seen to. They waited and watched with bated breath.

Veronica lived in a refurbished and extended cottage in Cloughran, a rural townsland in North County Dublin. Her house stands alone on a green site surrounded by high hedges to the front and green fields to the rear. Two rottweilers usually stood guard outside the house but on the night of 7 October 1994 they were asleep, locked in the house.

Graham was in the kitchen whilst Veronica typed away in her office, which lies to the rear of the house. Shortly before 10 p.m. she saved a file on her computer and walked to the kitchen. Minutes later, she heard the sound of a crack, then another. Wondering what the sound was, she walked back into the office and saw a bullet hole in the window. She then noticed a bullet lodged in a shelf above where she had been sitting.

She called Graham. They ran to Cathal's room and called the police. Detective Sergeant Cathal Cryan, a friend of the couple's, was alerted and raced to the house. The gunman, however, had long since gone by the time he arrived. Veronica was shocked but put on a brave face. Cryan inspected the damage, noting the gunman had fired a second shot through the house's gutter, he presumed, in a fit of panic. He considered what had happened. If the gunman had wanted to kill her, he could have.

Veronica's attitude was that the shooting was a warning. She later commented: 'I discussed it with Graham, my husband, because he had said, "Hang on a second, if this is the type of shit that we're going to be faced with . . ." And so we did think about it and it did frighten the life out of me. But I thought, what was the point in giving into them? That's just what they want. Then they'll think that they can just continue doing it to everybody else. So I carried on.'

The problem was Veronica did continue communicating with Traynor, not suspecting him of ordering the shooting. The Garda investigation didn't make any headway but one thing was for sure – it was a response to the Cahill revelations.

It was during the closing months of 1994 that Gilligan made contact with Martinus Maria Cornelis Baltus, a Dutch national from Zoetermeer in the Hague. The introduction came via Rahman who advised Gilligan to invest in a proposed holiday development scheme called Club la Costa. Baltus was seeking investors for the complex under construction in Rosendale, a town that straddles the Dutch–Belgian border. Gilligan saw the investment as a way of laundering cash while at the same time developing new connections in Holland. In the first week of December, he flew to Schipol Airport and made his way to a hotel where he came face to face with Baltus, who was with Rahman. In the bar of the hotel, the three men chatted about the proposed holiday scheme over drinks. Baltus provided Gilligan with the plans, brochures and other material.

Meeting Baltus was a blessing. Gilligan was in the right place at the right time. He was keen on investing cash in Club la Costa. In an effort to stay sharp and befriend his new-found acquaintances, he invited them out. A little while later, when they relaxed a bit more, they got down to real business. Baltus, a man never cut out for crime, became overtly friendly. Gilligan soon got him involved in the business, setting up deals, in particular laundering cash. When he returned to Dublin that weekend, Gilligan had effectively recruited a set of eyes and ears in Amsterdam.

Back home business was booming. Meehan ran the distribution business like a legitimate company. Bowden rented a lock-up premises to the rear of Emmett Road in Inchicore to distribute the drugs. At the request of Meehan, he used a fictitious name, Oliver Bond, to rent the store. From here, Meehan, Mitchell, Bowden and Ward offloaded more slabs of hash per week than other criminal gangs sold in a year. Gilligan found he had simply more money than he could handle. So by the end of 1994 he was forced to start smuggling cash to Europe to deposit in offshore accounts. This inevitably led to problems.

On 11 December 1994, Her Majesty's Customs and Excise (HM C&E) officers at Holyhead ferry terminal in Wales carried out a routine check of all long-haul trucks alighting off the Dublin ferry. One by one, they stopped each truck and questioned the drivers, asking about their business, destinations and cargo.

Customs officer Roger Wilson was on duty that morning. He stopped a Dublin trucker heading to Belgium. Wilson checked his cargo and registration, and had a quick look inside his cab. There he saw gift-wrapped parcels. Wilson, curious to know their contents, asked him to open the presents. When he did, he saw them stuffed with cash: £75,800 in punts and £2,000 sterling in total. Wilson didn't need anyone to tell him the money was hot. He detained the driver, who seemed taken aback, for interview. The driver explained that a friend he named as Denis Meredith had asked him to deliver the parcels to a truckers' café near Dunkirk in Belgium. A man called Martin would rendezvous with him there. That's all he knew.

Wilson notified his senior officer, Dave Winkle, of the find. Tony Cody, an investigator with the money laundering investigations unit of Customs and Excise in Manchester, was alerted. Customs are allowed to hold large amounts of cash found in such circumstances for 48 hours to establish the source. The money was taken from the driver and Customs waited to see who claimed ownership. 'Just 24 hours later,' recalled Cody, 'Gilligan put his head above the parapet and claimed the money was his.'

Gilligan always had nerve and when it came to his money, he had nerves of steel. He was also under pressure to continue dealing with Rahman and Baltus. He travelled to Holyhead the next day and presented himself to Wilson and Winkle, introducing himself as a horse breeder and professional gambler. The money, he said, was for Club la Costa. Customs were highly suspicious of his story. Winkle interviewed him but didn't believe a word out of his mouth. He consulted with Cody who instructed him to seize the cash under the Criminal Justice International Co-operation Act, Section 24, which allowed the seizure of monies believed to be the proceeds of drug trafficking. They went to Holyhead Magistrates Court who granted a detention order allowing Customs to hold the cash for a further six weeks to examine its origins. Gilligan attended the hearing. Cody met him outside the courtroom. 'Physically, he looked a scruffy git,' he remembers. 'He wore an ill-fitting suit, his hair looked like it needed combing, he was a dishevelled looking character.'

Gilligan went mad. In his criminal career he had not lost such an amount of cash and he wasn't about to start now. But more than anything, he feared losing face with the Dutch. He travelled home and contacted Baltus to explain the situation. He would send the cash as soon as possible. His appeal against the seizure of the cash from Meehan by Cherry was coincidentally due for hearing in the

Dublin District Court. When the case came up for hearing, it was adjourned to 22 December. He was furious but had no option but to wait.

The appeal was held in Court 31. Gilligan stood in the witness box and told the court he had entrusted Meehan with the money. 'He is a trusted friend,' he said. He won the case and the cash was returned. He couldn't believe his luck. But he was still one step behind. British Customs still had £75,000 belonging to him. He had tried smooth talking, which hadn't worked; now he reckoned a bit of straight talking might do.

In a moment of drunken impulsiveness, he called Winkle at 10.05 a.m. on New Year's Eve, pressing for the return of his money. He was amicable at first. But when it became clear that he was wasting his time, he resorted to his old tactics of issuing threats. 'I'm having grief. Give me back me money, I haven't caused problems here, with me family now, I can't get on with me business because I don't know where I stand with me money. I don't know how much money I have and I know where I stand, I know how much it would cost me for a barrister, and I know it will cost me to get satisfaction, if I need to get satisfaction,' he growled in gibberish down the phone.

'But I don't want nobody messing me family. I don't mind. If somebody robs my money, I'll have them shot. And I give that to the judge, I told the judge before in the court case if somebody messes my family I'll have them fucking shot. And then I'll go to jail on the consequences of it,' he shouted.

He then referred to Wilson. 'He's messing me about, he's robbing my money, I've accounted for it, I can't do it any more, the bank manager gets the fucking money, he faxed you, I've showed you where I got the money, what's the fucking problem? He's backed me into a corner, we can do all dirty things, it's not a problem for me to get somebody to shoot him, I know people that have been in prison. But I'm not going back down that road, I just want my money back.'

The threat was clear and noted. In the meantime, Cody was trying to gather information to prove Gilligan was a drug trafficker. All he needed was a drugs conviction or even proof that Gilligan associated with known dealers. He ran the Dubliner's name through Sedric, the Customs criminal database. This contained little information. His next port of call was the British National Criminal Intelligence Service (NCIS).

'NCIS referred us to the South East Regional Crime Squad in London. They had seen Gilligan at meetings with criminals in the Brighton area. They had an ongoing operation on these people and Gilligan had came into their operation fleetingly,' said Cody. Gilligan, in fact, had been secretly filmed in a hotel arranging a drugs deal. To confiscate his money, Customs would need to show the footage in court or produce any surveillance photographs taken of Gilligan. But to show this, they would expose the SERCS operation. They asked the rhetorical question. 'We asked whether or not we could use it. SERCS considered and said we'd prefer you not to. Because their operation was ongoing, we respected that. That was it. At the end of the six weeks detention order, we went back again to hold the money and lost.'

In a remarkable stroke of luck, Gilligan had dropped his Brighton suppliers just as the police prepared to make arrests. And in yet another bizarre coincidence, the fact that he had been monitored with them prevented the forfeiture of the seized cash. When the case came up for hearing on 19 January, the magistrates found in Gilligan's favour and ordered Customs to return the cash. Although he wasn't aware of it at the time, Gilligan's criminal career had came close to oblivion. He'd practically been caught but he saw the return of the cash as a reason to celebrate. He believed he'd outwitted the authorities by producing gambling receipts in court. He believed he had devised a fool-proof method of laundering hot cash.

Cody had exhausted every avenue in trying to get evidence. 'It was as simple as that. We couldn't show he had a previous conviction for drug trafficking,' he said. Cody later noted in his reports 'an aggression' in Gilligan's voice.

'He was a fella who suffered from mood swings. One minute he would be buddy-buddy with you. He'd say, "See it from my side" and all this, trying to smooth you over. Then he'd start to become a little bit aggressive and say the loss of this money was hampering his business. I think his manner fluctuated between being reasonable to being downright sort of irate and aggressive. He seemed to suffer from mood swings.'

CHAPTER 9

Drugs, Guns and Money to Burn

'I got a call from the Little Man who I know to
be John Gilligan. He told me that there was
something in the next consignment of hash.'
CHARLES BOWDEN TELLING DETECTIVES ABOUT ARMS IMPORTS

Veronica continued writing about crime, becoming more famous than her infamous subjects. The Cahills, meanwhile, were not on speaking terms with Traynor. Neither were his former comrades – all accused him of being a fool of a man. Not only had he disgraced Cahill's memory but he had spoken to a journalist, tantamount to informing to the police. The word on the street was that she had him wrapped around her finger.

It was no secret that Traynor was telling Veronica a lot more about the underworld than anyone thought. Not content with him giving her information, she started writing about Traynor himself. On 21 January 1995 she penned what can only be described as a deeply flattering article about him. She quoted him as saying: 'I'm the best in the country at fraud, and if I didn't live such an extravagant lifestyle, I'd be a millionaire.' The article didn't refer to Traynor by name; instead she called Traynor 'The Coach'. A lot of what she wrote was nonsense, tittle-tattle gossip that he wished was true. She even went as far as saying that his position in the underworld had grown since Cahill's death.

Traynor was secretly smitten with his new-found notoriety but the criminal fraternity now saw him as a threat. If that's what she was writing, how much did she know? He soon realised he was in serious trouble. He was given the benefit of the doubt on the previous articles, but Cahill's gang saw this as a step too far. Traynor needed to do something drastic to regain his respect. He decided to kill her.

The assassin called to her door at 6.45 p.m. on the evening of 29 January 1995. It was a Monday night. Veronica was speaking to her colleague Lise Hand, a society journalist, on the phone. The two were catching up on each other's lives when she heard a knock at the front door. This was unusual because everyone who knew the family home entered the house by a side entrance. Graham wasn't at home – he was attending the funeral of a former Lord Mayor – and Cathal was staying with his grandmother.

Veronica thought someone had got lost and was looking for directions. She opened the door and was confronted by a man pointing a large pistol at her head. She froze with fear; she could barely make him out. He was wearing a motorcycle helmet with a visor and a blue sports jacket. The gunman had screwed out the bulb over the porch light, making him more menacing to look at. She stepped backwards and he followed. She didn't break her stare but backed into a wall and cowered, putting her hands over her face in an effort to protect her face, pleading with him not to shoot her. She heard his gun discharge and felt a sudden pain in her right leg. With that, the gunman entered the house and ran down the corridor and out the back door.

'The first thing I saw was the gun,' she later said. 'And it looked huge and the light was shining on the thing. I didn't see him, I just saw the gun. The first thing that went through my head was that he meant it. I don't know why but I did it instinctively, I went into the foetal position. As he put the gun to my head, I began to roar – it wasn't a scream. And then I felt it at my thigh. I didn't hear it shoot. And then I heard his footsteps running out. And I just said, "Jesus, I've been shot."'

The hired killer had panicked and shot her in the leg. Why he ran through her house and out the back door is a mystery. But he did, past her guard dogs asleep in the kitchen. Adrenaline pumping, Veronica pulled herself to the phone and dialled 999. She struggled into a room at the back of the house where Graham had installed a bar and sat herself up.

Cryan was again the first to arrive on the scene. He had just finished work for the evening in Coolock Garda Station when he got the call. He walked into the bar and could see that Veronica wasn't that badly injured. They exchanged a few polite courtesies, harsh words spoken among friends, and he told her she'd survive. Within minutes, the area was swamped with armed police and an ambulance rushed Veronica to Beaumont Hospital. News of the shooting was relayed to media organisations who dispatched reporters to the scene.

The last time shots were fired at her house, her neighbour Patrick Buckley was sitting in the front room of his house watching television. When he saw blue flashing lights outside the house he realised something was wrong and went out to investigate.

'We did hear something the last time and it sounded like gun shots because they were so rapid they couldn't be anything else really. But I couldn't see anything when I went out,' he told assembled reporters. 'It was just after 7 p.m. this evening when I saw the ambulance and asked a Garda what had happened. Of course we are very shocked and hope that everything is all right. The way things are going in this country, I'm not surprised at something like this happening,' he said.

Cryan's officers sealed off the area, leaving two uniformed Gardaí standing outside the house. He telephoned Graham, told him what had happened and brought him to the hospital where Veronica was being examined. The bullet had entered her leg just below her right thigh, shaving an artery before lodging just beside the bone. The surgeon used the word 'miraculous' four times in his report on her wounds. It was a miracle that she was not more seriously injured.

After the initial shock, Veronica returned to herself. She welcomed hospital visitors and almost appeared to enjoy the attention. Journalists descended on the ward wanting news. Graham emerged and gave an impromptu press conference. 'Naturally, we're all horrified about what's happened, but I'm glad to say Veronica is very stable and in great form. I'm not a medical man, but as far as I am concerned she's talking away normally and she's fine.'

Her news editor, Willie Kealy, arrived minutes later and spoke to the media. 'We are aware, as we were all aware, that there was another shooting before, and to that extent she was cautious about her personal security,' were the only words he could think to muster. He was fond of Veronica and in shock. He felt it was too early to start talking about how she went about her job, but didn't think she would change her approach. 'She's a very courageous woman.'

The Minister for Justice, Nora Owen, arrived when everyone else was about to leave. 'I went up to her in the hospital without any great fanfare. The media were all in the front hall, I came in the back door and just went in to see her on . . . it was on a personal level. She said: "Well, they're not going to get me. They're not going to stop me." One part of me, as a woman in an occupation that is mainly male-dominated, one half of me said good for you, to have the courage to go on. And I left it at that.'

But that night Veronica spoke to Traynor on the phone. She did not know that he wanted her dead, that she was only alive because of his hired gunman's incompetence. Traynor, ever willing to lie, told her he had heard the news. He mentioned an article she had just published about another Dublin criminal, saying he had ordered the attack. But he hadn't – it was Traynor himself.

The next day, Gardaí searching the fields at the back of her home found a pair of black slip-on shoes stuck in mud. A short distance away, they found the gun – an old reconditioned .45 revolver. The gunman had also abandoned his jacket. Whoever he was he had literally got stuck and kept running, losing the gun in his ensuing panic. Forensic tests carried out on the bullet removed from her thigh showed it was an old piece of ammunition, primed for use. It was a dead lead slug.

Cryan did not need anyone to tell him that Veronica was now in clear danger. He wrote off the first shooting as a warning, but this was the real thing. He focused his inquiries on Traynor. But the truth was that no one knew. The investigation team made routine inquiries, all of which gleaned nothing new. Criminal informants knew nothing.

Veronica in the meantime had been released from Beaumont and put under police protection by Chief Superintendent Jim McHugh of Coolock. But determined not to give in to intimidation, she decided to personally visit each of the major gangland figures she knew. It was not a particularly sensible move but nevertheless she felt compelled to face down her fears.

She was still on crutches at the time.

'When I came out of hospital, I said, "This is it, I'm going to let those bastards see they didn't get to me." I went to them all, just to let them see me and let them know I wasn't intimidated. On the way to see the guy I thought had organised the shooting, I had to get Graham, who was driving the car, to stop twice, because I was physically sick at the thought of seeing him. But I felt I had to do it. I couldn't let them know they had frightened me.'

The next Sunday, she wrote an article for the *Sunday Independent*. 'I have already said, and I will say it again now, that I have no intention of stopping my work. I shall continue as an investigative reporter, the job I believe I do best. My employers have offered me alternatives . . . any area I wish to write about seems to be open to me . . . but somehow I cannot see myself reporting from the fashion catwalks or preparing a gardening column. I do not consider myself a brave woman. In deciding to continue, I am merely doing the same job as any of my journalistic colleagues . . . I am simply doing my job. I am letting the public know exactly how society operates.'

Traynor was arrested and brought to Coolock for questioning three weeks later by Cryan. He said he didn't know anything about the attack and gave an alibi. 'What else would he have done? We expected him to have at least that because we knew he hadn't pulled the trigger,' said the detective.

Veronica had made a mistake meeting Traynor but her errors of judgement continued. Her fatal mistake was her decision to keep in contact with him, not only keeping the lines of communication open, but affording him a degree of trust. She continued to place trust in him even after she learned he had ordered the shooting. They would meet for lunch in Fans Chinese restaurant on Dame Street. Traynor would later recall that she seemed completely fascinated and obsessed by crime and police work. He provided her with information she turned into exclusives.

She believed Traynor to be something he wasn't. He was a gangster but not the significant player she made him out to be. Not any more. There were bigger fish in the pond. It became a quid pro quo agreement. He helped Veronica because she heightened his profile and standing in the underworld. After all, how many criminals were close friends with respected journalists?

The agreement worked well until Traynor started talking about one John Gilligan. 'You think I'm big. He's fucking huge,' he told her. In the coming months he would tell her a great deal about Gilligan. Little did he know she would go straight to him.

By January 1995, Jessbrook was up and running. The secret to Gilligan's success was the way he ran his operation. Everything was run on a need-to-know basis. His gang was structured along the same lines as a paramilitary organisation. Gilligan appointed himself as chief of staff, Meehan and Ward acted as his directors of operations, Traynor his director of intelligence and confidant. He dealt with these one to one. No one else was allowed meet him, nor see his face. Like all good businessmen, he didn't invest all his cash in one single area of crime. The enterprise was divided into three separate units. One smuggled tobacco and contraband cigarettes into Dublin, another smuggled cannabis, a third collected and laundered the cash proceeds.

The burgeoning drugs culture sweeping through Ireland lent itself to the gangster. He simply couldn't import enough cannabis to supply the demand. Meehan recruited 'reputable' criminals involved. Reputable because they had convictions that ensured they were not Garda informants or had proved themselves as true criminals. In other words, they were under constant harassment by the law. Gilligan wanted to front the largest criminal gang in Ireland. But he knew the larger it became, the more vulnerable it was.

He spent most of his time laundering cash before lodging it in offshore accounts in Gibraltar, Morocco, Austria, England and the Netherlands. Baltus helped him in this endeavour. But while laundering his profits he also invested more cash into Jessbrook. On 20 January 1995, he bought a Land Rover Discovery 5-door for £29,500. He registered this to Jessbrook Equestrian Centre. Three weeks later, on 13 February, Geraldine, using her maiden name, bought a Land Rover for £5,290 from the same garage. This was also registered to Jessbrook Equestrian Centre. Gilligan spoiled those around him – especially his children. He paid cash for houses for them. In November 1994, he bought 1 Willsbrook View in Lucan for £73,000 as a present for Tracy. He paid £4,000 in cash for a deposit, followed up by another £3,000 in cash. The balance – £66,000 – was paid by way of bank draft. He didn't bother taking a mortgage on the house. In December 1995, it was Darren's turn. He got a spacious residence at 6 Weston Green, Western Park, in Lucan. They also got their own cars. Darren was fond of jeeps. Gilligan bought him a RAV-4 Toyota. Tracy got a Toyota Carina 1.6 GLI. Gilligan paid for both cars with hard cash.

As proprietor of the Jessbrook Equestrian Centre, he assumed the persona of a businessman. He no longer travelled economy class: instead he became a card-carrying member of Aer Lingus flying first class, mixing with the business elite. His Aer Lingus Gold Card number was 569210. The airline treated him as a VIP passenger and with good reason. He spent £27,091 flying between Dublin and Amsterdam. He flew 39 times on the Dublin to Amsterdam route and 33 times the opposite way and from Heathrow to Dublin four times. His spare change was lodged in 16 accounts held by Geraldine, Tracy and Darren in Dublin. Seven were opened in Geraldine's name, two in her maiden name, four in Darren's name, two in Tracy's and one under the name Jessbrook Equestrian Centre. The amount of money that passed through the accounts was huge by anyone's standards.

Geraldine controlled one of the accounts opened on 9 March 1995 at Bank of Ireland in Lucan. This account was used for the day-to-day running of Jessbrook. The total lodgements into this amounted to £338,484.60. Total payments out of the account were £373,595.15 Another account she opened under the name Matilda Dunne, A/C No. 52791983 at Bank of Ireland in Lucan, was used to carry out business. Lodgements into this totalled £839,689.73, the bulk made up of bookmakers' cheques. She instructed the bank to allow Gilligan to conduct transactions through it. They worked this account by transferring vast sums of cash, £286,939 in total, into the Jessbrook fund. Payments of £165,450 were also made to Gilligan himself while Geraldine withdrew £193,641 in cash over a period. The bulk of the money was lodged into the accounts in cheques made out to Gilligan, bookmakers' cheques. Later it would emerge he had laundered huge sums through bookmakers, who were unaware of Gilligan's nefarious activities.

The first bets were placed on 18 June 1994 when he sent his minions into Powers shops. Between this date and 11 April 1995, Gilligan placed bets totalling a whopping £1,052,282 inclusive of tax. He won £880,301, showing a loss of £171,981 which he wrote off. Between 3 March 1994 and 24 November 1995 he bet £342,650 with Coral Betting Group. He received a sum of £292,577, showing a loss of £50,073. Not only was he laundering dirty cash through some of Ireland's most respected companies but he was also fulfilling his addiction to gambling.

In April 1995 his messengers targeted Ladbrokes placing bets on his behalf. They bet £721,185 till they were barred the following year in April 1996. He received a return of £784,461, for once showing a profit of £63,276. Boyles Bookmakers were also used in the conspiracy. He started laying bets in their shops in August 1995. Gilligan bet exactly £1,444,333 with the chain the following June.

He received a return of £1,234,018. This showed a loss of £210,315. All in all, his total bets with all the bookmaker firms amounted to £5,371,696 inclusive of betting tax at 10 per cent. That left a deficit of £537,472.

The Criminal Justice Act 1994 came into force in May 1995, modifying how financial institutions handled cash transactions over £10,000. Among other things, it placed an onus on financial bodies to report to the Gardaí any transactions deemed to be suspicious. The act introduced by Fianna Fáil also put in place a series of procedures for banks and credit companies to follow if they suspected hot cash was being lodged with their institution. The act presented a huge obstacle to organised crime, particularly criminals like Gilligan. Crime was fast becoming a thorny issue which politicians could not afford to ignore. Politicians like Owen saw themselves facing a crisis in the next election and demanded that the agencies co-ordinate their efforts to tackle drug trafficking in particular. The Minister for Justice, and her ministerial colleague Ruairí Quinn, the Minister for Finance, demanded that all agencies tasked with tackling crime co-operate. 'The lack of co-operation between Customs, between Gardaí, between Social Welfare, between Revenue, was really negating the good work that each of the individuals were doing on their own,' she recalled. 'We set up meetings with Revenue, with Gardaí, with Customs. There had been some unpleasant and unnecessary spats between Customs and the Gardaí. I was very angry about it at the time and I spoke to the commissioner. I said, "This is ridiculous and we've got to solve this."'

Owen was breaking down traditional barriers between the Gardaí and Customs. Following her instructions, Patrick Culligan, the Garda commissioner, appointed Kevin Carty, the chief superintendent in charge of the Central Detective Unit (CDU) and Fachtna Murphy, a superintendent from the fraud squad, to represent the Garda at a discussion group meetings.

Owen had an idea. She wanted the Revenue to take a pro-active stance against crime by auditing criminals for undeclared or inexplicable wealth.

The Criminal Justice Act 1994 was only an enabling piece of legislation and none of the regulations had been written, or even agreed. Even though the legislation is dated 1994, the working bits of the legislation weren't there until Owen introduced new laws which came into effect that May. Even then, as the tedious negotiations dragged out, the law was worthless. The banks needed to train staff in declaring lodgements in what fell into the suspicious categories. In other words, the legislation would be useless until the banks trained their staff, which would take a further six months – a lifetime in politics.

Owen's own political career was coming under pressure. Drug dealing was evident in most towns. In Dublin it had reached epidemic proportions with dealers openly selling hashish, ecstasy and heroin on Dublin's main thoroughfare, O'Connell Street. In June 1995, Owen held a meeting in Garda headquarters with ten senior guards. Pat Byrne was there as a deputy commissioner. Carty was also in attendance. 'I said I don't want to hear when something goes wrong that you're hampered because of a lack of this or a lack of that,' she told them. 'I want to know what are the long-term annoyances in the system that you want . . . because I'm doing some housekeeping legislation every year when I'm here, that we gather together a number of things.'

The Gardaí accepted her frankness and told her out straight what was required. The Revenue, they said, needed to start investigating criminals. Drug dealing now represented the greatest threat to the security of the State. Without Revenue's co-operation, the Gardaí could continue investigating the dealers, identifying property owned by them, pinpointing their offshore bank accounts, but couldn't do anything about them. Owen listened attentively. She left the meeting saying she would do what she could. Carty took on board what she had said. He had his own ideas on how to tackle the drugs problem.

Gilligan meanwhile was encountering personal problems. He and Geraldine were legally separated that summer. But a new love entered his life. Carol Rooney was Gilligan's *femme fatale*. She grew up in Palmerstown. He found her strikingly attractive. At the tender age of 19, she had just finished her leaving certificate examinations and was working part-time in a bookmaker's office when Gilligan entered her world. He was gambling and noticed her working at a cashier's desk. He started flirting with her and asked her out. What she saw in him, only she can say, but the two became lovers. Gilligan, behind Geraldine's back, spoiled his young lover. He rented out a house for her in Cellbridge in County Kildare, took her on foreign holidays and wooed her with gifts including a $20,000 Cartier watch. Anything she wanted she got. Later that year, he took her to a garage and she picked out a Nissan Micra. He handed over a £1,600 deposit. Carol paid off the balance in cash.

His renewed lust for life spilled over into the drugs trade. He began streamlining his operation. One of the first things he decided to do was relocate his distribution base. After nearly a year of distributing from the Emmett Road lock-up, he felt this would be a prudent move and so instructed Charlie Bowden to find new premises. Meehan had promoted Charlie into the senior ranks of the organisation. Bowden himself made an unlikely criminal. He grew up in Finglas, a sprawling housing estate situated in the heart of North Dublin. When he left school after sitting his Inter Certificate exam in 1983, he joined the army and rose to the rank of corporal. He specialised in rifle marksmanship and the use of the 0.5 inch heavy machinegun. Such was his good aim that he won competitions for his shooting capabilities, including the Eastern Command Rifle Championships. Bowden, however, had violent tendencies. This character flaw surfaced in 1988 when he attacked two recruits. He beat them up so badly they were taken to hospital. He was court-martialled and asked to leave the army, whereafter he offered himself as muscle for hire. He began working as a 'doorman' at nightclubs, hired because he had a black belt in karate.

Working on the doors exposed him to drugs and dealers. Mitchell was his introduction to organised crime. Bowden soon started dealing ecstasy for him at £500 per week. If there is an art to peddling drugs and networking, he possessed it. He sought extra work. Meehan offered him work collecting and delivering slabs of hashish to his clients. He was paid £50 per kilo.

Although Bowden came from the working class, his people were respectable. He worried about the direction his life was taking and gave up dealing in September 1992, deciding to go back to school. He wanted to study history and philosophy at Dublin City University. But two years later, he had separated from his wife and two children and found himself under intense financial pressure because he could not keep up maintenance payments. The easy money that drug dealing provided beckoned once more.

So when Gilligan ordered him to find new premises, he scoured the city looking for a suitable place. His search took him to Unit 1B, Greenmount Industrial Estate, a small office space situated in

Harold's Cross in Dublin. Using the ficticious name Paul Conroy, he paid the required deposit and collected the keys. The Holland–Cork smuggling route was functioning unhindered. Rahman was freighting the cannabis to Cork where Dunne would arrange its collection and delivery to the Ambassador Hotel. 'This would be mostly on a Monday. We took the van from there to Greenmount Industrial Estate and transferred the drugs to the lock-up. We would then drive the van back to the Ambassador Hotel to the driver who would wait there,' said Bowden.

On each delivery, they would hand the driver an envelope with 'c/o John Dunne' scribbled on the side. Bowden soon became an equal partner in the Dublin operation. 'They increased my pay to £3,000 a week. At this stage there were five of us involved. From then on we split the profits five ways.'

What would later become known as the Greenmount gang would retail the product at £2,400 per kilo to dealers in Dublin, Cork, Limerick and across the border in Northern Ireland. 'Shay Ward and I would deliver the hash from there around the city. Each day I would contact Peter Mitchell or Brian Meehan and they would supply me with a list of customers to whom we were to deliver,' he would later say. 'I would write up the lists as I got the order over the phones and I ticked them off as the order was delivered.'

Carefully wrapped kilos of cocaine were sometimes delivered, providing Bowden with extra income. Sometimes weapons arrived with the shipments. Because Bowden was trained in their use, he was made the gang's quartermaster. 'Before the guns would come, Brian Meehan would tell us there would be something else with the hash. The first guns were two sub-machine guns and ammunition. I think 400 rounds plus spare magazines and a silencer for these guns. I unpacked them, cleaned them and oiled them.' He continued: 'I brought the guns in my car to Bridgit Burke's public house in Firhouse where I met Brian Meehan and Peter Mitchell. They got into my car and directed me to an old graveyard up the mountain near a convent.'

The location was the Jewish graveyard on the Old Court Road in Tallaght. Meehan and Mitchell hid the weapons in the grave of Mirium Norrcuip while Bowden waited around the corner for them. The machineguns were just the start. More weapons were imported.

'I remember another time Brian Meehan, Peter Mitchell and Hippo were away on holidays. I got a call from the Little Man who I know to be John Gilligan. He told me that there was something in the next consignment of hash. When this consignment came, I opened the box and found five nine-millimetre semi-automatic pistols with ammunition for them. They were also brought to the graveyard.'

On every occasion, Gilligan would call to enquire if the guns had come. 'In January 1996, another sub-machinegun came in with the hash. There was also a .357 Magnum and 12 rounds of brass casing ammunition with silver heads which were conclave. I cleaned that gun and oiled it and brought it up to the graveyard. Some of the guns were new and more of them weren't. The .357 Magnum was a new gun. I just wrapped it in clothes and put it in a tupperware box and it was put in the graveyard by myself.'

Bowden also took possession of a .38 snub-nosed revolver and a .45 semi-automatic pistol with ammunition. Bowden was the only member of the gang who knew how to use and service the weapons, but what Gilligan did know was that the weapons were a valuable commodity in dealing with the INLA. Traynor often passed guns to the terrorists as 'sweeteners'. Bowden recounted one story later. 'Sometime before Veronica Guerin's murder, John Traynor was looking for guns to give the politicals as a sweetener to keep them off his back. By politicals, I mean the IRA or INLA. I was told to give him a .9mm Browning semi-automatic pistol which had a faulty spring – this had come in in one of the consignments – and a .38 snub-nose, silver colour. I left these two guns at a little monument on the side of the road near the Jewish graveyard for Traynor to collect.'

The business ran like clockwork. There were no hitches. Indeed, for all the activity, they might not have even existed as far as the police were concerned. It was the deal of a lifetime for Gilligan. Everything was running according to plan until an unexpected visitor called at Jessbrook.

CHAPTER 10

Fight Fire with Fire

'It was only a tactic I used to try and
frighten her off, that's all.'
JOHN GILLIGAN

'If you do one thing on me or write about me I'm going to kidnap your son and ride him. I am going to shoot you. Do you understand what I am saying to you, I am going to kidnap your fucking son and I am going to ride him and I am going to fucking shoot you? I'm going to kill you.' The menacing tone of Gilligan's voice had the desired effect, although he could not see it from the other end of the phone line. Veronica's body trembled with fear: the possibility of her son being harmed numbed her senses. It terrified her. 'I'm going to kill you. Are you listening to me? I'm going to shoot you and your family.'

His threat had caught her unawares, coming as a complete surprise because she was attending a meeting with her barrister Felix McEnroy. That he would call her, introduce himself by name and threaten to kidnap her child threw her concentration off balance. McEnroy could see by her demeanour that the caller was threatening her. He stood up and walked around his desk to listen to the caller. Guerin turned up the volume on her phone. The barrister recognised the caller, having acted for Gilligan years beforehand. 'It was like an explosive burst down the telephone. Then he spoke in a more measured and controlled manner,' he later recalled.

Determined not to give in to intimidation, she turned off her phone. McEnroy took some contemporaneous notes of the conversation and wrote down the time and date: 1.05 p.m., Friday, 15 September 1995. This would be useful to the Gardaí. Veronica wasn't one to give in to intimidation but this time she really was afraid. Whether he was merely posturing she could not say, but she knew Gilligan was more than capable of violence. The bruises on her face and the constant pain in her lower back that caused her to walk awkwardly were proof of that. McEnroy thought she looked like someone who had been in a fight.

She must have thought back to the previous morning that started out like any other. She always considered herself a proactive journalist. She generated news – news did not arrive on her desk courtesy of public relations agencies. On that particular morning, she left her home and headed off on a special assignment. Not to meet a drug pusher in an inner-city flats complex or a fraudster sitting in the corner of a quiet café in downtown Dublin; no, she drove to the village of Enfield in County Meath. From here she travelled along the narrow country road that leads to the remote village of Mucklon. The signpost there pointed her in the direction of the Jessbrook Equestrian Centre. She arrived at its gates shortly before 9 a.m. and stepped out of her car. Perhaps at that moment Veronica was one of a few people in Ireland who realised why people turn to crime. Traynor was right. John Gilligan was huge.

In contrast to her own expectations, Jessbrook Equestrian Centre was a first-class riding school and showjumping arena. The impression she had been given by Traynor was one of an ad hoc horse farm; she could see this was clearly not the case. Jessbrook was an impressive set-up, worth somewhere in the region of two million pounds.

The main building comprised a showjumping arena built to international equine competition standards. This towered above the landscape. Adjoining this was the stable block, where the mares, foals and stallions were tethered and stabled. The centre was set against a backdrop of green pastures, where chestnut-coloured mares ambled about. To the right of the equestrian centre lay Gilligan's home, an old refurbished house linked to the main road by a long tree-lined avenue. Two electric gates kept out intruders and prevented the escape of the owner's collection of pedigree Old English sheepdogs, who bounded about the garden.

In part to let someone know where she was and in part to satisfy her journalistic urge to tell somebody that the owner, John Gilligan, was indeed a millionaire, she rang Chris Finnegan, a detective attached to the Garda Drugs Squad. The two were close friends and she knew he was always at the other end of a phone line.

He was having breakfast with his wife in the conservatory of their home when his mobile telephone rang. He remembers the morning vividly. 'Veronica called me at 9 a.m. She said, "You won't believe where I am. I'm looking at a mansion, Gilligan's place,"' he recalled. 'She said there were big gates and she was thinking of going over them. I told her not to, that would make her a trespasser. I thought she would go back to her office, that she wouldn't go in on her own, so I left it at that.'

Veronica had an irresistible curiosity and no matter what, no matter what the reason, nothing could have stopped her from pursuing Gilligan. Traynor spoke about him in an adoring way, revering Gilligan as an underworld hero. Those in the Garda who didn't subscribe to the belief that Ireland did not have an organised crime problem described him as a millionaire drug trafficker who lived between London, Amsterdam, Brussels and Ireland. Gilligan, they said, had a reputation for violence, and distrust of others formed part of his psyche. His criminal organisation was run along the same lines as a paramilitary organisation. He was familiar with the latest surveillance technology and was obsessed with surveillance and counter-surveillance techniques. He consulted with no one, just issued instructions and didn't take no for an answer. Much of what she had heard was gossip, but enough to spark off her interest.

On 7 September she had dispatched a letter addressed to Gilligan requesting a meeting, but had received no reply. The letter read: 'I would like to discuss your recent business success in the equestrian business. This is a tremendous achievement considering you have been working in this business for just two years.'

She knew if she wanted to meet him, she would have to go to him. After ending her call to Finnegan, she stepped out of her car and walked into the reception area of the equestrian centre. The time was approximately 9.10 a.m. There, the riding school's secretary, Patricia Murphy, met her. Veronica asked if Gilligan was there. Murphy said she didn't know. The Gilligans didn't mix with the centre's staff; hence no one working there had any idea about Gilligan or the source of his wealth. Veronica enquired where he was likely to be and Murphy answered: 'Try over at the house. They might know.'

'Can I go straight down there?' she asked, pointing down the field towards the house.

'No, go back out the road, turn right and go to the next big gate and ring the intercom.'

Veronica walked back to her car, drove the short distance and pulled up outside the gates. She stepped out of her car and pressed the intercom bell a number of times to announce her presence. She noticed a surveillance camera pointing in her direction and stood in front of this. Moments later, the gates opened. She waited to see if a car or person was coming out to meet her. When nobody emerged, she got back into her car and drove up the driveway.

She knocked at the door. Gilligan was inside with his wife Geraldine. The two had been out the night before, celebrating Darren's birthday. Gilligan was pottering around the house, wearing nothing other than a silk dressing-gown. He had seen her car coming and remarked to his wife, 'There's a car coming down the driveway.' When he opened the door, he saw a woman whom he didn't recognise standing before him. 'Yeah?' he said brashly.

Veronica asked; 'Mr Gilligan?'

'That's right.'

'I'm Veronica Guerin from the *Sunday Independent*. I want to ask you some questions.'

His facial expression changed and without any warning, he grabbed Veronica by the throat and started punching her in the face, throat and chest area. 'You write one fucking word about me and I'll fucking kill you, your husband, your fucking son, your family, everyone belonging to you, even your fucking neighbours,' he roared.

Veronica was paralysed with fear; Gilligan was beating her about the head with the skill of a professional boxer. She later recalled: 'He seemed to be physically carrying me towards my car. He continued to hit me in the area of my head, face and upper part of my body with his fists.'

He pushed her over the bonnet of her car, held her down with one hand and continued to punch her in the face. Moments later, he released her from his grip and she slid to the ground. She was dizzy from the beating and tried to scramble to her feet. 'Get to fuck out of here, get off my fucking property,' he shouted.

More than anything else, she wanted to escape and went to open the door to her car. As she did, he grabbed her by the arm and pushed her inside, whilst repeating his threats to murder her. The savagery of the assault sent her into shock and she fumbled for her car keys. But as she found them, Gilligan opened the door and grabbed her again. 'Have you a fucking mike? Where is the fucking wire?'

'No, I have nothing,' she screamed.

Gilligan reached in and pulled open her blouse. He then went for the side pocket of her jacket, ripping it open. He continued threatening to have her family shot if she wrote anything. Satisfied there was no tape recorder, he slammed her car door shut and shouted: 'Now get to fuck out of here.'

The beating had sent her into a deep state of shock. She sped away, accelerating towards the gates. Gilligan later acknowledged that he did frighten her. 'I lost the head. I don't know what happened but I must have frightened her because she flew up the driveway.'

The beating Veronica endured was savage. So much so that she drove in the wrong direction out of Gilligan's home, a course that brought her off into the countryside. Minutes later, when she had calmed herself down, she rang Finnegan. 'She was in a state of shock,' he said. 'She was distressed. She said, "Chris, he's after belting me black and blue."' Finnegan calmed her down, told her not to worry and to drive back to Dublin. 'I was now worried, I told her to go back to Dublin and ring the guards.' Remembering the morning in question, he said, 'That morning marked the end of the good days for Veronica. It was a defining moment in her life.'

Veronica contacted the *Sunday Independent* shortly afterwards to alert them to what had happened. She arranged to see her doctor, Stanley Buchalter, at 1.30 p.m. He examined her and noted in his report that she was complaining of a 'blinding' headache, pain across her head and soreness above her left eye. He diagnosed shock and extensive bruising and told her to put her feet up. She rested at home for the remainder of the day but, determined not to let Gilligan get away with the attack, rang the Gardaí.

Detective Inspector Thomas Gallagher of Coolock Garda Station was familiar with her line of work. He sensed urgency in her voice and drove out to her home in North County Dublin. He arrived at 7.30 p.m. and the injuries she had sustained caught his attention.

Veronica herself was visibly shaken and not in any state of mind to give the full details of the attack. Detective Inspector Gallagher reassured her and took possession of the clothes she had been wearing earlier: a black cotton T-shirt and a brown and black plaid jacket. He examined the clothing and took note the T-shirt was torn at the front, while one of the jacket's pockets had been practically ripped off.

The next day, Veronica met her legal team with whom she discussed the matter; she then drove to Coolock station to make a statement against Gilligan. Gallagher noted discoloration on her face around her left eye and the fact that she complained to him about pains in her chest and shoulders. He approached the case in a thorough manner and was meticulous in taking her statement, writing down her every word in order that charges could be proffered against her assailant. The search for Gilligan commenced days after the attack.

Sensing problems, Gilligan kept a low profile for a few days and avoided trouble at all costs. He moved into the city centre and started travelling by taxi in case one of the vehicles at his disposal would be stopped at a Garda checkpoint. He felt under extreme pressure. After months of working in absolute secret to arrange a new smuggling route, his entire operation was facing public scrutiny. Guerin, he felt, would be sure to highlight the attack. By the end of that week, he was proved right when the *Sunday Independent* published details of the attack naming Gilligan. A photograph of Veronica beaten and bruised accompanied the article. Now the general public knew what type of man he was.

On 25 September, he flew to Schipol Airport in Amsterdam where he booked into the nearby Hilton Hotel. It was not necessary for him to be in Ireland; Geraldine ran the Jessbrook Equestrian Centre while Meehan and his crew were taking stock of the cannabis trade. Instead of feeling he had escaped, he felt uneasy, for he knew the police would soon start asking questions about Veronica Guerin.

When the Gardaí arrived at Jessbrook looking for him, Geraldine was cordial and polite. Geraldine was far too clever to argue with detectives; a lifetime of answering the door to policemen had taught her that. She told the police her husband was out of the country but she would gladly pass on the message when he next called home. Days went by and the message was indeed passed to Gilligan. At this point he entered into a cat-and-mouse game with the investigation team, making appointments to meet them but failing to show up. It was not long before business forced his return to Ireland.

He arrived home on Friday, 10 November, and rang Detective Sergeant Michael Ryan from the Garda Special Branch, who had been seeking his whereabouts. The two made an appointment to meet on the following Monday, 13 November. Even if he was charged for the assault there and then, he would have no fears, safe in the knowledge that Baltus, Rahamn and Meehan were capable of looking after the business. The meeting place would be the car park of Scott's restaurant in Blanchardstown on the outskirts of Dublin: the time 12.20 p.m.

Gilligan was pacing up and down impatiently when the detectives pulled into the car park. Ryan was accompanied by Detective Garda Howard Mahony and they arrested Gilligan under Section 30 of the Offences Against the State Act, 1939, for the suspected commission of a scheduled offence under the act; the possession of a firearm within the State.

Gilligan was placed in the back seat of their patrol car and driven at speed to Santry Garda Station via the West Link road. The party arrived at Santry at 12.42 p.m. Detective Inspector Gallagher had in the meantime been made aware of Gilligan's arrest and he headed towards Santry. On arrival at Santry Garda Station, Garda Sergeant James Murphy took Gilligan's details and filled out his custody record.

> Name: John Gilligan.
> Address: 13 Corduff Avenue, Blanchardstown.
> Date of Birth: 29 – 3 – 52.
> Sex: male.
> Marital status: married.
> Nationality: Irish.
> Height: five foot five inches.
> Eye colour: hazel.
> Facial hair: none.

Gilligan was given notice of his rights. He declined an offer to ring a solicitor, saying he had 'already done that'. 'I have a mobile phone,' he remarked in a matter-of-fact way. The Garda took note that he was in good humour. At 12.50 p.m. he was brought into an interview room where Ryan cautioned him: 'You are not obliged to say anything unless you wish to do so. And anything you say will be taken down in writing and may be given in evidence.'

The interview commenced. Ryan asked about the assault on Veronica and the threats he had made against her. Gilligan answered that he had already been tried and convicted by the *Sunday Independent*. His answer was clearly rehearsed and designed to frustrate the line of questioning. In the meantime, Gallagher had arrived accompanied by Detective Garda James Phelan. They entered the interview room at 2.26 p.m. and took over the interrogation.

'You are not obliged to say anything unless you wish to do so but anything you do say will be taken down in writing and may be given in evidence,' said the detective inspector.

Gilligan sat motionless and listened attentively, his face expressionless.

'We are investigating an alleged assault on Veronica Guerin, which occurred on 14 September 1995 at Mucklon, Enfield, County Meath. Do you wish to give your version of the events as they happened or do you wish to make a statement?

Gilligan answered: 'On the advice of my solicitor, I have already been tried and convicted by the *Sunday Independent* and he has advised me to say nothing.'

An efficient and well-mannered policeman, Gallagher maintained his composure, in the knowledge that this was no ordinary suspect sitting in front of him. Gilligan was well used to police interrogations and was going to answer all his questions with this line.

'The day after the alleged assault, that was 15 September 1995, you telephoned Veronica Guerin on her mobile at approximately 1.05 p.m. and threatened to shoot her.'

'I have never had a gun in my life. I wouldn't know where to get a gun and I wouldn't want a gun.'

'Did you ring Ms Guerin on that day?'

'On the advice of my solicitor, I have nothing to say.'

'Do you know Ms Guerin's phone number?'

'I have already been tried and convicted by the *Sunday Independent* and on the advice of my solicitor, I have nothing to say.'

Gallagher tried another line of inquiry. 'Can you tell me where you were on the 15 September this year?'

Gilligan responded: 'As I said, on the advice of my solicitor, I have already been tried and convicted and I don't wish to say anything.'

'When you telephoned Ms Guerin on 15 September 1995, you identified yourself to her and made her aware of matter relating to the property at Mucklon, Enfield, that you were legally separated. All this could be confirmed by Hanahoe Solicitors, is that right?'

'I have nothing to say. I have already been tried and convicted.'

'Did you threaten Ms Guerin's son and family if she "wrote a word about you, that you would ride her son and kill her"?'

'That's all untrue.'

'Did you say, "I'll fucking shoot you" to Ms Guerin?'

'No, never in my life.'

'Did you say, you were "going to kidnap her son and ride him"?'

'No such thing, never in my life,' he answered.

The detective inspector proceeded to ask Gilligan more simple questions.

'Can you account for your movements on 15 September 1995?'

'On the advice of my solicitor, I have already been tried and convicted by the *Sunday Independent*.'

'On 14 September 1995 were you present at Mucklon, Enfield, County Meath, on the date of the alleged assault on Ms Guerin?'

'On the advice of my solicitor I don't wish to say anything.'

'Do you own or have access to a house and property at Mucklon, Enfield, County Meath?'

'That's my wife's house.'

'Were you there on the morning of 14 September 1995?'

'On the advice of my solicitor I have already been tried and convicted by the *Sunday Independent*. I have nothing to say.'

'Did you assault Ms Guerin at that address – punch her about the face and head?'

'No way. I never assaulted a woman and never will.'

'How do you account for damage to her T-shirt and jacket, both of which were torn?'

'Certainly nothing to do with me.'

'Do you recall Ms Guerin introducing herself to you at that address and you being asked if you were Mr Gilligan, you said "Yeah" on the 14 September 1995?'

'On the advice of my solicitor, I have been tried by the *Sunday Independent* and convicted. I have nothing to say.'

'Have you ever received a letter from Ms Guerin requesting a meeting?'

'No, never.'

'Did you ever meet her?'

'I have been tried and convicted by the *Sunday Independent*.'

'Do you know Veronica Guerin?'

'No.'

'Do you own a Land Rover vehicle?'

'I don't own any vehicle,' said Gilligan, wondering where this particular line of questioning was leading.

'Did you ever reside at Mucklon, Enfield, County Meath?'

'I lived there until myself and my wife happily separated sometime this year, early in the year, it was a happy separation, she received everything,' Gilligan said smirking.

'Are you saying you haven't been there since then?'

'As I've said, I have been tried and convicted by the *Sunday Independent*.'

'Do you own an Eircell telephone?'

'On the advice of my solicitor, I don't wish to say anything.'

'What is your permanent address?'

'I have lived at 13 Corduff Avenue since 1977. That was my first house and with the exception of a few weeks, I live there with my son.'

'You were aware that the Gardaí wished to talk to you concerning the alleged assault and threats to shoot Ms Guerin. You made a number of appointments and failed to keep them. Why? Was it because you had something to hide?'

'No, I have nothing to hide. My solicitor contacted the Gardaí and asked if they had a charge sheet or a warrant sheet there for John Gilligan and he was told that the Gardaí said they just wanted to talk to him and also on another occasion we rang to be told that the particular policeman was off for a few days. Twice that happened. Once I heard that there was no charge sheet or warrant. I didn't want to talk to the police. I had done nothing wrong.'

The detective inspector continued. 'Where have you been living since 14 September 1995, since the alleged assault?'

'I have been out of the country since 25 September 1995 on business and returned on Friday last,' said Gilligan.

At 3.40 p.m., Gallagher and Mahoney left the interview room to allow Gilligan to rest. A short while earlier, Garda Sergeant Michael McGarry had taken over as house sergeant in the station. He entered the interview room and offered the suspect dinner. Gilligan in his customary fashion asked if it would be possible to order a breast of chicken, a portion of chips and a can of Coke from a nearby fast food takeaway. He didn't want the Gardaí to pay and so offered some spare change from his pocket. The food was fetched and Gilligan wolfed it down.

At 4 p.m. his two interrogators returned. Gallagher continued to ask the questions.

'Are there any witnesses to the assault if it does get to court?'

'Yes, there is. I have six witnesses – none of them have previous convictions.'

'Can you give their names?' enquired the Garda, causing Gilligan to lose his temper.

'If there's a court case they will be in court. You can write this down, I am not going to open my mouth again. Charge me or do whatever you have to do, 48 hours or whatever, I don't care. I believe she abused a 70-year-old woman that day.'

Gilligan had become highly agitated and aggressive. The detective inspector was in no doubt that he had beaten Veronica and continued to ask relevant questions, much to Gilligan's annoyance. 'What evidence have these witnesses to offer?'

Gilligan remained silent and refused to speak.

At 4.40 p.m. the Gardaí stepped outside the interview room. They returned at 6.10 p.m. with two packages. Gallagher produced the plaid jacket and T-shirt which he had two months beforehand taken from Veronica. He showed them to Gilligan and asked him to comment on damage done to both items, pointing out the pocket of the jacket, which was torn, and the ripped T-shirt.

'I never saw these items before. I didn't tear them, I mean, pull the stitching out of the jacket pocket. That's what it looks like happened to me,' was Gilligan's only response.

In accordance with procedure, the notes of the interview were read out to Gilligan. This took place at 6.30 p.m. and he agreed with the contents. He then asked for the following words to be taken down by the Gardaí. 'I wish to add that since I left the country in September, I have contacted the Gardaí at Santry on a weekly basis. I gave them the number of the Hilton Hotel, Schipol Airport. As soon as I came back to Dublin Airport, I rang looking for Detective Sergeant Ryan and he rang me back there and we made an appointment to meet.'

Gilligan was released from custody without charge at 6.40 p.m. He made no complaints about his treatment and signed his custody record to that effect. He had been in police custody more times than he cared to remember and was well used to the routine. It didn't bother him too much and he went on his way, saying goodbye to the Gardaí on duty in the station before he left.

Gallagher submitted the file on the assault to the Director of Public Prosecutions. His work in pursuing Gilligan paid off when the DPP ordered that he be charged with two offences: the unlawful assault of Veronica Guerin; and criminal damage to a cotton T-shirt. The case would proceed on 14 May 1996 at the District Court in Kilcock in County Meath. Geraldine Gilligan was coincidentally one of the main witnesses, having overheard the exchange between Veronica and Gilligan.

John Gilligan put the impending court appearance to the back of his mind for the moment. More pressing problems were troubling him. He had come to the notice of the IRA. They were in the process of reorganising in Dublin and had taken a policy decision to start tackling drug dealing in the city. The Provisionals were under intense pressure to move against the dealers. The leadership of the organisation was not enthusiastic about fighting a drugs war in Dublin. But the grassroots membership had a utopian idea of ridding the streets of drugs by assassinating the dealers. None thought for a moment they could solve the problem, but they knew the IRA was more than capable of making life more than a little difficult for the pushers.

The republican movement's campaign took three different forms. Certain targets would be assassinated. Others would be abducted and questioned. The third policy was to afford protection to community groups and leaders who came out and marched on the homes of drug dealers. 'Ireland's not like England, where the criminals have only got the police or other criminals to worry about,' said one IRA man. 'There was a third force here.'

Thousands of people – parents, politicians, trade unionists – were turning out on the streets, holding vigils outside the homes of the pushers. Most of the bigger fish fled Ireland in fear for their lives. Gilligan was one of the few who stayed. The IRA operated by abducting criminals off the street and forcing them to talk. On other occasions, they would simply ask criminals to turn up and provide whatever information they had to assist in the inquiries. This created a climate of fear among the criminal class. Most didn't know who to trust or which way to turn.

Martin Foley was one of Cahill's gang and a one-time friend of Gilligan's. He was also a customer buying a kilo of cannabis each week. He had come under pressure from the Provisional IRA in bygone years. The IRA had kidnapped him in March 1984 but he was rescued by the Gardaí after they stumbled upon his kidnappers bundling him into a Hiace van. The IRA lost an entire active service unit, who were all subsequently jailed despite Foley's refusal to testify against them. The Viper, as Foley was known, was one of the first now taken in by the IRA. He pleaded mercy but offered to point his republican interrogators in Meehan's direction. He told the IRA the same story that Traynor told Guerin. Gilligan's firm, he said, was huge.

Foley was reversing his car into the driveway of his home on Cashel Avenue in Crumlin on the morning of 1 February 1996 when he saw Meehan and Ward approach in a car. Ward was driving while Meehan was sitting in the passenger seat looking anxiously at him. He thought nothing of it until it slowed down to a standstill.

Earlier that week, Gilligan had instructed Meehan and Ward to eliminate Foley. Meehan and Ward came up with a workable plan. Bowden, as the gang's quartermaster, decided the best gun for the job was a Sten sub-machine gun. He retrieved this from the gang's arms dump in the Jewish cemetery. He loaded and handed the would-be killer a .45 pistol in case the machine gun should jam.

Meehan was sure Foley had been telling the 'politicals' they were selling heroin and cocaine. If the IRA took him seriously, they would likely kill them all. There would be no backhander and the INLA would be no match for the Provisionals. Gilligan was right: Foley had to go. Although Bowden was by far the best member of the gang qualified to kill, he hadn't got the nerve. Instead it was left up to Meehan, though Bowden offered to teach him about the black art of assassination. The three went to a field at the back of the graveyard and test-fired the sub-machinegun. They tied a white plastic bag to a tree as a target. Meehan wasn't a very good shot.

After preparing the weapons for use, Bowden headed off to Ward's house in Crumlin and listened to a radio scanner monitoring Garda messages. Bowden would later admit: 'On the day of the shooting Meehan rang me and told me to go to Paul Ward's house. When I got there Peter Mitchell was sitting in the living-room listening to a scanner. Earlier that day Meehan had told me to get a gallon of petrol in a container and give it to Shay. I did this. When I got to Ward's house I joined Mitchell listening to the scanner. It was scanning police messages. After a while Shay Ward came in. He told me that Brian had arranged to meet Martin Foley to collect money off him for the hash and that they were going to shoot him at this prearranged meeting place. Shay also told me that he had delivered a stolen Honda Civic LS1 to Paul Ward earlier. It was going to be used in the shooting.'

Hours later, he heard there had been a shooting. When they spotted Foley, Ward and Meehan immediately jumped out of their car. Ward fired a number of shots through the windscreen while Meehan sprayed his vehicle. Foley put his car into reverse and bent down across the passenger seat while keeping his foot on the throttle. Meehan fired a burst of bullets at the car; one bullet struck the top of Foley's right ring finger. Foley scrambled out of the car and jumped over a wall into a neighbour's back garden, pursued by Meehan who continued firing at him. Foley then saw an open back door and ran for it. The family was sitting in the kitchen having dinner when he ran past followed by an angry Meehan. Foley made for the front door, then straight up the stairs, still being pursued by Meehan who was still shooting off rounds. He ran into one of the bedrooms; Meehan fired a volley of shots through the bedroom door. Realising he would certainly be killed if he didn't escape, Foley jumped through the window onto a flat roof. Meehan fired again, hitting him in the back. Meehan, fearing the Gardaí were on their way to the scene, ran back to the getaway car and made his escape. Shay Ward had the door open; awaiting the likely assassin's return.

Bowden later recalled: 'Almost immediately after the shooting, Brian Meehan and Paul Ward came into the kitchen. Shay also came in. He was carrying the guns and a black woollen balaclava and leather gloves. He put those in a plastic bag and went out through the house. Paul left the kitchen and Brian began to undress. He was wearing overalls and a jacket. He told me that he had fired off the entire magazine of the machinegun in one go at Martin Foley. He said Foley ran from the car into a house and he followed him there, he said he fired a shot from the .45 semi-automatic on a roof. He said the .45 had jammed. He was cursing. He said he hit Foley in the back and he was wondering whether he was dead.'

Gilligan would later taunt Meehan about the botched assassination. Gilligan believed assassinating his opponents was an essential part of being a criminal. 'That's the last time I'll send you to do anything. You couldn't hit an elephant, even if it stood still in front of you,' he roared afterwards. The next time he wanted someone shot, he would hire a professional killer who wouldn't miss.

Responsibility for the attack was blamed on the IRA by the media and the Garda. Gilligan's gang didn't even feature, which was what he wanted. If Gilligan thought he had escaped the IRA inquiries, however, he was mistaken. His now visible enormous wealth came to their attention quite accidentally. While Ward and Meehan by this stage possessed wealth beyond their means, they were still petty criminals. Ward was a heroin addict who would engage in thievery to get cash. Shortly after the Foley shooting, he and an accomplice attempted to rob a coal yard, holding a staff member to ransom with a knife. They escaped with a few hundred pounds, but after the scuffle Ward's identity was revealed to the Gardaí by a young man working in the yard. He decided to press charges and made a full statement to the Gardaí. Ward was arrested and questioned in due course and the Gardaí started to prepare charges against him.

News of this filtered back to Gilligan who arrived at the coal yard wanting to talk to the owner. Gilligan in his usual fashion was polite at first and sat down with the owner. He suggested the young man withdraw his statement. He said in no uncertain terms that he wanted the young man to back off, that the owner should sort it out. Gilligan was asked to leave. With that he produced a handgun and pointed it at the fuel merchant's head. 'Either you sort him out or I'll sort him out,' he roared before walking out. What he didn't know was that the youth was related to a senior officer in the IRA. The story was relayed to IRA GHQ staff in Dublin who decided to accompany the youth to Ward's court case.

Gilligan arrived and immediately recognised the republicans who eyeballed him. He stared at the ground and called Ward aside. To his relief, the Garda prosecuting the case didn't turn up at the court and the charge against Hippo was struck out.

The IRA now started making their own inquiries into Gilligan. The story recounted to them was too far-fetched for most to believe. Gilligan, according to just about every hoodlum in Dublin, was supplying tonnes of cannabis to dealers across Ireland, England, Scotland and Wales. His clients included loyalist paramilitaries, the INLA and just about every major Irish criminal. Not only did he command what was a sophisticated criminal organisation but he also had corrupted police, bribed officials and even recruited one or two of the IRA's own members into his fold. They simply couldn't believe it.

In mid-April, one of Gilligan's couriers, introduced one of his friends to the boss. Russell Warren ran a small industrial cleaning company called D & R. The company cleaned newly built houses and apartment blocks. It wasn't a very lucrative business but it paid the bills, keeping his head above water. Warren lived with his wife Deborah and her mother, Maureen Cooley. Gilligan's courier had mentioned Gilligan's name before, saying he knew him through betting. Warren thought nothing of the introduction. A few weeks later, Gilligan's courier arrived at his door with a bag of cash. '[Named courier] told me it was John Gilligan's money and it was money from betting. It developed from there,' he would later admit.

Warren was quickly inducted into the business of money laundering. The courier would deliver cash to his house on Heatherview Lawn in Tallaght. He would count it into bundles and repackage it neatly into a sports bag. Within weeks Warren was delivering cash to Schipol Airport where Gilligan or Baltus would collect it. 'At first I was told this money was from betting and the sales of smuggled cigarettes and tobacco. But as time went on and I got more involved I realised that this money was money from the sale of drugs.' By this time it was too late. He knew too much. The amounts of cash he counted were enormous. 'When I first started there used to be £20,000 to £30,000 in it. This figure would be the lowest amount. It would go as high as £160,000 sometimes, but most of the time it would be around £70,000.'

Warren wasn't cut out for crime. Instead of keeping his family in the dark about his new sideline, he inducted them into the business.

'I started to bring money to my father's and mother's house and I asked them to count it for me. The reason I asked them to count it was because it took me about two to three hours to count it on my own.' His parents never asked where the money came from. 'They were glad to get the few bob,' he said.

CHAPTER 11

Pineapple

'He was no criminal mastermind, just the right fella in
the right place at the right time.'
ASSISTANT COMMISSIONER KEVIN CARTY ON GILLIGAN

At 8.50 p.m. on 17 March, the feast of St Patrick, Gilligan walked into
the Scheveningen Casino in downtown The Hague. Beside him were
Meehan and one of his runners. Gilligan loved gambling and was
clearly in his element.

To the casino's patrons, he was an Irish businessman away from
home out celebrating St Patrick's night. The casino was packed to
capacity, which allowed the three to blend in before going their own
ways. Gilligan sat down at one table, Meehan strolled over to another
and the associate took a seat at a third. Gilligan smiled at the card
dealer, produced 150,000 guilders in 1,000-guilder notes and said he
wished to buy gambling tokens. Meehan and the associate did the
same.

Perched on a stool and sitting with thousands of pounds' worth of
gambling chips within arm's reach, Gilligan watched the game.
However, he didn't gamble, in fact he didn't place any bet. This drew
the attention of the security staff who kept him under discreet
observation. One of the security team went off and reviewed the
security footage to see who had arrived in Gilligan's company. Now
aware that the three were clearly not there to gamble, the security
men trained the casino's close circuit television system on them.
Slowly, one by one, Gilligan, Meehan and the associate left their
respective tables, taking their chips with them. None had placed any
bets. An hour later the three regrouped.

Later that evening, at ten minutes past midnight, Meehan walked
to one of the cash desks and presented tokens worth 250,000

guilders. He politely asked the cashier to have his 'winnings' transferred to a bank account. When requested by a player, the casino will transfer gambling profits to private accounts. To avail of this service, the player must submit written documents prior to gambling establishing his identity and bank account. When Meehan made the request, the cashier played for time while more checks were carried out. The security team in the casino confirmed that Gilligan, Meehan and the associate had either not played or hardly at all. Hence, the gambling chips were not gambling profits. A more senior member of staff stood in and explained to Meehan that the casino was unable to fulfil his request. Because he was not that clever, Meehan couldn't understand that the staff member was actually asking him to leave. Meehan persevered. If the casino could not wire the money to his bank, it could hold it on deposit for him. This request was also rejected, as deposits can only be made if it is reasonable to assume that the money to be deposited has been acquired by gambling. The staff member, who was by this stage highly suspicious, then suggested that the gambling chips would be cashed in the same form as they were purchased. Gilligan, surrounded by the casino's security team, watched as the tokens were cashed in 1,000-guilder bills. After their failed efforts to launder the money, they left.

If Meehan's request had been granted, he would have obtained a seemingly legal origin for 250,000 guilders by means of his bank statement. Alternatively, if the casino had granted his second request, he would have been able to prove at a later date that the money came from the casino deposit. Since only profits made by gambling are deposited, a seemingly legal origin could have been utilised here too.

Convinced that Meehan and his companions had wanted to procure a fake legal origin for the money, which they suspected had been acquired illegally, the casino's management decided to report the incident. All institutions where cash changes hands in Holland are obliged to report unusual or suspicious transactions to the Dutch Disclosure Office for Unusual Transactions (MOT). Despite its bureaucratic sounding name, the MOT is efficient in combating money laundering. The unit investigates all reported transactions and those deemed to be suspicious are referred to the public prosecutor's office. The report submitted by the casino caught the attention of the unit who decided to run Gilligan's, Meehan's and the associate's name past the Dutch National Criminal Intelligence Department. This is part of the National Criminal Intelligence Service (NCIS-CRI) which in turn is part of the National Police Force. The check did not yield any results.

The next step was to consult Interpol, the International Criminal Police Organisation, which is a world-wide exchange for police information. Established in Vienna in 1923, it was reconstituted in Paris in 1946, focusing on terrorism, forgery and the narcotics trade. Presently it serves more than 150 member nations, providing information about international criminals and helping to apprehend them. The MOT sent a file on the case through to the Dutch police and waited. Two weeks later, Interpol returned the file plus more.

Meehan, and strangely not Gilligan, was flagged as a criminal/drug dealer. Consultation of the Interpol register followed Meehan as No. 6.221.0.0/95.10122. The file contained a letter from the Netherlands Interpol to the Border Guarding Unit of Amsterdam-Schipol Airport dated 19 August 1995. It said, among other things, that Interpol Dublin had supplied the information that Meehan, born on 7 April 1965 (also using birth dates 8 April 1966 and 8 April 1960), was a well-known drug dealer.

Now what was originally treated as an unusual transaction was upgraded to a suspicious one. Given that Meehan was regarded as a drug trafficker, albeit not one with a criminal conviction for drugs, the file was passed to the National Public Prosecutor, then to the Financial Police Desk or FinPol, a unit within the Dutch Criminal Intelligence Service. The CIS asked the MOT to gather more information.

Officials there started trawling through bank accounts and reports dating back to 1994. The bulk of transactions took place at an exchange office of the GWK bank in the Hall of Amsterdam Central Station where Gilligan and an associate converted British, Scottish and Irish pounds into Dutch guilders. The associate was linked to two transactions where he changed foreign currencies into guilders worth £845,787.

Gilligan, as the MOT correctly suspected, had laundered a good deal more. From 1994, he had changed foreign currencies, which converted into 3,535,430 guilders in 13 transactions. Further investigations showed he used two passports, which are demanded as proof of identity, to carry out the exchanges. The passports, like everything else, turned out to be fake. Each carried a different date of birth, 24 March 1952 and 29 March 1952, but gave the same passport number.

Other members of the gang were drawn into the MOT inquiry. In one of the transactions reported by the exchange office in Amsterdam Square, Meredith showed up. Security checks were carried out on his name and date of birth. He had used his own passport bearing his name, Denis James Meredith, and his date of birth, 29 August 1958. His passport number, M034208, was confirmed as authentic. The GWK bank reported that he had made 37 exchange transactions in the period from 1994 to March 1996. Like the others, he had changed foreign currencies, mainly British, Scottish and Irish Pounds, totalling £10,297,025 into guilders.

Gilligan was now compromised. Not only was the MOT investigating his attempts to launder cash at the casino, but now they were examining the transactions that occurred in the GWK bank. The MOT requested details of all transactions carried out at the times when Gilligan's gang changed currency, particularly those which exchanged British, Scottish and Irish pounds at the GWK branch in the Hall of Amsterdam Central Station. The names of Baltus, Djorai and Rahman showed up.

The MOT knew of Baltus. They cross-referenced their own index files to find that he had changed large amounts of Irish punts into guilders on a regular basis in Amsterdam. Aszal Houssein Djorai was a Dutch criminal who was born in Paramaribo and was living in Gouden in Kent. Transactions by Djorai had also been reported by the MOT as suspicious. Since 1994, the MOT had recorded five transactions by Djorai that were regarded as unusual and 27 by Baltus. In nearly all cases it concerned transactions of British, Scottish and Irish pounds again exchanged in the hall of Amsterdam Central Station. In the six months prior to the investigation, he had changed into Dutch guilders Irish currency totalling a whopping £2.7 million.

In his negotiations with the Revenue Commissioners, Kevin Carty had sensed few signs of sympathy. Both he and Murphy left each meeting with the impression that it was all a waste of time. No matter what was said, the Revenue made one thing very clear, information relating to any citizen's tax was secret and confidential regardless of whether the subject was a criminal or not. Ministerial intervention, specifically from Owen and her ministerial colleagues, had failed to break what was clearly an impasse.

Carty was by nature a shrewd policeman and strategist who possessed an uncanny ability to foresee problems before they presented themselves. To combat crime, he knew the tax authorities had to come on board. Instead of feeling demoralised by the negotiations, he decided to set up an investigation that would involve Revenue and Social Welfare investigators.

Since joining An Garda Síochána, Carty had worked almost exclusively in the intelligence sphere, mainly against the IRA. A week after the IRA declared its cease-fire in August 1994, Carty had been transferred from Wexford, then into the Central Detective Unit in Dublin. CDU, as the unit was code-named, incorporated the drugs squad, serious crime squad and fraud squad. One week into that job, he set about restructuring the unit, breaking down old barriers. Instead of responding to crimes after they had been committed, he encouraged his officers to be pro-active, to recruit informants to glean enough evidence to make arrests and secure convictions. One of his more novel ideas was the creation of a Money Laundering Investigations Unit within the fraud squad.

The Chief, as he became known, surrounded himself with men he handpicked for various skills. Austin McNally, a superintendent who was stationed in Wicklow, was transferred to CDU. The two knew each other of old and most importantly of all McNally understood what Carty wanted to accomplish. In the next four months, CDU secured dozens of arrests and disbanded criminal networks using informants and covert surveillance to achieve its aims. In spite of the successes, Carty believed that a separate drugs squad, which operated independently, was required. His philosophy was that to tackle drug dealing, the force had to distinguish between street dealers and major players. Street dealers should targeted by local drugs units. Criminals who made the jump into the international scene required an international response, for they were behind the flow of drugs entering the State. 'We looked at how the drugs problem was being tackled and well, frankly, it wasn't working. We needed to be proactive, to go out looking for evidence,' he said.

Garda management accepted his advice and naturally appointed Carty to head a new anti-narcotics squad modelled on his own recommendations. At the request of Patrick Culligan, the commissioner, Carty was given the arduous task of fronting the Garda National Drugs Unit (GNDU) a year later. In reality, the move was part of an overall police strategy aimed at reducing drug trafficking. Within the ranks of the police, it was now time for Carty to show what he was made of.

It seemed clear to him what he needed to do because the Revenue's position was unequivocal. If the Revenue didn't wish to have the Gardaí joining them, they could join the Gardaí by way of invitation. Bearing in mind that the Government wanted the two sides to bond, Carty took it upon himself to invite the Customs National Drugs Team, which is a branch of the Revenue, to join, rather than assist, an investigation, the subject of which Carty himself was becoming all too familiar with.

The now awesome criminal cartel run by Gilligan, through a series of incidental timings, was brought to the GNDU's attention from the moment of its inception. Agent handlers were filing reports, which at the time were viewed with a degree of scepticism, stating that Gilligan through Meehan was smuggling the bulk of all hashish sold in Dublin, Cork and possibly Limerick.

Carty's clever decision to set up a Money Laundering Investigation Unit within the framework of the revamped CDU now validated itself. His decision hadn't generated much publicity or support at the time, but it came into its own the following year when the working elements of the 1994 Criminal Justice Act came into force. This made it obligatory for banks to report suspicious transactions. When it did, the financial intelligence squad was literally inundated with reports from the banks on Gilligan, Geraldine, their children, his brother Thomas, Brian Meehan and the rest of the gang.

More reports arrived via Europol, the European Law Enforcement Organisation. Agreed in the terms of the Maastricht Treaty on European Union of 7 February 1992, Europol's aim is to improve the effectiveness of the police in member countries in preventing and combating terrorism, drug trafficking and other forms of serious international organised crime. But like everything else created by the EU parliament, it took a further two years to get it up and running. On 3 January 1994, it opened its first offices in Raamweg, a leafy suburb in The Hague, where the Europol Drugs Unit code-named EDU is based. This office facilitates the exchange of data, personal and non-personal, between Europol liaison officers otherwise known as ELOs. It was from the Irish Desk that the reports on Gilligan's international financial dealings were dispatched to Dublin.

The reports confirmed what many were starting to suspect. Gilligan was not pumping all his cash into Jessbrook – the construction costs only represented a fragment of what he was earning. Although he couldn't read or write properly, had a limited view of life and didn't strike those who knew him as in any way intelligent, he had transcended himself. He was no longer a Dublin criminal who occasionally did business in Europe. He was now a European criminal who did business in Ireland. The financial reports confirmed this. These proved that he was banking money in Austria, Holland, Britain, France and Belgium. Carty, never one to underestimate or overestimate criminals, was made aware of this intelligence. Carty approached his superior, Deputy Commissioner Noel Conroy, head of the crime and security, seeking permission to mount his joint investigation. It was a bold move because it broke with tradition. Permission was granted.

At 11 a.m. on the morning of 23 April, Carty delivered a speech to a team of some 50 detectives gathered in the conference room that adjoins the GNDU offices on the fourth floor of Harcourt Square Garda Station. To Carty's left stood McNally. The head of the Money Laundering Investigations Unit, Detective Inspector Terry McGinn, was present. At that time, she knew more about Gilligan's money laundering activities and wealth than perhaps anyone else. She had examined case-loads of financial documents, she had analysed his modus operandi, cross-referenced suspects' names and investigated them one hundred times over. But she might as well have had her hands tied behind her back, for to try to press charges would have proved futile without knowing details of Gilligan's tax affairs.

'We brought in as many units as possible,' said Carty. 'It wasn't just the sole domain of one unit. Special Branch got involved because they're good at generating criminal intelligence. They had people active in that area, so they came on board. Then we got Gardaí from the Louth/Meath division and Naas because Jessbrook lies on the border and officers from Store Street because they were dealing with Meehan, and he obviously played a big part in Gilligan's operation. Basically we got as many people as we could involved.'

There was a strange face in the room. Carty introduced him as

Higher Officer Finbar O'Leary from the Customs National Drugs Team on behalf of the Revenue Commissioners. Carty outlined his plan. He believed it was pointless trying to secure a drug conviction against Gilligan. 'The problem we had was that he didn't physically touch his product, therefore we were looking at a conspiracy or money laundering charge. So we concentrated our efforts on that.'

Carty spoke in no uncertain terms. Gilligan, he said, was the biggest criminal in Ireland. He made Martin Cahill and anyone else who went before him look like a boy scout. He said the incident room for the investigation would be open at any time to anyone involved. He wanted the entire squad to act in co-ordination. 'Basically I wanted to make his life hell in every way possible, come at him from all sides,' he recalled.

If nothing else, this would make Gilligan acutely aware that he couldn't bully or intimidate the State, that for his actions he would learn there would be a measured reaction from the State. When the conference ended, someone asked what the operation was called. Carty looked quizzically at McNally. One of the special branch delegation interjected. 'What about Operation Pineapple?'

From what he had heard so far, the officer reached the conclusion that looking at Gilligan's organisation was like looking at the layers of a pineapple. It was a curious comparison, but one they understood.

If Carty didn't know much about Gilligan on that day, he soon did. His suspicion that Gilligan couldn't possibly be declaring his wealth to the Revenue Commissioners was on target. Not only was he not paying tax, but he had his own peculiar way of returning his tax remits. One sent to him for the tax year ending 1994 seeking his predicted earnings was sent back with a personal note scrawled in red crayon on the letter. It read: 'I'm just out of prison, I have no fucking money for you, leave me alone.'

Towards the end of April, the team had built up a comprehensive picture of their target. Carol Rooney's relationship with Gilligan was of particular interest although she was barely out of school. Carty continued approaching other State agencies looking for help. Officials from Kildare County Council were asked to assist. 'Gilligan had no planning for Jessbrook. There had been huge intimidation of council officials after he illegally put ramps on the road, so we invited all the different agencies that had competency in this area, so we could make life as difficult for him as possible,' he said.

The thrust of the inquiry focused on the cash Gilligan was shifting through unsuspecting bookmakers. The team approached the large bookmaking firms who reported how much money he had gambled. In his career, Carty had dealt with serious crime, but was aghast at the wealth Gilligan was collecting. 'I had dealt with subversives and the like, so nothing shocked me. But I was a bit taken aback with the sheer scale of his operation. We had intelligence that he was bringing huge amounts of hash into the country, so we knew he had to be making serious money. But I don't think anyone thought it was that big.'

The Garda team started approaching locals who lived near Jessbrook. John Gilligan, contrary to what Geraldine would have you believe, was despised by their neighbours. He bullied his way around and shouted and screamed at people who crossed him. One neighbour whom Gilligan wanted to buy land from was beaten up when he refused – Gilligan urinated on his face. Another who needed Gilligan's permission to use part of his land to supply water to his home was refused. He was hated in the rural community.

An essential part of the investigation was keeping Bowden, Meredith, Geraldine and virtually all of Gilligan's associates under surveillance. Rooney and Geraldine, the latter blissfully unaware of the former, were also tailed.

Slowly the team began to put the jigsaw together. The incident room would remain open till midnight each night, busy with people filing reports. 'We worked 12 hours a day on the case, 24 hours some days, as late as necessary,' said Carty.

In the first weeks of the inquiry, Carty had made sure the CNDT were involved in the decision-making. The CNDT assumed responsibility for tracking the movements of Gilligan and his associates through Dublin Airport, vehicles flagged to the gang and the ferry terminals. Brendan 'Speedy' Fegan was identified dropping off Meehan at Dublin Airport to catch one of his many flights abroad. Pineapple soon outlined the nucleus of people associated with Gilligan. Carty asked Special Branch for a report on Gilligan's links with the INLA, who were beginning to feature in the inquiry. Twelve of their number found themselves implicated. Information from taps on their phones confirmed the INLA was handling hashish worth £10,000 a week, as well as carrying out shootings on Gilligan's behalf.

Every one of the team was aware of Gilligan's connection to Traynor, and the charges relating to the Guerin assault. Carty knew the journalist personally – the two were unrepentant Manchester United fans. Midway through the inquiry, he warned her to be careful. Gilligan, he said, was dangerous, perhaps more so than anyone imagined. 'I think she thought of it as just intimidation on Gilligan's behalf. She would say, "What else would you expect of John Gilligan?"'

Gradually, Carty came to understand that Gilligan was a fool, but a dangerous one. Reading report after report on everything about his life, he gained an insight into Operation Pineapple's target. 'He was a fella who achieved what he should never have achieved,' he later reflected. 'If he was anything, he was a two-bit handbag snatcher from Ballyfermot, who started out doing the dirty work, then started paying others to do it when he got the money. Gilligan was no criminal mastermind, just the right fella in the right place at the right time.'

Even before linking Meredith, Baltus and Djorai to Gilligan, the Dutch MOT were convinced they had uncovered a serious money laundering operation. If they had needed confirmation of this it came on 9 May when a criminal investigation team tapped Baltus' and Rahman's names into the Dutch national criminal system. By a stroke of good fortune, Baltus had been arrested the day before in a hotel in The Hague collecting an envelope. This envelope had been posted from Dublin and marked for the attention of one Mr Simon Rahman. When Rahman failed to collect the letter, the hotel's manager opened the package and found it contained 31 counterfeit US dollar notes. One of the notes was printed on one side only. The rest were of good quality and bore the serial numbers B70161620K and B26466264L. The manager called the police. One detective stayed in the hotel while his colleague took the forged notes away for forensic examination. Back in police headquarters, the detective learned that a similar amount had been seized from Baltus' son the previous October. Not only that, but Interpol had circulated bulletins on the counterfeit cash. The detective went looking for the bulletin, reference number 12 A20305. Meanwhile back at the hotel, Baltus turned up to collect Rahman's letter and was promptly arrested.

Forging any currency is a serious offence, but printing US dollars is far more serious because they belong directly to the American Government. Once the embassy was alerted to the find, the pressure would mount on the local police to locate those responsible. To be seen to have done everything possible, the detectives asked the hotel to let them know if anyone called about the letter. A day later, the hotel staff received a call from a young woman inquiring about the letter. She rang three times and asked if it had been collected. Each time she got more anxious, demanding to know if anyone had showed up. On the fourth call, she left an Irish phone number. Her name, she said, was Mrs Ollie. The hotel passed the number to the police who in turn contacted Garda headquarters. The phone number was traced back to Carol Rooney.

Ever cautious of his phone calls being tapped, Gilligan had asked his girlfriend to call on his behalf using a friend's phone. When she failed to find out what was happening, he called the hotel himself. The call was traced. Baltus was arrested pursuant to article 209 of the Criminal Code, which refers to counterfeiting. Ever willing to cut a deal, he told the investigators he had received his orders from Rahman. He then volunteered Djorai's name. The police picked him up a short time later. They couldn't press charges due to lack of evidence.

A week later, after cross-referencing the telephone calls and security footage of Gilligan taken in the casino, the Dutch police were told by their Irish colleagues that 'Gilligan belongs in the top three criminals in Ireland. He deals in drugs and firearms and maintains contact with subversive groups.'

After a year of chasing the Danish 'Mr Big', the Danish serious crime squad decided to involve Europol. The investigation had started on 4 February after the Spanish police seized 1.8 tons of hash hidden in the roof of a Danish-registered truck. The driver, Rene Thor Andersen, under interrogation had given away the specific details of Mr Big's role in the haul. Back in Copenhagen, the police didn't need anyone to tell them it was their suspect. They code-named Mr Big 'Target 1'. Realising they were chasing an international criminal group, of which Gilligan was a member, they decided to seek assistance from their European counterparts. This was arranged through the official channels of Europol, which arranged a meeting to be held in the Swedish Embassy on Thursday, 6 June. In attendance were liaison officers from Belgium, the Netherlands and Denmark. A UK detective seconded to Brussels to liase with police there was also present.

The delegates were told that the Danish Serious Crime Squad

believed Mr Big was supplying drug traffickers across Europe with hashish and, of late, ecstasy pills. This information, the representative stated, was gleaned from several telephone interceptions. The latest news from the telephone interceptions was of a conversation between Mr Big and an associate, which took place on 30 May. In the conversation, the two discussed the sale of hashish. Mr Big, a rancorous dealer by any standards, bragged that he only dealt in quantities that weighed over one ton. Mr Big then suggested to his associate that he send in a ton from his 'stock' in Spain to The Netherlands – from where it, in smaller portions, could be distributed to Denmark. Another associate, Otto, was then mentioned. Telephonic intelligence suggested that he was now running an amphetamine and ecstasy laboratory, located somewhere in Belgium.

Unknown to Mr Big, his every move had been monitored since March. Police tailed him while he travelled to Otto's home in Lanaken once a month. His mode of transport from Spain to Belgium was his BMW. The only precaution he took was to change the plates as he crossed international borders. Making sense of the long distance travel, the police concluded that Otto was supplying ecstasy to Mr Big, who they suspected was smuggling it back to Spain for sale on the Costa del Sol. Copies of Otto's photograph were handed to the delegates as they sipped coffee and consumed biscuits. Accompanying the photograph was a document listing his associates. It read: 'RAHMAN, Simon Atha Hussain, d/o/b: Surinam 09.01.42. The police in Den Haag/Netherlands are having an ongoing investigation against RAHMAN because he is suspected of money laundering, drug trafficking and other criminal offences.' The document gave the code-name for the investigation as Operation Aerial. It continued: 'RAHMAN has close contact to: GILLIGAN, John, d/o/b: unknown, living in Dublin/IRELAND. The Dutch police suspect RAHMAN to launder huge sums of money for GILLIGAN, and up to now it seems that RAHMAN has changed approximately 14 mill NGL. The Dutch police have also got information about smuggling of boxes from Rahman to Gilligan using trucks. There is nothing certain about the containment of the mentioned boxes.'

Most of the delegates agreed the sheer scale of Mr Big's drug-dealing syndicate required the co-operation of possibly several countries. The Danish representative suggested the information exchange in the case, code-named Operation Wedge, should be co-ordinated by the ELO-network in Europol. All agreed. The Danish team made another important suggestion, after requesting that Wedge utilise analytical support from Europol Drugs Unit in order to make a better overview of the case. 'We should really get Ireland and Spain involved,' they said. They all left the meeting, agreeing to regroup in Europol headquarters on Tuesday, 18 June, at 11 a.m.

On 10 June, Carty received correspondence from the Irish desk at Europol inviting him to send officers. When he saw Gilligan's name mentioned, he gave the go-ahead.

Meanwhile, the MOT was working at cross-purposes to Operation Wedge. Like the Danish, it realised that Gilligan and Rahman were part of a larger, nefarious organisation. Linking Rahman, Gilligan or Baltus to drugs was not their function and they knew well that they would never get enough evidence to press charges. They also deemed the inquiry far too problematic, given that most of the suspects were living in Ireland, outside their own country. They too decided to enlist Europol. On 12 June, John Van Wijk, from the MOT wrote to Robert Tjaikens, an officer in the planning and development section of Europol Drugs Unit, seeking his help in investigating Gilligan. Van Wijk recounted the casino story, how the MOT had learned about Meehan's links to the drug trade and of course, Gilligan's role. 'On the basis of the above information,' he wrote 'there are justifiable suspicions that there is a connection among the persons mentioned. Additionally it can be said that in view of the criminal backgrounds of Meehan and Gilligan the amounts of money exchanged were acquired in drugs traffic and/or arms traffic and/or terrorism.' The MOT, he wrote, suspected that Baltus, Rahman and Djorai were linked to Gilligan. 'It is important for us to find out whether transactions by the persons mentioned were reported to your institution or whether you possess any other information relevant for the MOT. Trusting I have sufficiently informed you, please keep me informed about the progress you make.'

By the time Europol notified Carty about the MOT's inquiry, Operation Pineapple was well under way. In less than a month, the Irish end of Gilligan's operation had been documented, extensive reports on his financial dealings compiled and above all his most trusted lieutenants exposed. The squad started making life decidedly uncomfortable for Gilligan although he didn't know it was a co-ordinated effort.

Carty's decision to concentrate on his finances inevitably caused his officers to visit accountants and investment brokers, a necessary move that was unheard of. 'We had hit maybe 20 investment brokers and accountants offices, People were kind of looking at us, asking what were we doing. This sort of investigation was new. But it was what we needed to do,' he said. And this is how the investigation progressed.

The team also utilised the information that was now flowing in from Europe. To get more concrete evidence, Carty sent Eddie Rock, a superintendent in the GNDU, with McGinn to the Operation Wedge meeting in The Hague on 18 June. The two officers returned with even more information.

Finally, after weeks of hard work, liaison meetings and sleepless nights, Carty told his crew they had enough evidence to start making arrests. At midday on Monday, 23 June 1996, the team gathered in the incident room. 'I gave out the orders to arrest those around him, anyone who was close to him to get more evidence, to build up a stronger case,' he recalled. 'We had picked the interrogation teams, search teams and we were going to bring in Geraldine, Tracy and Carol Rooney. She, in particular, had a story to tell that would have opened other doors.' The meeting lasted less than an hour. After it had finished, Carty left in the company of McNally. As far as they were concerned, Gilligan's days were numbered.

CHAPTER 12

A Time to Kill

'I thought he was only going to fire one or two shots at
her, but he emptied it into her. Fair play to him.'
BRIAN MEEHAN SPEAKING TO CHARLIE BOWDEN

The problem Gilligan faced was how to stop Guerin from proceeding with the assault case. In contrast to his expectations, the threats hadn't intimidated her to the extent that she dropped the charges or even temporarily ceased writing about crime. On the contrary, she continued writing, producing stories that would be posthumously described as her best work. Gilligan did not possess such inner strength. The prospect of incarceration in Portlaoise unsettled him. He looked on the journalist as an inconceivable woman. 'Who does she think she is?' he asked Meehan rhetorically. That she would dare arrive at his home, ignore his threats, name him on the front page of the *Sunday Independent*, then attempt to press charges against him, he could not understand.

For the first time since his release from Portlaoise, he was running scared. He became 'more intense', Warren would later say. This behaviour soon turned to obsession. Like his father, Gilligan had an explosive personality that shaped his life. He would strike out at anything that threatened or annoyed him without a thought. There was no calming him. He became prone to mood swings. Geraldine's harsh but tranquillising words had no effect on him. Neither had Rooney's. He could not sleep at night, enjoy himself or relax to any great extent. The mere mention of Guerin's name agitated him.

In March, two summonses had been delivered to Jessbrook notifying him that he was to appear before Kilcock District Court on 14 May charged with the assault. On the morning of the trial, he arrived at the court accompanied by Geraldine and a gang of young men, all clutching mobile phones that rang incessantly. Michael Hanahoe, one of the finest criminal defence solicitors in Dublin, was at his side to represent him.

In the months that followed the attack, Guerin developed an outright animosity towards Gilligan. The Operation Pineapple team and the IRA were not the only ones inquiring into his wealth. She had made it her business to learn more about him, his criminal organisation, his henchmen and the crimes they engaged in. Outside the courthouse, she came face to face with her attacker for the first time since he assaulted her. There were no words spoken but there was a sense of tension in the air. Graham had brought his wife to the courthouse along with a colleague from the *Sunday Independent*. Gilligan could not hide his contempt and eyeballed her. Geraldine was more direct in her approach; she walked up to Veronica and told her she would not forget her. All this went unnoticed in the hustle of the court sitting.

The case was adjourned when it came up for hearing due to a legal technicality. Judge John Brophy fixed a date for mentioning the case, 28 May. Gilligan walked away from the court a free man. It was at this point that he noticed a photographer taking his picture. He despised cameras, never mind photographers armed with telephoto lenses. The photographer took only one picture as he walked away. Gilligan stared back defiantly, not knowing whether to cover his face with his hands, or pretend he was innocent and walk away smiling. The media bothered him. Where would his photograph appear? Would his legitimate business acquaintances recognise him? He felt a deep sense of rage. Apart from members of his family and a select group of acquaintances, he had never allowed anyone to point a camera in his direction. Now his photograph could appear on the front of Irish newspapers alongside articles about how he attacked Guerin, threatened to rape her son and murder her family. He had spent the last few years trying to conceal his criminal background – the convictions, robberies and links to paramilitary outfits. He considered himself a businessman whose wife ran a highly successful riding school and socialised with the high flyers of Dublin's social scene. In truth, he was a gangster and Jessbrook represented the proceeds of crime. Now, the house of cards he had spent years cleverly constructing was about to be exposed for what it was.

Gilligan was deadly serious when he said he was not going to allow Veronica to destroy him. At a party held after his first court appearance, he stood in a corner surrounded by former inmates of Portlaoise. One joked that he would be back in his cell soon enough for beating Guerin. Gilligan was not amused. 'I'm not going back to prison, no matter what. That bitch is going to be sorry she ever messed with me,' he growled. Coercion had not scared her. Threatening to rape her son appeared not to have any effect. There was only one way to stop her as far as he was concerned. The Gardaí believe he decided to murder her at this point and what follows in the rest of this chapter is what they believe happened and what the prosecution was subsequently to allege in the Special Criminal Court concerning John Gilligan.

A week after his first court appearance, Warren visited Gilligan in Jessbrook. Gilligan collected him at the Spa Hotel in Lucan. During the drive, they spoke about money laundering and the enduring success of the business, which was going from strength to strength. An invitation to Jessbrook was an important occasion for Warren, still a relative newcomer to the cartel. His criminal credibility was not particularly impressive, so when the opportunity arose, he bragged that he had broken into a house and stolen a motorcycle. This aroused Gilligan's interest.

Warren recounted how he and one of his friends had been drinking in the Speaker Connolly pub in Firhouse on the outskirts of Dublin. His friend's name was Paul Cradden. He lived on the Corrib Road in Terenure. When they left the pub, the two headed towards Dun Laoghaire where Cradden's employer, Ian Keith, managed a large house on Royal Terrace. Keith was a motorcycle enthusiast. His most prized possession was a Kawasaki racing bike. 'Paul showed me where the garage was. I jumped over the wall and got into the garage. I then opened the door. He pulled a cover off the motorcycle.' Warren examined the bike. It looked valuable. He noticed a sticker affixed to its windbreak. It read Genuine Oxford Grip. They decided to take the bike. Warren had parked his small van in a nearby lane way and the two pushed the bike into the van. 'We didn't know where to go with it or in fact what to do with it,' he said. He rang a friend, Steven McGrath, who lived on St Enda's Road in Terenure. McGrath was a hackney driver and owned a garage. 'We gave him some story about repossessing a bike.' They brought the stolen bike to his garage and stored it there.

After they arrived at the equestrian centre, Warren walked the land with Gilligan who gave him a guided tour of the arena and livery facilities. Workmen were installing seats in the showjumping arena. Gilligan brought up the subject of the bike. He seemed interested in it. 'Just keep it,' he told Warren. 'Don't do anything with it, I may need it,' he said.

John Traynor was encountering similar difficulties with Veronica Guerin. Their relationship had turned sour, if not bitterly hostile. In talking about Gilligan, The Coach had unwittingly implicated himself in the drug business, though not by design. In due time, she realised that virtually everything he had told her was lies. With Traynor, she concluded, it was impossible to distinguish between the truth and lies. Yet what seemed most dreadful to her were his sexual perversions, which she accidentally learned of. Finally seeing Traynor for what he was, she decided to write about him. She made one mistake though – she kept her line of communication with him open.

There is no doubt that she thought this was a shrewd manoeuvre. Rather than lose what was clearly a good source of information on Gilligan, she continued meeting him, but recorded each conversation using a tiny dictaphone she carried in her pocket. Traynor certainly knew the type of reprisal Gilligan's gang had planned for Guerin and, with a degree of irony, hinted as much to her in an obscure way during their last meeting. For the first time since the two had met, Traynor warned her about Gilligan. 'Even last week, when you were saying about Gilligan and what he's capable of, and trying to stop me going to court, it makes me more determined. It's the way I am,' she told him.

He said: 'If he never done anything, at the back of your mind, you know what he's capable of.'

The Coach's engagement in the narcotics trade caught Guerin by surprise. But once she had ascertained his specific role in Gilligan's operation and the cannabis trade, he became a legitimate target for her investigations. Her mistake was to tell him about what she knew and that she intended to name him in the *Sunday Independent*. There is a suspicion that he toyed with the idea of murdering Veronica himself. The windows of her car were smashed around this time in what appeared to be an act of vandalism. Traynor, however, admitted responsibility and paid for the damage. Veronica confided that she suspected that Traynor was testing the car windows to see if they were bullet-proof. But rather than resort to violence or use intimidation, he turned to the courts.

On Thursday, 13 June, Traynor arrived at Hanahoe's office on Parliament Street, where he spoke to Michael Hanahoe. That day he displayed all the hurt of an innocent man who was about to be wronged. He said Guerin had called him to say she was preparing a story for publication that would link him to the drugs trade. The article was due for publication the following Sunday, 16 June.

Traynor, who had a noteworthy ability to charm, said he was at the end of his tether with Guerin. She had threatened and tried to cajole him – legal redress was his only solution. The lawyer listened attentively and in proper fashion advised an injunction. Traynor accepted his opinion and told him to do whatever was necessary. Hanahoe picked up the phone, called the law library and arranged a consultation with a senior counsel for 9 a.m. the next day.

Traynor explained his predicament once more. What he told his lawyers was a mixture of lies and half-truths. For obvious reasons, he denied any association with the 'narcotics trade' as he called it. He concocted a story about how Guerin had, two weeks earlier, lunched with him in the Greyhound bar in Harold's Cross in Dublin. Minutes into the meeting, he said, Guerin announced that her editor had received a Garda report together with a photograph from a Garda file. The photograph was of him. The report, she suggested, linked him to Thomas Mullen and another criminal, two heroin traffickers from Dublin, though he didn't mention either by name. 'This confidential report was never produced to me, nor was it ever offered to me, nor was it ever subsequently forwarded to me at any stage by her, or by anybody,' he said. By that afternoon, he had secured the injunction impeding the publication. Traynor kept Gilligan fully briefed on his case, which the latter viewed as a good way of disseminating black propaganda against Guerin. Anything to damage her reputation would do.

While Guerin was a brilliant journalist in many ways, she was ignorant of the criminal psyche. She did not understand the danger Traynor represented, or his ability to double-cross. The likelihood of Gilligan mounting an attack had crossed her mind, but she saw her own well-founded fears as a weakness in herself. This was her first mistake. Her second oversight was that during one of her many casual conversations with Traynor she told him she was due before Naas District Court at 11 a.m. on 26 June to be judged on a speeding offence.

If Gilligan ever decides to speak about his knowledge of the killing, he would probably say his gang began plotting the journalist's murder at the moment he left Kilcock District Court. Fear of jail was one reason they had to want her out of the way, but Gilligan was also apprehensive in regard to losing power. Meehan was the son he always wanted, unlike his own heir Darren. But if Gilligan was convicted, given his criminal record, the likelihood of prison was not a prospect but a certainty. Meehan was more than capable of taking control. This, more than anything else, preoccupied Gilligan's mind because it would not only destroy him financially but also dent his ego. Expecting more journalists to attend his next court appearance on 25 June, he focused his mind on a grand plan to sort Guerin out once and for all. The court fixture itself was a routine affair. He knew the case would not proceed, giving him plenty of time to execute his plan, which he decided to discuss with Meehan.

One of Gilligan's inherent character flaws was that he surrounded himself with a band of fools. The two discussed shooting the journalist, yet neither could see the inevitable chain reaction it would cause. On the contrary, Meehan agreed with Gilligan's general outlook – he too reckoned Guerin had to go. Meehan steadfastly agreed with Gilligan's thwarted view of his predicament. God hadn't blessed him with intelligence or a conscience, nor was he a cunning criminal. A more ambitious criminal would have seen Gilligan's return to jail as something of a probability rather than a possibility, and as an opportunity for him to take control without sparking off a bloody feud. Whether it was lack of self-confidence or devotion to his boss, he stood firm behind Gilligan, believing the business would certainly fall apart if the boss was jailed. This was the worst scenario imaginable for Meehan. Without Gilligan to organise regular cannabis deliveries from Holland, he saw his career as effectively finished. This encouraged Gilligan's gang, who saw no distinction between attempting Foley's murder and assassinating one of Ireland's best known public figures. On the contrary, they thought such an act would heighten their standing in the underworld. They had not the slightest comprehension of the consequences their actions would have, no matter which way they rationalised the situation. In spite of his crimes, Gilligan also had a passionate hatred for Guerin. He despised what she stood for; his business was no business of anyone else's. This was his rationale.

On 19 June, Gilligan rang Warren asking whether he had possession of the stolen motorcycle. 'Do you still have it?' he inquired of the bike. Warren confirmed he did. 'Is it where anyone would see our faces? I have Brian Meehan with me.'

Warren sensed the urgency in his voice. He said the bike was in his friend's garage at the rear of St Enda's Road. 'No one will be around, you can have a look,' he promised. They arranged to meet in the car park of the Terenure House.

Thirty minutes later, the two gangsters arrived. Warren sat in Gilligan's car and directed them to the garage. He looked over his shoulder to see if he was being followed. They pulled up outside the garage and scuttled in. Parked inside was the powerful-looking Kawasaki.

Working like a mechanic, Meehan commenced an examination of the bike, methodically checking its suspension, brakes, indicators and balance. He saw the keyhole on the fuel tank had been drilled to allow a refuel. The back indicator lights were also broken. Some farings were missing. Should the bike break down, it would mean certain trouble.

Warren couldn't help but wonder why Gilligan was on edge. His body language was that of a man possessed. Never before had the little man seemed so distracted. But the months Warren had spent working under Gilligan's tutelage had given him an unnatural ability to keep his mouth shut and not to ask questions that he didn't want to know the answers to.

Happy with his cursory examination, Meehan said the bike would do. Gilligan then ordered Warren to fit it out with new plates and indicators. They left in Gilligan's car. He offered to drop Warren back to the Terenure House where he had left his car. Gilligan drove, Meehan sat in the front passenger seat and Warren sat in the back. Then, out of the blue, Gilligan turned to Warren and in a matter-of-fact way said: 'I have been told not to trust you, but I will.' Warren was astonished. Gilligan then said he would murder him, his family and parents if he ever made a statement against him. Warren thought it was a joke but Gilligan didn't smile. Neither did Meehan, who looked directly at him with an expressionless face. His voice steady, Warren mustered up the courage to ask if he had done anything wrong. 'Just keep it in mind,' answered Gilligan. 'Just keep it in mind. Don't think I won't do this. No matter where you are I'll get you.'

He dropped Warren off and said he'd be in touch. Warren immediately returned to McGrath's house and started repairing the bike. Warren bought two new rear indicators for the bike in a motorcycle shop for £16. He purchased new number plates. He also got petrol. Finally it was fitted with modern Euro plates.

On the evening of 21 June, the five principal members of the gang assembled in Meehan's apartment in Clifton Court. They often met there on Friday nights to discuss business, how much money they had made and the events of the past week. Gilligan rarely attended these criminal conferences. Afterwards the gang – Meehan, Mitchell, Bowden and the two Ward brothers – would usually retire to a nightclub, snort cocaine with cheap women and generally act out the part of gangsters. On that night Hippo wasn't present. Meehan, however, had other pressing issues on his mind. 'The little fella', he said, was 'pissed off'. They all knew what he meant by this. 'Gilligan's upset about her, something's going to have to be done about her. If he's sent down for the assault, the whole operation will fall apart,' he said with authority. 'He's the only one that knows the people to get the gear.'

Bowden said nothing. Mitchell nodded in agreement. Ward fidgeted and his brother Shay remained silent. They left it at that. Bowden shrugged it off. He'd heard such talk before. Every second week, either Meehan or Gilligan would plot someone's murder. The conspiracy however would inevitably be made redundant within a few days. 'It was,' as he would later remark, 'the way they went on.'

Except this time the gang were deadly serious. A reputable assassin had already been hired. Meehan had in fact offered to carry out the shooting but this was decided against; Meehan had already botched Foley's execution. If Guerin survived, it would be a disaster. However Meehan would oversee the assassination and was entrusted to arm, collect and deliver the killer to the scene.

That weekend, the gang met to finalise their plans. Meehan drove towards the Phoenix Park, up the back roads along the Liffey valley into the Strawberry Beds. The talk was of cannabis and guns. Meehan asked Bowden where the Magnum was. He said he'd searched the hiding spot, in a grave in the Jewish cemetery, but it wasn't there. 'I told him that we were using more than one grave,' Bowden would later say. He directed Meeham to another grave.

At 10.30 a.m. on Tuesday, 25 June, Gilligan attended what was to be his last appearance before Kilcock District Court. He arrived in the company of his solicitor. It was supposed to be a routine fixture where Judge Brophy would mention the case as arranged. It lasted no more than a few minutes. After Judge Brophy had finished dealing with the case, Hanahoe emerged. The trial now looked as if it would proceed sometime in July. The solicitor was concerned about aspects of the case. If he familiarised himself with Jessbrook, he could get a clearer picture of what happened with his own eyes. Could he go there at once to look around? Gilligan said he'd take him there. The two drove in Hanahoe's car to Jessbrook where the lawyer viewed the scene and its surroundings.

Gilligan, always the opportunist, said he had to catch flight EI 608 from Dublin Airport leaving at 3.35 p.m. for Amsterdam. He had purchased the ticket to depart nine days earlier. Rooney was flying with him. Hanahoe offered him a lift. He was heading back to Dublin anyway. That night Meehan, accompanied by Mitchell, arranged to meet Warren in the car park of the Terenure House. They collected Warren and drove to St Enda's Road. Meehan wanted to test drive the Kawasaki. They arrived as it got dark. In one arm, Meehan carried a new motorcycle helmet. 'We drove up to the end of the lane. I went to the garage and Brian joined me later. Brian had a new silver full-face helmet and gloves. He put those on and drove the bike away for a test drive,' said Warren.

The bike was ready as ordered; Warren had fitted it out with new lights and false plates should any passing police car notice it. But Mitchell wasn't impressed. 'It wouldn't be my first choice but it will have to do,' he said.

While Meehan was gone, Gilligan called Warren on his mobile phone. Warren was due to fly to Schipol the next morning to deliver money. Even before he could ask where in Amsterdam Gilligan wanted to meet, he was interrupted and told that he was needed in Dublin instead. 'I want you there,' said Gilligan. His words came as a complete surprise. Now he knew that something serious was going on.

Meehan returned minutes later. When he dismounted, he asked Warren if he knew what Veronica Guerin looked like. Warren said he didn't. He said nothing as Meehan gave him a description. 'He said that she was between 30 and 40 years old, small build and I think he said greyish short hair. I didn't know who she was and he didn't mention anything about her being a journalist or anything to do with papers,' he recalled. Warren felt he was sinking into a mire, but he remained clear-sighted. He listened to Meehan attentively and said goodbye. As soon as they left, he took a can of petrol and wiped the bike of his fingerprints.

Meehan drove straight to Greenmount where he rendezvoused with Bowden. The moment Bowden walked in the door, he noticed the Magnum. It was placed on a shelf with six individual pieces of ammunition. The gun looked dirty. Bowden picked it up, wiped it clean, rubbing off excess oil from the polishing he had given it before hiding it away in the grave. 'I loaded it with six rounds and left it on the table with six other rounds.' He didn't need anyone to tell him Guerin was going to be shot.

Meehan woke the next day at 7 a.m. That morning was bright and sunny with little cloud cover. The sky was clear, bright blue. He called Paul Ward's home at 8.14 a.m. His telephone wasn't working properly and the line broke down. The call lasted just 17 seconds. Fourteen minutes later, he called again. This call lasted just 48 seconds. He called Ward's house another 17 minutes later. He was anxious. The line broke down. The call lasted just nine seconds. Perhaps this was to make sure that Ward, a chronic heroin addict, was out of bed. His role in the conspiracy was to monitor the airwaves. At 8.56 a.m. Ward returned his calls using a mobile telephone. He couldn't get through. He made a second call at 9.08 a.m. Both calls lasted just five seconds each.

Meehan was using an ear-piece plugged into his phone. He bought this for the murder. The device was designed to allow him to take calls while driving. It was a great device but it didn't work.

Mitchell had collected him around 8 a.m. at his apartment and drove him to Terenure to collect the motorcycle. He was due to rendezvous with Warren at 9 a.m. Warren was already waiting to meet them when they arrived at the rear of St Enda's Road. 'As far as I can remember I got a telephone call on my mobile telephone from

Brian saying that he was delayed and would ring later. I went into Stephen's house and I had a cup of coffee.' McGrath had no idea what the gang was planning.

Meehan arrived between 9.20 a.m. and 9.45 a.m. He looked at the bike. It was in perfect running order, just as he'd left it the night before. He said he'd be back later for it. Meehan then ordered Warren to drive to Naas. Without asking Meehan himself, what happened next can only be surmised. After he drove away from St Enda's Road, he either went and collected the gunman chosen to pull the trigger or returned on his own, then linked up with the hired killer.

The caretaker at Naas District Court, John Kelly, had, like Meehan, risen early that day. He arrived for work at 9 a.m. The caretaker for more years than he cared to remember, he made his usual rounds, opening the relevant offices and doors. One of his chores was to erect the tricolour that flies from the top of the court structure; 26 June 1996 was just another day.

Veronica Guerin had risen early that morning in preparation for her court appearance. She arrived at the courthouse around 9.45 a.m., giving her plenty of time to get her story right for the judge. She parked outside a hotel next door to the courthouse.

Back in Crumlin, Ward was in the early stages of a nervous breakdown. He was not made for murdering journalists, nor anyone else for that matter. He was tense and desperately needed to know what was happening, if only to convince himself that no one would get caught. He called Meehan again at 11.02. There was no answer.

Traynor knew about the plan. He didn't care one way or the other. He too had had enough. Whether Guerin died or not was irrelevant to him now. At that moment he was racing at Mondello racetrack. Always mindful of giving himself an undeniable alibi, he decided to stage a crash. Minutes after 11 a.m. he overturned his car. When rescuers ran to the scene, he asked that an ambulance collect him. He was rushed to Naas General Hospital. Warren set off for Naas. He drove down the Long Mile Road and turned off on to the Naas dual carriageway. He arrived in the town about 10.30 a.m. 'I drove through the town and parked up near the centre of the town. I got out and walked looking for the courthouse and the red sports car.'

Meehan called him, wanting to know if he had found Veronica's car. The calls lasted only a few seconds. Warren shouted into his mobile phone, which was conspicuous by its large size. A passer-by noticed him making the call. The size of his mobile phone caught her eye. It seemed strange to her that anyone would carry such a clumsy device. As she continued about her business, Warren walked off in the direction of the Newbridge Road. He parked his vehicle in a position that allowed him to monitor Veronica's Calibra.

Her case was called around noon and by 12.30 p.m. it was over. She was fined £120. She walked out of the building elated, for the prospect of losing her driving licence would have been too much to bear.

'I then rang Brian Meehan on his mobile. He asked me who was in the car. I told him there was only one person. He told me to follow the car,' Warren said. When she pulled away, he picked up her trail. Minutes later he called Meehan, who by this stage was parked on a lay-by on Blackchurch Road, outside the village of Rathcoole. 'She's on the way,' he said.

Warren followed the car as it headed towards Dublin City, along a route that cut short her trip by avoiding traffic lights and traffic. Warren noticed that she drove at a steady speed, making telephone calls as she did. But he was more interested in ingratiating himself with Gilligan's gang. He pressed his redial key as she passed the Airmotive complex on the Naas dual carriageway. 'She's at Airmotive, passing now,' he said, his voice raised to compensate for the lack of volume.

Meehan, catching his first glimpse of Guerin's car, said: 'I see it.' He sped off.

Ward was still fidgety and growing more and more nervous. He called Meehan again at 12.49 p.m. The call lasted just three seconds. Meehan couldn't answer. He was driving at high speed following Guerin. He followed Veronica for about four miles from Rathcoole to Clondalkin.

Warren maintained a discreet distance behind Guerin's car, following at the same speed in the same lane but keeping a distance of four cars. A red light appeared at the junction to the Boot Road in Clondalkin, forcing the traffic to stop. When it did, he saw Meehan drive past. The bike pulled up alongside Guerin's car and the pillion-rider produced a gun. What happened next was a bloody carnage.

Although it all happened in the space of a few seconds, it seemed like an eternity for Warren. 'I froze. I went to get out as if I could help. I just stopped. It was like slow motion. I realised what we were after doing.' He drove away at speed. Witnesses mistook this for blind fear.

Gilligan called him minutes later. He called from Amsterdam where he was with Rooney. She overheard the conversation, which lasted no more than ten seconds.

Warren went home, then arranged to meet a friend for a drink to give himself an alibi. Meehan, in the meantime, made quick his escape, driving up the Belgard Road, on to the M50 roundabout and down a slipway which brought him to Walkinstown Road in Crumlin. Eleven minutes after the shooting, at 1.06 p.m., Meehan called Ward's phone again. This call was the second longest of the day, lasting 37 seconds. He was just about to arrive and wanted the garage door open. Ward had not the nerve for murder. He was a trembling wreck. Meehan, of course, did not recognise this and started boasting seconds after he walked in the door. He threw the Magnum into the bathroom sink and said in a most casual way to the killer: 'You emptied that into her.' He didn't waste time with conversation – speed was of the essence in order to establish an alibi.

Peter Mitchell and Shay Ward were waiting in the house. The latter was given the job of driving Meehan into Dublin. Mitchell had a similar role, but he was charged with getting the killer to Crumlin. The news was still not on the airwaves. Trying to stick to their original plan, which had so far been carried out with military-like precision, they left.

Mitchell, although no one thought it, was in shock. He wasn't cut out for murder. Nerves caused him to drive with the skill of a lunatic, overtaking cars and honking his horn. Some minutes later, at 1.25 p.m., he was seen by an off-duty policeman who spotted his car heading towards Walkinstown. The Garda gave chase but could not keep up without endangering the lives of fellow motorists. He took note of the time and driver.

Shay Ward delivered Meehan into Dublin City in quick time, dropping him off on Angier Street at 1.30 p.m. By chance, Detective Sergeant John O'Driscoll, the head of the North Central Drugs Squad, was sitting in a car parked across the street waiting for a colleague. When he saw Meehan jump out of a small van driven by Ward his first instinct was to reach for his notebook. He took note of the registration and of the fact that Meehan was talking into his mobile.

Mitchell made his way into the city where he regrouped with Meehan. They made straight for Bowden's hair salon on Moore Street and, according to plan, were seen by a Garda patrol. Two minutes later, at 1.32 p.m., Meehan phoned Paul Ward to reassure him everything was going according to plan. The call lasted 29 seconds.

News of the murder hadn't reached the general public and so life inside the hairdresser's was normal, with no talk of the murder among the women inside. Meehan knocked on the window through which he could see Juliet Beacon working. The time was now 1.40 p.m. She stepped out through the door. He asked where Bowden was. She didn't know, but said he shouldn't be long. Meehan smiled and said he'd be in Fallon's restaurant and to tell Charlie.

He had just sat down when Bowden arrived. They ate nothing, just sipped tea and coffee. The aftershock of the adrenaline caused by the shooting was still affecting them. He was excited. 'It was a good job this morning,' he told Bowden. 'I thought he was only going to fire one or two shots at her but he emptied it into her. Fair play to him. We legged it up the Belgard Road on the bike.'

To evade prosecution, it was essential that each showed no emotion, especially when the subject of Guerin's murder surfaced. Back in Crumlin, Ward was scanning the police airwaves for information on the murder. He learned nothing that was of benefit to him, not that the police were careful about what they said over their porous communications network. But they knew nothing. He relayed this back to Meehan in three short phone calls.

As one might expect, the details of Guerin's ghastly execution impacted hard on the staff at Naas Court. John Kelly was particularly reminiscent. Guerin's murder preoccupied his mind as he untied the tricolour and pulled it down for the night. 'Who would do such a thing?' he thought to himself while he carefully folded the flag. Turning to walk back into the court, he noticed through the corner of his eye that someone had been on the roof – the slates were disturbed. There had been a second person monitoring Guerin's movements.

That night, Meehan, Mitchell, Bowden and his girlfriend Juliet

Beacon, and Vanessa Meehan assembled in the Hole in the Wall pub on Blackhorse Avenue. The European Championship games were playing on the television. Meehan was in particularly jovial form. When Ward hadn't appeared by 11 p.m. Meehan telephoned him to see where he was, but the line broke down after six seconds. Ward called him back to say he was on his way. The beer flowed and Meehan took some cocaine to sedate any anxieties he possessed.

Meehan, however, was putting on a brave face. He was worried. When he went to the toilet, he got into a fight with one of the bar's other patrons. They all left and went to the Turnstile pub, located a short walk away. The pub lies adjacent to the Phoenix Park and was situated a short distance away from Bowden's home in the Paddocks. They stayed until closing time and headed for the POD nightclub, coincidentally located across the road from Garda headquarters.

After the club had closed, they went on to Bowden's home. The party got into full swing. Senan Moloney lived next door to Bowden. He was the crime correspondent for the *Star* newspaper and had spent the day writing about the murder. He had seen his colleague's limp body and felt physically sick. The day had proved too much for him. So he finished early and made his way home. As he was walking through his front door, he had noticed Bowden lugging trays of beer into his house. 'I formed the opinion there was going to be more booze and music that night,' he later said. And he was proved correct.

That night the music blared and the beer and cocaine flowed. In one corner, Meehan sat drinking a can of beer, his eyes glazed from the cocaine in his bloodstream. In another corner sat Ward with his arms around his girlfriend Vanessa Meehan, Brian's youngster sister. Bowden and Beacon danced. Gilligan had called earlier, telling them to have a good night. Away from the outrage that was quickly enveloping Ireland, he felt relieved. That was the end of her, or so he thought. What Guerin couldn't do to him in life, she certainly wouldn't be able to in death.

CHAPTER 13

Public Enemy Number One

'I'm finished in Ireland. They're saying the Provos will
get me.'
JOHN GILLIGAN

The gangster's name was catapulted into the national consciousness within 24 hours of the murder. Gilligan had predicted a public outcry but postulated that any outrage would soon subside – that Veronica's murder would become nothing more than another statistic. But this was no more than an arrogant hope. The next morning the storm broke when his photograph was published alongside lengthy articles which made no attempt to disguise the fact that he was the prime suspect.

The Government and the police had not a minute's peace, as it became clear the public had lost all faith in their ability to tackle organised crime. Radio programmes were inundated with calls and the letters pages in the morning newspapers were saturated with angry correspondence.

The killing had huge ramifications for the Government, especially for Owen, who found herself defending her stewardship as society vented its anger. She was in no frame of mind to deal with the onslaught, distraught at having lost a close friend. The frenzy reached fever pitch in the Dáil where the feeling of malevolence towards organised crime was now firmly a political issue. Owen's trustworthiness was not being gauged on her notable initiatives to streamline the judicial system but on the absolute disregard Gilligan held for the law, which had now made the headlines across the English-speaking world. Therefore it was only natural that the opposition capitalised on the public unrest. They demanded action against the now famous drugs barons; the ones who had Mafioso status through Gilligan's action.

GANGSTER

John O'Donoghue, the Fianna Fáil opposition spokesman on justice, was Owen's nemesis. During the previous year, he had carved out a career for himself highlighting the various faults in the criminal justice system in a highly vocal manner. He didn't hold any personal animosity towards the minister; it was just the way Fianna Fáil did business. He did, however, see that Ireland required new laws to tackle criminals like Gilligan. With great political acumen, he had months earlier drafted novel legislation with a barrister friend Eamonn Leahy. He called it the Organised Crime (Restraint and Disposal of Illicit Assets) Bill 1996. The legislation was rudimentary in that it reduced the standard of proof required to seize the proceeds of crime. Instead, it tied the offences to the assets, as against an individual's liberty. The idea had been conceived with a burst of inspirational genius the previous Easter in a place called Cuascrom: 'A beautiful place overlooking the Blasket Islands off the Kerry coast. It came to me there,' O'Donoghue would later say. The law was modelled on a case he remembered when funds collected by Sinn Féin, the political wing of the Provisional IRA, were seized. A subsequent challenge in the High Court found the seizure was within the constitutional parameters.

Fianna Fáil had published the bill but decided to withhold pressing for its enactment until an election was announced. The time was right. O'Donoghue had reason to believe the Government would have no other option but to accept the bill, which would represent a political goal. He went to one of his colleagues, Mary O'Rourke. Because she was a senior party member, who had a fearsome reputation for smiling while denouncing her opponents (an art she probably learned from her days as a school teacher), he believed she would be instrumental in persuading Bertie Ahern, the opposition leader, to move the bill. She agreed with his assessment of the situation.

The two went immediately to the party leader's office on the fifth floor in Government buildings. Here O'Donoghue outlined his case. Ahern didn't need convincing and without haste ordered his officials to withdraw another piece of legislation on contempt the party had planned to move. This effectively gave O'Donoghue free rein. 'Looking at it from the perspective of democratic accountability, I felt that when the stage had been reached in any society that they could now gun down an investigative journalist in the streets, then there

151

was something rotten in that society which had to be rooted out.' He presented the legislation to the Government on the evening of Thursday, 27 June. Jim Higgins, the Government Chief Whip, accepted the bill with a degree of caution. He sent a copy to the Attorney General, Dermot Gleeson, for examination.

For her part, Owen was fighting an impossible war. Not only had she lost a close friend, but she was effectively being blamed for allowing crime to get out of control. Most of the criticism was blissful ignorance but it affected her personally. She would remember that week as one of the hardest of her life. The experience, however, left her resolute. She pressed ahead with her plans to create a multi-agency unit to target crime. She formally unveiled her plans on 2 July to a packed press conference in Government buildings. Accompanying her proposal was a comprehensive package of anti-crime measures. Drug dealers, she said, were not invincible. The Government would hold a special debate on organised crime on 25 July. That gave her four weeks.

Those entirely familiar with the story all agreed that Gilligan was the most likely culprit, but none could understand his senseless logic. The motive was too obvious; he was the only person that would benefit from her death. Traynor's hand in the slaying was another distinct probability. This was a view shared by the police officers tasked with bringing charges against the killers.

Tony Hickey was the chief superintendent in charge of the Serious Crime Squad. He was on holiday in the Portuguese village of Alvor when the gunman struck. Standing in a shopping queue, he overheard a conversation between two Irish tourists standing in the same line. They were talking about Veronica's murder. He said nothing. But when he returned to his apartment, he rang Lucan station and asked if the unthinkable had happened. He took command of the inquiry when he returned home that weekend.

Hickey was a proficient murder investigator, a man who had spent much of his career chasing villains and who possessed all the accompanying mannerisms – he chain-smoked and always looked expressionless. He surrounded himself with a coterie of officers whom he trusted emphatically, and consulted with no one, not even officers attached to other units. Hence he spoke about the investigation only when he needed to. He had joined the Gardaí in 1965 and since that time had avoided the media at all costs, believing that much of what was written about drugs was exaggeration and conjecture.

The problem he faced was how to link Gilligan to the assassination when he was over in Amsterdam at the time of the killing. There was also the possibility that Gilligan was not responsible, a real prospect. To solve the case he hand-picked a team of detectives he trusted. Most were drawn from the Serious Crime Squad, though at the beginning of the inquiry over 100 officers from all divisions in the city got involved.

What Gilligan could never have known was that the police had a head start on him. The Operation Pineapple squad had gathered a mass of intelligence on the gangster. This was shared with the Guerin investigation in accordance with orders from Carty, who learned of the murder whilst standing in the offices of the National Surveillance Unit in Garda headquarters. Privately, he concurred with Hickey's view that Gilligan might be innocent. 'No one could be that stupid,' Carty said. Working from this information, which was big enough to fill several crates, the Guerin team got to work collecting statements from witnesses. Police informants were grilled for anything that would lead to the assassin. The dragnet started.

Even from his hideaway in Amsterdam, Gilligan could see the public reaction to the killing was inspiring an anti-crime wave the likes of which had never been seen before. There was nothing he could do. He was having enough problems keeping his fellow conspirators calm. Warren appeared to be suffering from post-traumatic stress, waking in the middle of the night shivering with fear. If arrested he would be easily seduced into making a statement. Shay Ward found that he too couldn't forget the terrible events. He couldn't bear to hear Veronica's name mentioned. He would walk out of a room if her name was referred to in his company. Paul Ward was in the same state of mind. Bowden, Meehan and Mitchell, however, were unaffected.

But what caused Gilligan most worry was Geraldine. The sound of her voice told him that she was under tremendous pressure. And it was his fault. The press was not yielding. When they couldn't find him, they turned on her, writing about Jessbrook, in the process destroying the reputation afforded to its excellent livery facilities. The business she dearly loved collapsed overnight. The showjumping arena had been due to host a number of equestrian events – all were cancelled within 24 hours of the murder. He was somewhat sheltered from the consequences of his impulsiveness, but she wasn't.

In the foolish belief that he could alleviate the campaign, unexpectedly, he decided to talk to the press. Liz Allen was a journalist with the *Sunday Tribune*. Like many of her colleagues, she travelled to Jessbrook in the hope of contacting Gilligan there. Everyone carrying press identification was refused admission, but she persisted, eventually managing to speak directly with Geraldine, who said she couldn't help, but if her ex-husband rang, she would gladly pass on the message. She sounded so genuine that Allen was taken aback.

The journalist received a call from Gilligan within hours. She made arrangements to fly to Schipol Airport on Monday, 2 July, for an interview. She was accompanied by photographer Bryan Meade. Before the flight departed, she went into the ladies' toilet to use her mobile telephone. 'It was quite noisy in the departures lounge,' she said. As she went to dial, it rang. It was Gilligan. 'I know you're on your way. I know what you are wearing, you have long blonde hair and you're wearing a red jacket,' he said. She thought it was her boyfriend joking and was about to ask him to stop fooling around until she recognised the voice. She looked at herself in the mirror, as much as to confirm what he said was true. She did not panic and said she'd speak face to face in a few hours. Meehan, she would later learn, had been directed to the airport by Gilligan to see if she was travelling alone. He was sitting in the same departure lounge, waiting to catch a flight to London and had phoned through her description.

On arrival in Amsterdam, she made her way to the Hilton Hotel where, as promised, Gilligan was waiting with a bunch of white lilies. He smiled as if participating in a civic lesson and assured her she would come to no harm. He said he didn't want to speak in the foyer, so the party checked in. The interview was conducted in a hotel room where in the most convincing language she had ever heard he proclaimed his innocence. 'I had no hand, act or part in her murder. I swear to fucking God I don't know. If I knew I would go after them myself.' He ran his hands over his face, acting out the part of an innocent man. 'I'm finished in Ireland. They're saying the Provos will get me. They've set me up. Jesus, I've been blamed for this and I am finished now.'

There was purpose in the interview. Earlier that day, as expected,

Traynor won his case prohibiting the *Sunday Independent* from publishing Veronica's story. That she was dead was irrelevant. The Coach stayed away from the court, allowing his solicitors and barristers to represent him. In his affidavit, he made himself out to be a victim, though no one believed a word of it. His affidavit quoted from imaginary conversations he claimed took place. Veronica was portrayed as a self-serving manipulator; he an innocent victim. 'I know you're not involved in heroin but I have to print it,' he said she said. 'It's your lifestyle. You have a boat worth a quarter of a million pounds and a string of race cars in Mondello.' Mr Justice Barron, with no other option, granted the injunction the following day.

Gilligan was kept informed of the events as they unfolded. Offering outright lies in one hand and truths in the other, he began to fight back through the medium of the press in a pincer movement that complemented the bogus allegations levelled by Traynor.

After the interview concluded, Gilligan asked Allen if she wished to go gambling in a nearby casino. 'He said he'd show me just how much money he could make in one night,' she said. Smiling, she declined the offer and said goodbye. He thanked her for giving him the opportunity to put the record straight. The evening ended in the same strange circumstances it had begun. After he had left the room, Allen noticed her interviewee had forgotten his briefcase, a metallic Samsonite. Tempted as she was to inspect its contents, she decided to leave it untouched. She handed it in at the reception desk.

That weekend, John Gilligan, criminal par excellence, introduced himself to the Irish public for the first time. The portraits Meade took made him look suave, almost Italian.

The interview was a foolish decision, for later that week the assault case against him collapsed when it came to court on 9 July. It never occurred to him that the public would now have a face to put to the name of the defendant in the assault case, which was destined to collapse because of the untimely death of the principal witness

The Garda prosecuting the case, Superintendent Brendan Quinn, stood up before Judge John Brophy and asked that the charges be struck out. When the matter was concluded, the judge asked the court and the journalists in attendance to stand for a minute's silence in memory of the 'lady who was the principal State witness in the case'. 'The reason why it can't go ahead is because there is no effective evidence that could be offered in a court of law because of her untimely death within the last two weeks,' he said. 'Remember the hymn at Dublin Airport church, "Be Not Afraid". If you are afraid then the barons and the major gangland people in this country will take away your rights and freedoms which this country has fought for over decades.' The judge didn't name Veronica until making his closing remark. 'I hope other people in the media will follow on in her tracks.' The case ended on that note.

Months before the murder, Patrick Culligan, the Garda commissioner, had announced his retirement, sparking off a covert contest among his senior officers for the job. None of the competitors showed the ability that his deputy commissioner, Pat Byrne, did to canvass for the job. Byrne was appointed deputy commissioner in May 1994, taking control of all anti-terrorist and drugs operations. From the outset, he made a point of making the right impression with anyone that crossed his path, particularly political representatives, whose thoughts he scrutinised. In another life, he could have been a theatrical performer or indeed a politician, such was his ability to entertain a captive audience.

Weeks before the murder, he addressed the cabinet, delivering a polished speech on drug trafficking and organised crime in preparation for Ireland's presidency of the European Commission. Owen would later say he used the opportunity to interview himself for the job. 'He made a very clear presentation to the cabinet when we were coming up to taking the presidency, because we knew we were making the whole fight – international drugs and crime – one of our major planks in the presidency. His briefing to the cabinet was very frank and upright. In a way he gave information to my colleagues that I would have had, but they wouldn't have had – the networking of the drugs – and he gave facts and figures. It was a very graphic display of understanding and knowledge of the situation.'

His endeavours paid off on 10 July when Owen announced that he would succeed Culligan. With the new commissioner ready to take control, Owen put the Revenue and Garda under pressure; she wanted them to work together. At the same time, officials in her legal department were working unnatural hours rewriting O'Donoghue's bill, which they renamed the Proceeds of Crime Act. Other laws enabled the Revenue to disclose information on tax and contribute to the envisaged agency which she called the Criminal

Assets Bureau, CAB for short. The necessary laws were drafted in preparation for 25 July. Then just days before the emergency debate, the Government decided that a separate bill would be required to establish the bureau on a statutory basis.

The crime debate commenced that afternoon in the Dáil with virtually every TD in attendance. It was a heated exchange in which the police and judiciary came under attack. Gay Mitchell, the minister of State in the Taoiseach's Department, was the most vocal. Many of his constituents had suffered at the hands of the drug barons; he was enraged. The crime problem, he said, was associated more with order than with law. 'While the police should be fully supported we are entitled to require from it that its members behave in a totally impartial, non-political manner and keep their noses out of politics, whether they are members of Garda management or Garda trade unions. I would say publicly to the new Garda commissioner that I wish you well. You have a very difficult job, but please keep away from high society receptions. We do not want to see you there. I want to see you out meeting the ordinary people in the community.'

The drama didn't end there. 'The judges have got away with murder for long enough. They have a well remunerated, difficult job and are honourable, but they must be called to account. They should get out among the people whom they do not live among. We have had enough of their interfering with the legislature and the executive. The tail will have to be wagged a bit and judges will have to change the way they do their business,' he said.

There was no visible show of support for his speech, but there was a general consensus that what he was saying was what everyone thought, but hadn't the courage to say. Across the road, in Buswell's Hotel, the Dublin City Wide Campaign Against Drugs had gathered. Drug addicts and their parents from the communities worst ravaged by heroin made themselves available to meet the Oireachtas and explain the roots of the crime problem. The meeting was a sincere and honest gesture wasted on the political establishment. Only 56 of the 226 legislators – a quarter – made the 30-yard walk across the road to the hotel.

Inside the Dáil chambers, things were a little more productive with six pieces of anti-crime law processed without any opposition. Four were passed, making the day's sitting the most productive ever.

O'Donoghue, never a man to miss an opportunity – a common

Fianna Fáil trait – reprimanded Owen. The Minister, he said, had made so many promises that 'her long finger resembles Pinocchio's nose'. Perhaps when he opened the next morning's papers, where it was announced that Fachtna Murphy, the former head of the fraud squad, would front the CAB, he felt slightly embarrassed. Murphy was one of the few policemen capable of investigating serious financial fraud, though at that time his expertise was being wasted. In the age-old tradition of police bureaucracy, when he was promoted to the rank of chief superintendent, he was dispatched to Dun Laoghaire, where his talents at dissecting complex financial frauds were all but wasted. He only learned that Owen had earmarked him for the job when he opened the morning newspapers. He made a great effort not to enquire with his superiors to see if the reports were true, should they view this as blind ambition.

Barry Galvin, the State Solicitor for Cork, had already been approached to act as a legal advisor to the new squad. He had a satirical sense of humour, a typical trait for a lawyer, which masked a true sincerity for the victims of the drug epidemic. He had spent much of the previous two years campaigning for more Customs patrols of the south coast and for Garda management to deal competently with the drug barons. His correct analysis of the prevailing crime problem had made him a thorn in the side of police management, who were more than content to write him off as an agitator. For this reason, the Department of Justice reckoned he would be invaluable because he genuinely believed in retribution. His practice also specialised in debt collection.

The investigations into Veronica's murder were meanwhile upping pace. Gilligan knew this was happening. His men on the ground scrutinised all media reports, they watched television bulletins and collected newspaper reports, which they phoned through to the boss daily. The object of the exercise was to establish the identities of who was taken in for questioning. Once their identities were confirmed, Meehan would pay them a visit to ascertain what was said. The visits were also a form of intimidation and sent out a clear message. Gilligan may have been miles away in Amsterdam but he was still in control, albeit from the shadows.

The Guerin investigation had developed a high profile in the media through leaks to selected journalists aimed at putting the fear of God into the prime suspect. The truth was, it was going nowhere. Hickey was exhausting every avenue of investigation and getting no results. Then at the end of July it came together, accidentally.

Meehan had dumped the bike used for the assassination in a shallow stretch of the Liffey along the Strawberry Beds. He followed instructions to the letter and broke up the bike. In the summer months, the river swells and submerges with the release of water by a hydroelectric plant upstream. Notwithstanding this, wildlife flourishes on the river, which draws walkers, anglers and joggers who spend their spare time on the banks. On the morning of 29 June, the river was particularly low and a habitual walker who strolled down the riverside paths saw a motorcycle immersed below the waterline. When he got home he rang the Gardaí in Lucan. They took the details, thanked him for the call but did nothing. After two weeks of police inaction, he decided to take the bike out himself. He went down to the river on 9 July, entered the water and lifted the parts on to the bank. Someone saw him and, suspecting he was up to no good, called the Gardaí who arrived minutes later. He recounted his story to them. They took the bike away to see if it had been reported stolen. Tracing the bike's owner in the police stolen vehicle register took time.

More important than this development, though, was the secret work being carried out by detectives from the Special Branch. They were charged with tracing calls made from Gilligan's mobile telephone in the days proceeding 26 June. There were hundreds of calls, some to local numbers, others international. The detectives sifted through this labyrinth of numbers, eventually compiling a comprehensive picture of the people Gilligan talked to.

This element of the inquiry was kept secret from the press, as were the workings of Operation Pineapple, which had gathered so much intelligence on Gilligan that Carty decided to mount an all-out strike. He was aware that Geraldine had started withdrawing hundreds of thousands of pounds from her various accounts before they could be frozen. The Pineapple team had served orders under Section 3 of the Criminal Justice Act on the Bank of Ireland in Lucan obliging them to reveal details of the accounts. The documentation the detectives received made shocking reading. Between 24 and 29 July, Geraldine withdrew in four transactions £85,000 from one account she held in her maiden name, Matilda Dunne. This left a balance of £472.69.

She withdrew £10,000 and £40,000 from two separate accounts on 26 July. Three days later, on 29 July, she withdrew £21,000 in two transactions from the same two accounts.

After four months of working in absolute secret the Pineapple team arrived at the gates of Jessbrook at 9 a.m. on 30 July. They cordoned off the roads, took over the equestrian centre and prepared for an assault. When everyone was in place, one detective pressed the intercom button at the main gates, awakening Geraldine from her sleep. When she answered, a small convoy of unmarked patrol cars flanked by squad cars flew up the driveway. At the same time, a dozen officers entered the house without saying a word or giving her time to ask questions. They began sifting through every drawer, box and cupboard. They found financial records, account files, commerce books, diaries and bank statements – items of significant importance. The equestrian centre was rummaged. Accounting files and receipts were removed and put in clear plastic bags marked 'evidence'.

Geraldine didn't make any attempt to interfere. She decided her best course of action was to play the fool. When one Garda noticed a photograph of Gilligan and Traynor pinned to a wall in the kitchen, he asked Geraldine if she knew Traynor. She fumbled for her glasses before asking, 'Who is it?' For good measure, she returned to the Bank of Ireland the following morning and transferred £49,988.11 into one account opened in the name of Jessbrook. She then closed down the account.

The money laundering investigation unit took the papers found during the search because CAB was not functioning as the Government wished. For one, Murphy didn't even have an office. With Galvin by his side, they wandered like lost souls around Garda headquarters working out of cardboard boxes. He also had no staff although he knew the type of team he wanted. He approached the commissioner and asked if he could hand-pick a team. This was a bold move, for in the Garda senior officers rarely make demands or seek autonomy. Byrne, however, obliged. The list Murphy had compiled was made up of detectives who worked in the Money Laundering Investigation Unit. Others were taken aboard because they happened to be in the right place at the right time.

Officials from the State's Social Welfare and Revenue services were not that enthusiastic about joining. Revenue found it difficult to get applicants for the job, which civil servants contemplated as dangerous. The Department of Finance offered a financial incentive of £1,600 annual allowance to encourage people to apply.

But these were only teething problems. The CAB still had no statutory powers, its role was uncertain and the laws under which it operated had still not been passed. In other words, Murphy could investigate crime and collate financial intelligence on Gilligan, but always with his hands tied behind his back. On hearing about the possibility that her accounts might be frozen, Geraldine effectively cleared them out. Murphy went directly to Owen and outlined the problems he foresaw. If he thought there was a problem, there was none, for Owen set about drafting the extra legislation needed to make the bureau work.

When Donal Ó Siodhacháin read the newspaper reports tying Gilligan to Veronica's killing, he was intrigued. From his conversations with Gilligan in bygone years, he could not believe the man possessed the capability to run an international drugs cartel, although if there was ever a graduate in the science of criminal cunning, Gilligan would have a first-class degree. Ó Siodhacháin had watched the story unfold step by step in the press with great interest. He could not reconcile himself to the notion that the man he had fought a civil rights case for years earlier was now a drug trafficker, nor that he had colossal wealth, judging by the most recent reports which disclosed that the police had seized £21,000 from Gilligan's brother, Thomas, that week.

Out of curiosity more than anything else, he called Jessbrook and asked to speak to Geraldine. 'Tell her its Donal and Pat,' he said. There was a long silence as one of the workers left the phone unattended. Minutes later, she picked up the phone. The two parties spoke little, aware the call was probably being intercepted, but agreed to meet the next day in the Green Isle Hotel. Geraldine arrived, followed by a plain clothes detective whom O'Siodhacháin and his partner Pat Herron quickly identified as they mingled in the hotel lobby. They went over to a quiet corner. She ordered tea and sandwiches.

Before he got the chance to speak, she declared that John was innocent. 'He's been framed. Why would he kill her if he was due in court with her?' she declared.

Her analysis seemed reasonable, and he urged her to talk to the press and recommended that John do likewise. He suggested that she return to the hotel the next day at the same time where he would be waiting with a journalist.

She did. That journalist was this author. The next day, she repeated her assertions that Gilligan was an innocent man. She then dialled her mobile phone, walked six steps away, mumbling into the phone, then handed the phone to me. Gilligan then spoke: 'I'm doing this because Doney is the only one who ever done anything for me for nothing,' he said.

That weekend on Sunday, 11 August, the *Sunday Business Post* carried an interview with Gilligan. Far from being shy, he was upfront about his life as a gangster, nearly bragging about his life in crime. 'Anyone with big money can order an assassination. You don't have to be a criminal. I could have ordered it but I didn't. I had no hand, act or part in it.'

He was still furious about the cash seizure from his brother. 'The Gardaí may have won round one, but they won't win round two in the courts. That money came from a bank account in Lucan. It was to pay the builders because they didn't want cheques in case the accounts got frozen. I have no doubt in my mind, I will get that money back for my wife.'

Then he dropped a bombshell when he said he had amassed a personal fortune of £15 million, which lay in offshore bank accounts. 'The Gardaí will never get their hands on it.'

That same morning, as Geraldine read over the interview, Carty received a fax message from the headquarters of Europol in The Hague. The correspondence was telexed from the Dutch Desk, which was relaying a report from its domestic National Criminal Intelligence Service. The fax read: 'After the successful CD-Operation in WEDGE-case last weekend we have more good news. This time it's the PINEAPPLE-case. Last Thursday, August 11, Mr Simon RAHMAN was arrested by the special police-team of The Hague. Mr RAHMAN was driving a car in which was hidden 204 kg hashish and 20 false banknotes US 20 dollars. In a shed, situated in Zoetermeer, that belongs to Mr RAHMAN, the investigators have found another 1.040 kg hashish. Mr RAHMAN was accompanied by a man, who is living in Rotterdam. In his house the investigators have found 45 kg hashish and DM 17,000. Also this man was arrested. At this moment the investigators are examining the administration of Mr RAHMAN and all the other papers. When we get more information we inform you asap.'

CHAPTER 14

Breaking the Code of Silence

'I might as well tell you everything.'

CHARLES BOWDEN

Traynor relocated to the Costa del Sol. He saw the writing on the wall and pulled away from Gilligan and the cartel. In less than two months, his entire life fell apart. He was living away from his wife, mistresses and children. More than anything else he was bored. He was the epitome of the Dublin criminal; a creature you could take out of the slum, but you couldn't take the slum out of him.

He missed the city. He was also afraid of Gilligan who instructed him to talk to the press, to distract attention away from him if nothing else. Traynor knew the power of the press. In fact, he decided to talk to as many journalists willing to listen to him as possible. His lies were impossible to distinguish from the truths. He told the *Sunday Business Post* how he learned about the killing.

'I was in hospital when my phone rang. Someone rang to say a woman had been shot. I took no notice of the call. When something like that happens, the lads just make a few calls to let everyone know what's going on. Ten minutes later a man rang to say a woman had been shot in a red Calibra. When I heard about the car I started to get anxious because Veronica drove a Calibra. I was walking back into casualty when one of the lads phoned to say Guerin was dead. He had heard it on the news. I just thought, "Shit, this is going to be ten times worse than the injunction." That's why I left Ireland.'

He conducted this interview in downtown Malaga in a small coffee shop off the Alameda Principal. 'I didn't do it. I've never organised a shooting in my life. You can't go shopping for it. I couldn't order that sort of intimidation because I'm not that well connected in the underworld. I have a fair idea who was responsible and I know the reason why, but that's my business. I'm a straight businessman. I think they think I shot her to stop her writing a damaging story about me, but it wasn't me. I'm straight. I'm not involved in crime any more. I suppose that doesn't tally because I know John Gilligan and was friendly with Martin Cahill, but I grew up with those people. They were just my friends.'

For the first time since the abduction, he acknowledged he knew what had happened. But his foolishness knew no boundaries. Those pointing the finger of responsibility for Veronica's murder at him were all wrong. 'If I was going to shoot her I would not have spent £3,000 on an injunction before I ordered it. I haven't seen this J-district report or heard this tape. Veronica told me that I was involved in heroin dealing because she had read it in a Garda report. She quoted the report, which is now known as the J-district report, as saying that I was laundering money for Robert Murphy and Thomas Mullen. I wouldn't have anything to do with those scum. I don't know why I was being mentioned in the report because I'm not a drug dealer and I've never been questioned about drugs by the Gardaí.'

He slammed down his hands on the table. He was agitated. He continued to lie, saying the IRA had never questioned him. 'The tape recording is nonsense. She was going on about this confession which she couldn't produce. The IRA was supposed to have interviewed me after the Widow Scanlon's attack. I was never questioned by the IRA.'

He was equally convincing in his denials of ordering the first shootings of Veronica at her home. 'I was arrested under Section 13 and questioned about the attack. When the guards picked me up I said I'd answer everything, which I did. I was released about nine hours later. They know I had nothing to do with it. If they thought I did it they would have kept me in for the full 48 hours.

'I did tell people I ordered it because they started ringing me up congratulating me for it. I told some people that it wasn't me but before I knew it everyone believed that it was, so I let them. You could say it improved my street credibility. If people sit back they should see that I didn't want the publicity and people would have known that getting her killed would bring the house down. I had nothing to fear against the allegations because they were untrue. Why go to court and get an injunction when the obvious thing would have been just to get her killed and have no injunction?

'To be honest I did feel hard done by and I still don't know why she turned on me but I wouldn't kill her for that. I didn't know her movements, I hadn't spoken to her in six months. I didn't know she was in court on a speeding charge. I was not involved.'

He did his best to sound honest. He recounted how he first met the journalist. in September 1994. 'She wanted a copy of a Garda file, which Martin had stolen before he died. I thought she was a naïve journalist, nice but naïve, but in some ways streetwise. She knew what was going on but her stories were based on rumour. Dublin's underworld is like a rumour factory – you can't believe anything you hear. She was nice but had two personalities, one was righteous, the other one was friendly. I used to meet her every few weeks, sometimes three times in one week, then I might not see her for a month.

'I did supply her with some stories, though not the ones the papers claim. For example I introduced her to a chap who was kidnapped by the UVF in Walkinstown after clearing it with him first. I knew the lad. I also cleared it with the IRA. It made a good story. I also gave her other stories, always with the consent of the people involved. I never discussed hard information with her. In fact she told me far more than I ever told her. I gave her the story on the Garda running business with criminals. Some journalists got that mixed up and made out that the Garda was working with me or having a gay affair with me. Then she started coming out with all the drugs stuff and I went for the injunction. You know the rest.'

This was his life. Denying and lying. Weeks of hearing fumbled and exaggerated reports of what was being said about him had slowly turned him into a fantasist. Although he followed the story from afar, watched the television, read newspapers and wrote letters, he believed the press was calling him a child molester and publishing stories of his sexuality.

'I'm not a child molester. I'm not homosexual. I never had a sexual affair with a Garda and I did not make videos of prostitutes with businessmen. Where are the people who are making these allegations? Let them come forward and show their faces. Where are these videos of prostitutes and children? It's funny no one is able to produce them because they don't exist.

'I regret 100 per cent that I ever got involved with Veronica. Her death has put me out of business. It has brought shame on my family and friends. I don't want to be thought of as a scumbag who murders women. Newspapers have jumped the gun. What they print one day is taken as fact the next. I believe the police are plundering to break through the investigation because they are being led by the media.

'The Gardaí never called me a suspect or ever requested to talk to me about the murder. Now I'm a suspect because of newspaper reports.'

September marked the beginning of the end for the cartel. The CAB was fast turning out to be a great white elephant. The Gilligans transferred all their liquid assets out of the State. Geraldine in particular cleared her accounts of cash. All that was left was loose change. This agitated Fachtna Murphy. Moreover, Gilligan himself bragged in his *Sunday Business Post* interview of having transferred £15 million to offshore accounts at a secret location where he said the Gardaí would never lay their hands on it.

Garda management wrote off the remark as wishful thinking. They tried to fight back, leaking dubious information to the more faithful journalists following the story, who duly reported that Gilligan could not have amassed any significant wealth. The truth contrasted starkly. The force knew Gilligan was a multimillionaire. They also realised that as long as the Proceeds of Crime Act was not incorporated into Irish law, they were powerless to intervene. The following logic prevailed; if headquarters repeated the myth that Gilligan wasn't asset rich, eventually someone would believe it. 'It was all about PR,' recalled one officer later.

It was a desperate situation, exacerbated because it was clear to all that Gilligan was winning the battle. Murphy viewed the situation with an astute eye. The CAB could not freeze any bank accounts, especially ones they did not know about. The bureau had no powers. The Proceeds of Crime Act was due to become law within weeks, but this was of no use. He did his best to improvise. The CAB may not be able to apply the draconian Proceeds of Crime Act but they could pursue the Gilligans for tax evasion under the existing laws. It was the only solution.

The bureau took possession of the financial intelligence gathered by Operation Pineapple. Murphy looked through the paperwork. His detectives searched through records held by the Department of Social Welfare and Revenue Commissioners. There was an injection of life into the department. The appraisements were made under section 19 of the Finance Act, 1983, in respect of earnings, the sources of which were not known to the inspector or which were known to have arisen from an unlawful source of activity. It was a simple solution but a novel idea.

They calculated that Geraldine owed over £800,000 income tax for the year 1994–5. John owed £1.75 million for the same period. If they didn't pay, the bureau would seize their belongings in default. However, at that moment, just when everything appeared to be going according to plan, trouble presented itself. Murphy was told that not one of the tax inspectors seconded to the bureau would sign the demand, which was obligatory. This was a real crisis. The assessments were dependent on an inspector's signature No one thought to ask if the civil servants were worried for their own safety. Murphy was placed in a grave dilemma. He would not order any member of his staff to do something they didn't want.

Murphy was always decisive but this time he felt as if he was trying to achieve the impossible. Galvin came back at him with an inventive solution. He said he would sign the demand, after he was appointed a temporary inspector of taxes. Murphy picked up a phone and called Cathal MacDomhnaill, the chairman of the Revenue Commissioners. He outlined the problem and said he needed to talk urgently, face to face. They arranged to meet later that day in MacDomhnaill's office in Dublin Castle.

Galvin went along. He articulated in simple words the course of action needed. The urgency in his voice convinced MacDomhnaill. Later that same day, on 16 September, Barry Galvin, chief legal advisor to the CAB, attached another title to his name, inspector of taxes. He signed the two giant assessments and they were dispatched to Jessbrook. The game was on.

Geraldine could not comprehend the bill. She called John at once on his mobile and told him what had arrived in the post. He exploded with rage. He rang the author and screamed down the phone. 'You're not going to believe what they just did. They sent me and Geraldine bills for tax,' he said. 'How can they say that my firm earned this and that and then tax me on it? What's the fucking world coming to?'

'Are you going to pay it?' I enquired.

'Am I going to what? Do you want to come over and take pictures of me burning it? They're gone fucking mad.'

Geraldine was decidedly more grounded in her response. She sought legal advice from Michael E. Hanahoe & Co. The solicitors wrote to CAB querying how the amount was calculated. The lawyers pointed out correctly that their client had been unable to lodge a return of income for 1994–5, or even appeal the assessment because her accounts had been seized. The matter rested there.

No one thought for a moment that Gilligan would dare return home at the height of the murder investigation. But his arrogant nature and the fact he was homesick did not allow him to stay away. He chose to sneak back into Dublin in time for Geraldine's birthday, which fell on 21 September. He took a senseless route, flying into Belfast Airport, then catching the train to Dublin. He decided it would be foolish to attend a small drinks party Geraldine's friends planned to throw in the Spa Hotel in Lucan on the outskirts of Dublin. The Gardaí would be watching, he reckoned. So he went to Carol Rooney. His next port of call was to Jessbrook. Geraldine was ecstatic, the children overjoyed.

Earlier that morning, Donal Ó Siodhacháin and Pat Herron travelled to the capital, arriving from their Kerry home in Scartaglen. They arrived in Dublin shortly after 10 a.m. Like most days in Ó Siodhacháin's life, it was long and arduous and involved several meetings with people he chose to help fight complex legal cases. Without any invitation, he decided on impulse to pay Geraldine a visit. He pulled up outside the avenue, stepped out of his Volvo and pressed the intercom. Geraldine answered. 'Come on up,' she said. Her voice sounded jovial on the crackled intercom line. The gates swung open and he drove in. She was waiting at the door with her Old English sheepdogs. These jumped on Ó Siodhacháin when he stepped out of the car. It was a cold night, so he headed straight in the door without waiting for a verbal invitation.

Standing there before him was Gilligan with his hand extended. 'Hello Doney.'

Not knowing what to say, he exclaimed in amazement: 'Jesus, what are you doing here?' Ó Siodhacháin didn't know how to react. He didn't delay in asking the questions that troubled his mind.

They sat down in front of the fire, Gilligan answering each one methodically but denying everything. His version of what happened was entirely different. Of course he said he was a criminal. 'There's not a good bone in my body,' he declared 'but I didn't do it. I'm not involved with drugs. If she thought I was involved in heroin or drugs she'd kill me herself,' he said about Geraldine who, overcome with excitement, went to bed. According to Gilligan, Veronica's murder was an elaborate ploy to destroy him.

They talked all night, till sunrise the next morning. Ó Siodhacháin did not know what to believe, but for the first time allowed a shred of doubt about Gilligan's innocence to enter his mind. He left the next morning. Gilligan shook his hand and wished him well. Exhausted, he walked to his car under the watchful eye of Gardaí from the National Surveillance Unit camped out among the hedgerows. Gilligan left later.

Days later, Gilligan received a call from a man he didn't know. It was Father Peter McVerry, a Jesuit priest from Dublin, famous for working with young homeless boys. He was one of the best known charity workers in Ireland. He had dialled Geraldine's number, but was redirected to Gilligan. The priest had a message for Geraldine and asked Gilligan to pass it on. The IRA, he said, were going to harm her or kill her. It was imperative that she leave Jessbrook at once.

'I had been contacted by someone, who said she was going to come to harm. I explained to Gilligan that I was not a member of the IRA. I was just a messenger,' he said later.

Gilligan didn't know what to believe. He rang Geraldine and implored her to leave the family home. The priest's message terrified her and she left at once. She moved into a friend's home in Tallaght where she stayed for two days before coming home. Weeks later, after a suitable time had elapsed, she called the priest to verify that it was he who had called. He said it was and she thanked him.

That same day, Owen announced the promotion of Tony Hickey to the rank of assistant commissioner. His elevation could have been seen as a celebration of what was to come. The Lucan Inquiry, the name afforded to the murder investigation team, was making deep inroads into the cartel. The Garda have at their disposal an array of sophisticated devices that can intercept and trace dozens of calls made to and from mobile phones at the touch of a button. These systems can operate anywhere and trace all telephone traffic on selected lines. The team traced all the calls made to and from Gilligan's mobile and listened to both sides of the calls. The calls were recorded digitally. This allowed the Gardaí to keep abreast of his plans.

GANGSTER

The telephone traffic that took place on 26 June, the day of Veronica Guerin's murder, unravelled. Numbers attributed to Brian Meehan, Paul Ward, Shay Ward and Peter Mitchell were documented. But there were two others. The first was someone the investigation hadn't heard of. It was Paul Conroy, a fictitious name. The second number belonged to someone they all knew: Garda John O'Neill. His number appeared on Paul Ward's itemised bills.

Hickey, a man who had unquestioned allegiance to the police, welcomed the news. He thought O'Neill had recruited an informer within Gilligan's gang. He asked the team to trawl discreetly through police intelligence files. This exercise was aimed at establishing whether O'Neill was contributing information on organised crime to police files. He wasn't. He was placed under surveillance.

On Sunday, 29 September 1996, Warren was standing in the arrivals lounge of Dublin Airport when his mobile rang. It was Gilligan. He started berating him for not collecting cash from Paddy Holland, a close friend of Gilligan's and one of the gang's customers.

Gilligan had met Holland in Portlaoise. Holland stood out among the other inmates. He spent much of his time alone, weight training and exercising. He didn't need reassurance from anyone. He didn't ask anyone to sort out his problems; he handled everything himself. He was his own man and answered to no one. He stood just under six feet tall. He was blocky and bald. He wore a wig to disguise his hair loss. Some of the inmates called him The Wig. Others called him Dutchy because of his surname.

When Holland was released from prison in September 1994, Gilligan quickly indoctrinated him into the narcotics trade. Bowden and Shay Ward would deliver 30 kilos of dope to his cronies at various points around the city. He got rich beyond his wildest dreams. Gilligan taught him about money laundering – one area of crime he was unfamiliar with. Dutchy soon amassed too much wealth. Like Gilligan, he set up a money laundering operation, but this time in the form of a publishing company which he called Holpat made up of the first three letters of his names. It published an alternative to the RTE Guide. Another venture was the publication of a second-hand car trade magazine. Holland did his best but he was not a publisher and the two ventures failed, with considerable losses.

GANGSTER

Holland was not like the rest of the gang. He had no inclination to show off his wealth. He preferred to live a solitary existence in a small holiday home at Lissadell, near Brittas in County Wicklow, which he bought for £30,000. The only thing that mattered to him was his wife, Angela.

Like Gilligan, Meehan treated him with unreserved respect. They all saw in Holland a man they privately wished they could be. He was afraid of no one. He was the nearest thing Gilligan had ever met to a professional mercenary. He also had a proven track record for crime. And he was certainly not an informer. The ageing gangster had spent most of his life in jail.

Holland grew up in Chapelizod in Dublin. His best friend was a youngster called Pat Culhane. They had ambitions of travelling the world and joining the American Marines. They followed this dream when they turned 18 but were sent to different platoons after they joined. The young Holland became homesick two weeks later and returned home. Culhane stomached the training and spent the next four years in the military. When he finished his contract, he joined the Gardaí. In later years, he rose through the ranks eventually becoming a chief superintendent. Holland simultaneously rose through the ranks of Dublin's underworld. Easy money attracted him; crime attracted him. In June 1965 he was caught with stolen goods and sentenced to six months. He lost his job and his family disowned him. So he became a burglar and then an armed robber. In 1981, he was caught with the proceeds of a bank robbery and was sentenced to seven years' imprisonment.

Jail did not alter Holland's criminal inclinations. He was just out of prison four years when he was arrested with seven sticks of gelignite, detonators and fuse wire in a flat in Dublin's north inner city by a young police officer, Tony Hickey. The explosives were not for subversive use by any paramilitary organisation. The materials had been stolen from the Arigna Mines in County Leitrim. Holland intended using them to crack safes. He was serving this sentence when Gilligan arrived in Portlaoise.

Gilligan's temper couldn't be calmed. He had told Warren to collect the cash from Holland the night before. Warren, surprised by his own insolence, told him he had tried to collect the cash but Holland hadn't got it. He said he'd call. Gilligan said he'd better. Holland, who could be relied upon like clockwork, rang 15 minutes later and arranged to meet outside the Virgin Megastore just off O'Connell Bridge.

Warren went straight there and found Holland waiting. They nodded at each other. Holland handed him a sports bag and said there was £70,000 inside.

Warren went straight to his parents' home in Tallaght. He was due to collect other monies from Meehan but when he rang him, Meehan said they wouldn't have their money until Tuesday. He wasn't bothered.

'If I had collected more than £100,000 on Monday I was due to fly out to Schipol Airport, Amsterdam, with it. As I hadn't that amount I waited and was due to go on the Tuesday night or Wednesday morning when I would have collected the remainder of the money,' he later explained. However, things didn't go according to plan. At 9.05 p.m. that Monday he was arrested. At the same time, a team of detectives entered his parents' home where they found the money. Warren went into a state of shellshock. He was driven to Lucan Garda station where his interrogation began. He said nothing.

When news of his arrest reached the gang they panicked. The arrest was unexpected. They met in the Hot Pot Restaurant in Sundrive shopping centre in Crumlin the next day. Meehan was particularly astonished at the arrest. The Gardaí were not supposed to know about Warren. He decided the time had come to clear out the lock-up at Greenmount. He told Bowden and Shay Ward to take care of this.

They sat down and ordered tea and coffee. Meehan and Mitchell said they would take care of the drugs orders. 'This would ordinarily have been done by phone but as we knew Russell Warren had been arrested we didn't want to use the phones,' Bowden would later say. They relaxed. Then Peter Mitchell recognised a man sitting on his own at the next table. He said he was a cop.

Meehan looked around. He recognised the man's face but said he was a fellow he went to school with. Bowden grew uneasy. They all left. As they did, Bowden looked around and saw the same man speaking into his mobile phone. Meehan and Mitchell left by car. Ward and Bowden went to a nearby hardware shop and bought plastic bags. Mitchell was right, they were under surveillance.

Their car was followed. Mitchell, out of fear more than courage, did a U-turn and drove up behind the unmarked car. They went straight to Meehan's apartment in Clifton Court. For the first time since the murder, Meehan was scared. He rounded up the cash they were owed.

At 3 p.m. Wednesday, 2 October, detectives attached to the Operation Pineapple squad arrived outside Sunlight Chambers, a historic building on the corner of Parliament Street. Inside were Michael Hanahoe's offices. That morning Terry McGinn had obtained a search warrant from Judge Gillian Hussey in Kilmainham District Court. Three detectives from CAB were present. Galvin had advised the squad to get a search warrant because, in his opinion, Hanahoe would have been legally obliged to contact Gilligan before disclosing any information to the Gardaí. This way, Hanahoe would not be compromised. In any event, he and his staff co-operated fully with the court order. When the Gardaí had finished, they left carrying several briefcases.

On exiting the building, McGinn noticed a number of photographers standing across the road. They were taking photographs. Afterwards, journalists called Hanahoe direct asking him to comment. A spin was being put on what was effectively a routine piece of police work. Hanahoe was taken aback. The visit was being portrayed as a raid. He told the *Irish Times*: 'I'm only unhappy that it might be misinterpreted by people in the wrong light.' Asked by the newspaper if he felt the visit breached the traditional code of confidentiality between solicitor and client, he said: 'I don't want to discuss it now. There will be a time when it will be addressed.' The solicitor subsequently successfully sued the State for a six-figure sum in damages arising out of the manner in which the search had been leaked to the media.

Warren was released from Lucan the same day. He was exhausted and got into a taxi. He was not handling himself properly. Guilt was written all over his face. His mobile telephone rang seconds later. It was Gilligan. 'I said give me 20 minutes and I'll be at home.' He stopped off at Molloy's liquor store in Tallaght where his phone rang a second time. It was Gilligan again. He screamed at him to go home. 'Give me another five minutes,' said Warren. As soon as he stepped through his hall door, Gilligan called a third time. He wanted to know about the interrogation. Warren's wife and mother-in-law were in a near state of panic. He walked out of the house and took the call on the roadway.

Gilligan got straight to the point. 'I'm now going to tell you, you're dead and your family is dead and everybody around you will be dead. I want the truth, tell me exactly what was said and what your family said.'

Warren was terrified. The only thing he could think of saying was that it was all about the money. He explained that he hid the cash in his mother's home, which prompted a fierce argument about why he hadn't delivered as instructed.

'When I tell you to do something you do it,' Gilligan roared. He asked if his wife had made a statement. 'Get on a plane tomorrow.'

'I can't, everybody is upset,' said Warren.

'Come over or I'll go over to ye and I'll kill ye all.'

He hung up.

One of Gilligan's couriers then arrived, wanting to know if Warren had implicated him. Warren's mother-in-law walked into the room and told the courier to leave. She had had enough and was appalled.

Gilligan telephoned the next morning at 8 a.m. He wanted to know why Warren wasn't in England. 'If you're not fucking over here I'm going over to you and I'll kill you and I'll kill you if you tell me lies.'

The only excuse Warren could invent was to say he had no money.

'Ring Brian and he'll give you money.'

Left with no other option, he called Meehan at once and arranged to meet him at his mother's home on Stanaway Road. Meehan answered the door. He looked up and down the street before ushering Warren inside. He handed him £1,000. Warren couldn't decide if Meehan was more relaxed or just more scared. He asked what questions the investigation team raised. Warren offered the same story. He appeared to believe him. Meehan offered to drop him off at Rosie O'Grady's pub in Harold's Cross. On the way, he asked if Debbie, McGrath or Cradden had said anything. 'I have to know,' he said in a friendly way.

Warren left for London the next morning. He took a taxi to Dublin Airport to avoid surveillance. Before he got onto the plane, he rang Debbie and told her he was going to meet Gilligan, in case he didn't return. He arrived in Heathrow at 2 p.m. and called Gilligan straightaway. 'He told me to take the train to Russell Square, and to meet him at a hotel there. I got off the train and went to a phone box to ring Gilligan. There was a man at the

phone box. He approached me and said, "Russell?" I said, "Yeah."
"Follow me."'

The stranger escorted him to a nearby hotel. The two entered a
lift and pressed the button for the second floor. He was led to one
of the rooms. Gilligan was waiting inside. He walked in and sat on
the bed.

'You and your family are dead and Debbie, no matter how long it
takes, I'll get you all. I want the truth. Now put "I'm going to kill" at
the back of your mind. You have to answer the questions for me and
don't tell me lies.' Gilligan paced back and fourth. Warren, trying to
compose himself, told him that no one had said anything. But
Gilligan wasn't convinced. He kept screaming and shouting. The
mood then changed. 'I want you to go to Calais tonight. '

'I don't have a passport. The police took it,' Warren said.

Gilligan screamed. He ranted and raved about Warren not telling
him this earlier.' 'I have £300,000 in there,' he yelled, pointing in the
direction of a wardrobe. 'Who is going to bring this for me now? I
will have to do it myself.' He resumed questioning him about his
arrest. 'What did they ask you about?'

Warren told him that the police had lists of telephone calls made
by Warren, Brian Meehan and himself on the day of the murder.

'Don't worry about that. That could be anything, that could be us
talking about collecting money,' Gilligan said.

Warren felt slightly more confident. Gilligan was slowly calming
down. He was struck by the unalloyed calmness in his voice. When
Gilligan had been given sufficient time to cool off Warren plucked up
the courage to ask if he regretted ordering the killing. He later told
Gardaí that Gilligan said, 'Are you joking? I even tried to ring Brian
to call it off, but I couldn't get through to him.'

Warren might as well have been trapped in a surreal world for he
agreed that it was a pity that Meehan's phone hadn't been working
properly. 'I had the same problem getting through.'

Furthering the conversation's descent into the sublime, Gilligan
nodded and agreed. 'It wouldn't have made a bit of difference,
because she was dying of cancer anyway.'

The murder investigation found itself caught in a whirlwind of
activity. They knew they were striking at the heart of the cartel
although they didn't realise just how close they were to cracking one

of the murderers. They were informed that Warren had been summoned to meet Gilligan. He was under surveillance from the moment of his release from Lucan station. The time had come to arrest Bowden. He was preparing to leave the State, taking his mistress with him. The Gardaí arrived outside his home on Saturday at 7 a.m. He was barely awake when he was handcuffed and driven at speed to Lucan where Detective Inspector John O'Mahony and Detective Bernie Hanley began an interrogation. At the same time, Gardaí knocked on the door of Bowden's brother Michael's home and started searching it. Back in Lucan, Bowden was cautioned and told his rights.

O'Mahony, a stout-looking detective, led the interrogation. 'Will you tell us what you know about the shooting of Veronica Guerin?'

'I know nothing about it, I had no involvement in it. You can ask Juliet. I was in the shop that day with her.'

'Do you know Brian Meehan, Peter Mitchell, Shay Ward?'

'I know Peter Mitchell. His mother Eileen gets her hair done in the shop,' answered Bowden.

'In the searches of your house and your brother's house this morning, there was evidence of you having a lot of money, and there was a lot of money found which is connected to you.'

'This money was savings I had from the business.'

'What about the money found in Michael's house?'

'I know nothing about that,' Bowden said.

'Michael states that you handed him that money outside Joe Wong's restaurant in Clontarf last Sunday night.'

'That's not correct.'

'There was a hell of a lot of money found which we believe belongs to you, and which couldn't be savings if, as you say, you get £150 a week out of the shop.'

'It's all savings.'

'Your brother Michael is going to say that the envelope we found in his possession this morning, he got from you to mind.'

'He's right. I gave it to him to mind.'

'I am putting it to you that you know Brian Meehan, Paul Ward, Peter Mitchell and Shay Ward and that you were in contact with some of them by telephone on the day of Veronica Guerin's shooting.'

'Okay, I know them. I know them through Peter Mitchell. Look I want to tell you about the money, I know nothing about Guerin's murder. I would have nothing to do with anything like that, it would scare me shitless. I have been working with Meehan, the Wards, Mitchell. That's where the money is from. If I was talking to them on the day of the shooting it was only about business.' Bowden, a master at the art of deceit, guessed the Gardaí had followed him. He resorted to making lies between truths.

'What business do you mean?'

'Selling drugs, that's my only involvement with them.'

'How long were you at this?'

'About two years. I got to know Peter Mitchell first through his mother, Eileen. She gets her hair done in the shop. Peter helped me out with a spot of trouble I was having with a sign writer from Gardiner Street.'

'What do you mean by this?'

'The sign writer was threatening me, saying I owed him money for a job he had done for me. Peter talked to him and warned him off. After that I got involved in selling a bit of hash for Peter, through the hairdresser's, just a bit – about a kilo a week.'

'How do you know Brian Meehan and the Wards?'

'They were involved with Peter, they were all working together. We would meet regularly in the POD and System. We would hang out together.'

'How much money have you made altogether?'

'I don't know, a lot. Lately I couldn't handle the amounts. It was getting in on top of me.'

'Where is it all now?'

'I will show you, I have it offside, it's in a flat near Lesson Street Bridge. I don't know the address, it's a friend of a friend of mine who has it. He doesn't know anything about it. He was just asked to mind a bag.'

Bowden made his first direct reference to the murder but attempted to give Meehan and Mitchell an alibi. He said he saw them outside Klips when Veronica was shot, but conveniently left out the details. 'I was in the shop at the time, I wasn't talking to them.'

'Are you agreeable to bring us out and show us the flat where the money is?'

'Yes.'

'How much is there?'

'I couldn't tell you, there must be about £100,000. I haven't counted it,' he added. The cash was that week's takings.'

The suspect returned to the question of the murder. He explained where he was on the night of the killing. 'Now I remember, when I was talking to them on the phone, I arranged to meet them that evening in the Hole in the Wall pub in Blackhorse Avenue, to see the football match between England and Germany. We all met there that evening. There was Brian Meehan, Peter Mitchell, Paul Ward, my girlfriend Juliet.'

At 10 p.m. Bowden was driven into Dublin city by O'Mahony and Hanley. They pulled up outside Klips before heading across the Liffey to the financial district where Bowen directed them towards to a flat off Mesipil Road. On the way he engaged O'Mahony in conversation. He said he lied about how he first met Mitchell. It was a conversation of half-truths. The pressure was on and Bowden knew it. He could take a fall or save his own skin. He chose the latter.

Unknown to him, the investigation team had discovered Greenmount through surveillance on Meehan and Mitchell. The investigation team procured a search warrant and went into Unit 1B, Harold's Cross the next morning. It was a Sunday. Inside they found 25 cardboard boxes of hashish. There were seven bags of white powder and electric weighing scales. The workspace was littered with cannabis. There were drugs everywhere – wooden boxes full of hashish slabs. There was a black Nike sports bag containing 115 bars of vacuum-sealed dope ready for delivery. Bars of cannabis sat neatly beside the claw hammers and jemmy bars used to prise open the wooden crates the drugs arrived in. There was rubbish strewn everywhere. Amongst the debris was a green covered file containing the tenancy agreement. A list of names was found pinned to a partition wall.

Bowden was blissfully unaware of the find, not that his interrogators knew he was stringing them along. He had slept well the night before. He was brought back to the interview room at 1.55 p.m.

O'Mahony asked him to be honest. 'Tell us the full truth about Veronica Guerin's murder.'

'I am not involved in the murder. I am not a heavy. I just do the drugs for Meehan and Mitchell, for the money.'

'Where do you get these drugs from?'

'They are delivered to me or else I meet Meehan or Mitchell and they give the drugs.'

'Do you know where the drugs are stored?'

'No.'

'Do you know where they come from?'

'No, I don't ask any questions, I just deliver the hash to the list of customers given to me by Meehan or Mitchell.'

'Charlie, the Gardaí have located a warehouse at Greenmount Industrial Estate, Harold's Cross, and they are searching it. They have discovered a large quantity of cannabis and other suspected drugs there.

'Have ye found it? I should have told ye last night. Fuck it, I was going to tell ye when we were stopped at Harold's Cross lights. Now ye have found it I will tell you everything. I am sorry for not telling ye about it already.'

'Charlie, all we want is the full truth, we want you to tell us all you know about the drugs operation and give us whatever information you have regarding the murder of Veronica Guerin.'

'I will tell the full truth now. It is not true to say that Brian Meehan and Peter Mitchell deliver the drugs to me for delivery. I have over the years organised a few lock-ups where we store the drugs when we get them.'

'Where do you get the drugs from?'

'I will tell you that too. I am scared if Gilligan hears that I have ratted, I am dead. I rented the lock-up in Greenmount about a year ago.'

'How much did you lease it for?'

'£500 a month.

'How did you pay for it?'

'By cash. I have the key for it on my keyring. Shay Ward and I delivered the drugs from there. We had a blue Kadett van which we used for the delivery. It is parked up on St Peter's Road, Walkinstown. I was making up to £3,000 a week on the drugs. Brian Meehan and Peter Mitchell were in charge of the drug operation, but I know that John Gilligan was in overall charge.' Bowden said that the drug consignment found in the warehouse was hash which had been returned because it was poor quality. The last supply was delivered to the lock-up on the previous Monday. Drugs came in from Cork. They were imported as a legitimate cargo by Seabridge Freight, Little Island, Cork. The fellow in charge of the company was a John Dunne who was originally from Dublin but now lived in Cork. Gilligan knew him from way back. It was Gilligan who arranged the importing of the hash.'

'Tell us how the drugs are taken from Cork to Dublin?'

'It is delivered by a courier in a white van. Shay and I meet them at the Ambassador Hotel and drive the van to Greenmount where we unload the drugs and then bring the van back to the Ambassador. The driver used to stay in the Ambassador. I know that the boxes of drugs were addressed to a company in Little Island, Cork. I used to take the labels off the boxes in Greenmount.

'I also want to say that there is a cover for a machine gun in the lock-up. That was a cover that was on a gun that came in with the hash. We got a good few guns in on different times. Firstly, the sub-machine guns and ammo for them. I put these guns in an old graveyard up near Bridget Burke's pub. Brian Meehan and Peter Mitchell told me where to put them. I will show you the place.'

'Are those two guns in the cemetery still?'

'Yes, one of them was used to shoot Martin Foley. I took the gun back up to the graveyard after the shooting. Meehan and Paul Ward (Hippo) were involved. Meehan did the shooting and Ward drove the car.'

Neither O'Mahony or Hanley could believe their ears. 'Martin Foley was shot at twice – which one are we talking about?'

'The one in Cashel Avenue. They made a bollocks of it. They allowed him to reverse the car and he got away. Meehan couldn't handle the gun. I had shown him how to fire it in a field out at the back of the graveyard. I got the gun ready for them and collected it afterwards.'

'Why was Foley shot?'

'Because Foley mouthed to all the politicals that Gilligan and Meehan were selling heroin.'

'Does Foley know it was Meehan who shot him?'

'He does. They have patched it up and Meehan is now supplying hash to Foley. I will show you which gun was used for the shooting.'

'What other gun did you get?'

'I remember another time when Meehan, Mitchell and Hippo were on holidays a box with five 9mm semi-auto's came in with the hash. I put those in the graveyard too. John Gilligan told me that these were coming in and he asked afterwards if I had got them. In January of this year another sub-machine gun and a .357 Magnum and 12 rounds came in.'

'Where is the .357 gun now?'

'I know that is the gun you are looking for for Veronica Guerin's murder.'

'How do you know what type of gun we are looking for?'

'I got it wrapped up and put it up in the graveyard too. Right. I might as well tell you everything. There is a name you haven't mentioned at all, the person who shot Veronica Guerin. Can I trust you? I have told you so much now I might as well tell you all. Pat the Hat, do you know him?'

'No I never heard of that name for any criminal.'

'You must know him, he has done a few hits around town.'

'Do you know his correct name?'

'He is called Pat the Hat but we call him the Wig. Be careful of that, there is only a few of us that know him by that name, only five of us.'

'Who are the five?'

'Meehan, Mitchell, the two Wards (Shay and Hippo) and myself.'

'What is the correct name?'

'Don't know it, call him The Wig.'

'Give us a description of him.'

'He might be called Paddy too. I am not sure.'

'What's his description?'

'Forty-five years approximately, maybe more. Bald on top, sandy kind of hair, about 5 foot 8 inches or 5 foot 9 inches. He has a bent nose. I met him often. I used to give him some hash.'

'How can you be so sure that the .357 Magnum was used for the murder of Veronica Guerin?'

'Because I cleaned it and got it ready before the murder. There were refill bullets in it. Brass with silver heads, the tops were turned in, rather than coming to a point.'

'Where did you get this gun when you cleaned it?'

'Shay Ward brought it down from the graveyard.'

'Who did you give it to?'

'I left it in the lock-up with Brian Meehan, Peter Mitchell and Shay Ward. They had been talking about shooting Veronica Guerin. Traynor had told them that she was up in court in Kildare.'

'Tell us everything you know about Veronica's murder.'

'Well, I knew they had planned to shoot her and when I cleaned the gun I knew that that was the gun that was to be used in the shooting.'

'Why was she shot?'

'John Gilligan wanted her shot. I often heard Meehan and Mitchell talk about her and how upset Gilligan was about her charging him for assault. I didn't know where she was to be shot, I had nothing to do with it. I am telling the truth about that day. I was at work, they wouldn't involve me in it. I am not into heavy stuff, they never asked me to do anything else in the murder. I met Brian Meehan, Peter Mitchell and Hippo Ward that night of the murder in The Hole in the Wall pub. Meehan told me about the murder, he said that he drove the bike on the job and The Wig did the shooting. Shay Ward told me afterwards that he was in Paul Hippo's house in Walkinstown Avenue that day. They were listening to a scanner. Meehan and the Wig were to call back to Hippo's house after the murder and they were there waiting for them. They put the bike into Hippo's garage after the shooting and Shay drove Meehan into town. Meehan changed into his clothes in the Greenmount lock-up. The Wig was real cool. Shay said that he said something about his fine house. Shay didn't tell him how The Wig went away. Hippo took the gun away, then left it behind in his house after the shooting. I heard that Russell Warren got the bike for them.'

'Do you know if John Traynor was involved in the murder?'

'The only thing I heard about him was that it was he who told them that she was in the Court in Kildare. I don't know anything else about him. I gave him two guns – this was before the murder. Traynor wanted to give the guns to politicals as a sweetener for something. I gave him a .38 snub-nosed and a Browning semi-automatic. I was told to give these guns. I left them on the roadside near the graveyard.'

O'Mahony and Hanley eased back into their chairs. It was over.

CHAPTER 15

The Usual Suspects

'John's only answer to everything
was "I'll bump him off".'
MICHAEL GRIMES

When Veronica Guerin was shot, Gilligan's world changed irrevocably. He could only spend a few days in any one place at any time. He correctly suspected that every police force in Europe was looking for him. His instinct, a trait he heavily relied on, told him he was being followed. Paranoia consumed him. The criminals he listed as friends now shunned him. He was fast losing control of the gang at a time when he needed them most. He found himself trapped in London with hundreds of thousands of pounds, which he needed to smuggle to Amsterdam. With no one available to transport the cash, he was put in the position of doing the unthinkable – carrying it himself. This was risky. Ever since he had threatened the staff in Holyhead, he was wary about making a mistake on British soil. Her Majesty's Customs would be looking for him. Although he didn't know it at the time, this assumption was correct. Roger Wilson had made sure Gilligan's name and passport number remained on the intelligence database. He believed that it would only be a matter of time before the pint-sized Gilligan made a mistake.

Gilligan did just that on the morning of Friday, 4 October, when he presented himself at the KLM ticket sales desk wanting to purchase a ticket for a flight bound for Amsterdam the next day. He paid for the ticket in cash. There was no problem. The next day he checked in late, just 30 minutes before his flight was due to depart. His only luggage was a metallic, hard-backed suitcase, which he pulled along with little difficulty. He said he'd carry it on board as hand luggage. It weighed just 23 kilos. His decision to check in late sparked off a security warning on the airline's computer, which immediately alerted Customs intelligence staff at Heathrow. The names of all passengers who arrive late for outbound flights are referred to Customs for security checks. The intelligence staff didn't pay too much attention to the referral until one recognised Gilligan's name. He took the flight details and logged on to Sedric, the customs database of criminal intelligence. Gilligan's name showed up.

A surveillance team was mobilised. By the time Gilligan was located, he was already boarding the flight. They learned that he was due to return on another flight later that day and decided to wait. He never showed up then, but he did the next morning, on 6 October, when he did the same thing. Obviously he had re-entered the UK by another means of flight and perhaps under another name. He made his way towards the KLM fight desk and purchased a ticket for flight No. KL120. It was bound for Schipol Airport. He handed over a fistful of notes. With the ticket in one hand and the suitcase in the other, he checked in late. The receptionist glanced at his photograph and smiled before handing him a boarding card. She looked at the suitcase but before she could say a word, he interjected: 'That's hand luggage.' She said it was necessary to weigh it to make sure. It weighed 23 kilos. He went to the departures lounge. This time, Customs were waiting for him. He didn't notice the officers staring at him from the security gate until it was too late to turn back. One stepped forward and asked him if he had anything to declare. He said he didn't.

They took him aside into a small room. He still had a firm grip on his suitcase. He was asked to open it, which he did. Inside was a pillow and a shirt. There was an anti-bugging device and a loan agreement for £4 million from a Lebanese man, Joseph Saouma. There were also bookies' cheques. The officer searched further, moving his hands about. In the bottom, he felt soft plastic. He gently removed the pillow to uncover a package enfolded in bubble-wrap. It was filled with notes. Inside was £330,000 in sterling, Northern Irish sterling and Irish currency.

The blood drained from Gilligan's face. Alone in the room, he knew he was in the hands of the same security agency whose members years before he had tormented and threatened. He was placed under arrest for concealing money in order to avoid a drugs charge. More Customs staff entered the room. He was then taken away for interrogation which lasted two days.

With audacious calm, Gilligan started explaining that he was on his way to Amsterdam to go horse racing and to look at property. He pointed at the suitcase. 'It's all legal and above board,' he said.

The interrogation continued with various teams of officers coming and going. They carried with them bundles of files, listing names, passenger and flight details. He asked to call his solicitor but was told he could not. The day passed with more officers arriving. These were more senior and clearly knew more about him than the others. During one of the changeovers, he rang Geraldine using his mobile, which had not been taken from him. 'They've got the three hundred grand . . . tell Terry . . . ring Terry.' He was interrupted midway through the call and hung up.

Two days later, he was not in the frame of mind to answer any more questions and he asked if he was going to be charged. 'Yes, Mr Gilligan, you are,' said one of the Customs men. He went pale. The next day, he was brought before Uxbridge Magistrates Court on a charge of concealing or transferring his proceeds of drug trafficking under Section 49(1)(a) of the Drug Trafficking Act 1994. It was a routine court appearance. He was remanded to Wormwood Scrubs Prison.

Across the Irish Sea, the cartel was slowly being dismantled. Bowden was brought before Kilmainham District Court surrounded by tight security. He was charged with various offences and remanded to Mountjoy Prison. It was a theatrical act played out by both sides to fool the others still at large. It worked, sending them all into a fit of panic. In reality, they knew their days were numbered. They prepared to flee. However, if their passports were presented at Dublin Airport, they would surely be arrested. Meehan and Ward knew a friendly Garda who could solve their problem. In the meantime they vanished, moving out of their homes and into hotels or friends' houses, never sleeping two nights in the one bed.

Hippo sought refuge in the Green Isle Hotel on the Naas Road. By chance, Ronanstown Gardaí were searching for a man with a similar name in connection with an armed robbery. A tip-off to detectives resulted in him being arrested at gunpoint while he slept at the hotel early on 8 October. He was taken from the hotel and driven to Ronanstown Garda Station, arriving at 1.50 a.m. Overcome by shock, he said nothing, waiting for the inevitable. Then he was released at 2.45 a.m. He was told he was the wrong man.

GANGSTER

The next day at 7.15 p.m. he rang John O'Neill at Tallaght Garda station. They agreed to meet later that night. Ward gave him two passport forms and four photographs of his brother Shay, whom O'Neill immediately recognised, having charged him years before. Hippo told O'Neill he believed he was going to be arrested for the murder of Veronica Guerin. They agreed to meet four days later at the Cuckoo's Nest on the Greenhills Road at 8.20 p.m.

O'Neill did as he was told. He arrived for the meeting in his Land Rover. Hippo was waiting inside and on seeing O'Neill, walked out and sat in the front passenger seat. O'Neill, never a man to worry about security, switched on the car's internal light and handed some papers to Hippo. Ward threw his eyes over the paperwork. O'Neill had stamped the passport applications as instructed. Neither of the conspirators took much notice of the people coming to and from the pub. They should have done.

When they finished their business, Ward jumped out and O'Neill drove home.

It was the least he could do for Gilligan's gang. They had completely corrupted him. He had solicited bribes and allowed himself to plunge into criminality. When it was established that O'Neill had abandoned his moral senses Hickey instructed the team to intercept the passport applications through the Department of Foreign Affairs. If the gang managed to reach the continent, they could disappear, possibly forever. He wanted to avoid a lengthy extradition process at all costs. He had another message for O'Neill and Ward – he ordered his officers to arrest them both.

The morning of 16 October was cold and overcast. Ward's miraculous release from custody the week before had, if nothing else, given him a sense of false security. The surprise that day was that he had returned home where he was found. Elizabeth, his mother and Vanessa Meehan were also detained at exactly the same time. Ward was placed in a squad car and driven to Lucan station. His lover was sent to Ballyfermot, his mother driven to Cabra.

The suspect was formally registered 20 minutes later. He demanded to speak to a lawyer and requested medication. He told the police he was a heroin addict. He needed physeptone. With no preparatory talk, the police called a doctor. His name was Lionel Williams. He arrived later that day after the interviews had started. When he arrived at the station, Ward asked to be examined to see if he had injuries. The doctor did as requested but found nothing. He gave 40 milligrams of sedative in liquid form to a Garda to give to the prisoner. The interviews commenced.

O'Neill heard through the grapevine about Ward's detention but thought nothing of it. He was the most surprising of men for it never crossed his mind that he too was in trouble. Over time, he had managed to hypnotise himself into a surreal world. He was quickly brought back to reality when at 7 p.m. the next night six Gardaí arrived at his door armed with a search warrant. Detective Inspector Jerry O'Connell knocked at the door of his home in Kingswood Heights in Tallaght. A stunned O'Neill answered the door. O'Connell asked him if he had anything illegal in the house, as detectives made their way in. 'No. No, I don't have anything in the house. Why would I have anything in the house? I've only got a sawn-off shotgun. It's upstairs in the wardrobe,' he said. Minutes later, the search party found the weapon. It was an air pistol. Beside it was a file marked 'courts'. Wearing plastic gloves, detectives opened the file. Inside was a bench warrant for Fiona Walsh, a girlfriend of Meehan. O'Neill was arrested and brought to Naas Garda Station. He came clean.

Ward's interrogation was getting nowhere. He said nothing. Vanessa Meehan was also refusing to co-operate. One detective said later: 'It was a constant answer she gave us, "I don't know."' At 10.30 p.m. they brought her to Lucan to see him. They put her in a cell and brought him into her new cell. The distinction was important. It was an emotional reunion, which proved futile from the investigation team's perspective. His mother was brought to visit him at 2.27 p.m. the next day. This did not work either.

Then O'Neill was brought to the interview room. 'I've told them everything,' he said.

'Fuck off,' Ward shouted. 'There was no need to do that. He didn't tell me fuck all about the murder. The money is his fucking problem. I am saying nothing else to you.'

Later that Friday night, shortly before nine o'clock, Ward became the first member of the gang to face charges for Veronica's murder when he appeared before Dublin District Court. The offence was harbouring persons knowing that they had been involved in the murder, and with possession of drugs with intent to supply. He wore black shoes, blue denims and a yellow, blue and green jumper with a diamond pattern. He carried a blue anorak. He sat with his legs crossed and the anorak across his knees.

The Gardaí proceeded to arrest others who they suspected might have information about O'Neill's dealings with criminals. More than anything else, police management feared a scandal emanating from within their own ranks. There were persistent allegations of corruption, which through an assortment of friendly journalists were denied. They were now in the precarious position of having to charge one of their own officers with offences linked to Guerin's murder. O'Neill had sung like a canary, naming the criminals who bribed him. He said he met Ward through Martin Ryan, a nightclub manager he once worked for. Ryan was arrested and taken to Terenure Garda Station where he was interviewed, throwing further light on the Gilligan gang. Though he was not suspected of being involved with the murder of Guerin, Sergeant Cormac McGuiness and Garda Pauline Reid, the officers conducting the interview, got straight to the point. 'Why did Paul Ward call to your house on Tuesday, 15 October 1996?' asked McGuiness.

'He just dropped in. He said he was meeting someone in the Cuckoo's Nest. He was very agitated. He said he was meeting a bloke and he wanted to leave him dangling. He said he had five minutes to spare. He appeared to me to be in a bit of limbo. He didn't seem to know whether to keep the appointment. He appeared to want to come into my house.'

Ryan managed the System Night Club on South Anne Street in Dublin. Meehan, Ward and Mitchell were regular patrons. He was held overnight. The next day Sergeant Michael O'Leary and Garda Andy Manning took over the interrogation. This proved more productive. He inadvertently linked Holland to the gang. 'There's another guy, they call him "Gene Wilder". He's about 50 years. He's very thin, about 5 foot 5 inches. His name is Gene. He's very grumpy and I tried to stop him at the door one night. He was with Aidan, Brian Meehan and a few other girls and I think "Git". Aidan said that he was with them so I let him in. He used to come in on his own after that but he would always be with Brian Meehan and Paul Ward. Ward would come in at least once a week. They always got on well, having the *craic*. Sometimes "Gene" would come in with a guy called "Kellyer". He looked like a junkie.'

'Why did they call him Gene Wilder?'

"Cause he looked like him when he had the hair out frizzy. He normally has his hair tied back in a ponytail. The ponytail is shoulder length, so when it's out it looks real frizzy.'

'Can you tell us anything else about Gene?'

'No, not really but he's easy to pick out. He has a fat nose – it's lumpy, very red and pointy. He wasn't very clean, always T-shirts and jacket, navy or black, and trousers.'

The officer asked Ryan if he knew any Gardaí. He wasn't aware that O'Neill was in custody. 'I know another guard from Tallaght, he's known as "Buffalo". He's John O'Neill. I was at his house in Kingswood. We called to his house to get a parking fine fixed. He wasn't in when we called but I met him on the Greenhills Road near the Cuckoo's Nest.'

'How many times have you been in contact with John O'Neill?'

'About six times.'

'What was the reason for these contacts?'

'He was always asking me for money. I'd give it to him sometimes. He'd call to my house.'

'What is your connection with Paul Ward and John O'Neill?'

'John O'Neill is a great friend of Paul Ward. I don't have anything to do with them. They have an arrangement with them and Brian Meehan. They look after him for whatever, information I suppose. I don't like O'Neill, he's dirt, a sponger.'

O'Neill was charged the next night at a special sitting of Dublin District Court. He had resigned from the force while in custody. The hearing took less than ten minutes. Three charges were proffered. Meehan, Mitchell, Ward and Holland left the State immediately. The Gardaí had put the Passport Office under surveillance to see if they would collect the passports O'Neill had stamped. But they never showed up.

News of the charges was communicated to Gilligan. He was trying to fight his own battle. The British authorities moved him from Wormwood Scrubs to Belmarsh High Security Prison. He made an application for bail on 23 October but lost. The Crown Prosecution Service objected to bail and won. He was further remanded to 14 November.

The sheriff arrived with his men outside the gates of Jessbrook at 9 a.m. on 20 November 1996. His men were burly and wore masks and overalls. Some of them wore dark glasses, baseball hats and scarves to conceal their identities. The number plates on their vehicles had been removed. Behind them stood half a dozen Gardaí drawn from the Louth/Meath division. They were there as back-up. A small number carried firearms. When John and Geraldine failed to respond to their respective tax bills, the CAB instructed the county sheriff to seize their property. The day had come.

Geraldine was at home with Darren, Tracy and her daughter Shannon. She saw them coming but there was nothing that she or anyone else could do. Frank Lanigan, the county sheriff, knocked at the door and explained his business. His men entered the house. The Gilligans put up no fight.

They took everything, lifting furniture and everything else as if they were removal men. Geraldine was lost for words. She spent much of her time during the raid sitting on the floor. At other times, she was possessed by a strength that made her appear outwardly unwavering in the face of such adversity. What affected her more than anything was the removal of her beloved horses. When she saw the sheriff's men lead them one by one into horse trailers she broke down. For the first time since the murder, it became all too much. She was stunned. All they left was a child's pony and four horses that she didn't own. The seizure of the animals brought her back to her senses and in a bold move she walked out the gates and spoke to the media for the first time. The dogs followed.

She had only one message. 'I couldn't answer any tax assessments because the police have all my documents of returns, and everything else, so I didn't have any documentation to answer with,' she said. Asked how much was sought in the tax assessment she received, she said: 'Mine was £882,000, but the one that I got on the 14th of this month has gone up with interest to £1,292,000.' She came across as a genuinely wronged woman, almost breaking down crying.

The sheriff's men left at 5.10 p.m. It was bitterly cold and almost dark by the time they had removed everything. During the course of the day, detectives from the CAB made an inventory of the property seized. This was handed to Geraldine who ran her eyes down the list. There she noticed a Nissan Micra car. She remarked to the detective that no one in the family owned a Micra. 'Oh, that's John's girlfriend's,' the detective responded, with a smile.

She said nothing. Once inside the door of her bare home, she fell to the floor and started crying. She had no choice. There were no seats or furniture left to sit on. Everything was gone. Darren and Tracy comforted her and her friend Jean Bolger wiped away the tears.

The press were everywhere outside. Eventually, they started calling to the door. She refused to answer it. She cried all night. She couldn't believe that Gilligan had a young girlfriend, young enough to be her daughter. She asked how he could do this to her. Then when sense began to prevail, she asked how he could have a relationship with such a young girl. 'It's not her I'm annoyed with. It's him,' she said.

Tracy was more direct. She wanted to go straight to Carol's house and tell her what she thought of the relationship. 'My ma's been crying all night because of her. I could kill me fucking da.'

In reality Carol Rooney was the least of her worries. Public unrest began to manifest itself with vigilante attacks on Jessbrook. Her car windows were smashed. People started sending her pornographic hate mail in the morning post. The gates to Jessbrook were vandalised. 'Drugs bitch out' was sprayed on the walls. In an attempt to give her side of the story, she spoke to the press, painting a rather bleak picture of her existence.

'All that's left for me to do is die, then everyone will be happy. I still believe John had nothing to do with the murder. The papers have made him out to be a killer,' she told the *Sunday Business Post*. 'My life has been turned upside down, so much so that I can't describe it. It's just all gone. All that's left for me to do is just die, then everyone will be happy. I've even lost my brothers and sisters. It kills me to think that my family wouldn't even stand by me, even though I've done nothing wrong. You know last week a newspaper article said my life ended when the sheriff and police came but my life really ended when Veronica Guerin was killed.'

Though her interview was polished, she could not explain her wealth. She carefully avoided mentioning the cash withdrawals, or where the money was now. 'I'm not interested in what people think. The money came from gambling as far as I am concerned. I don't believe John was involved in the drugs trade. If people believe that you can't win money gambling there would be no bookies' shops. Are the people of Ireland telling me that you can't win money gambling? John even had limits placed on his bets in some bookies. I have never seen any evidence, which made me believe that John was involved in drugs.'

Making herself out to be a victim, she said her separation was legitimate: 'I wish it wasn't because I still love him in some way. The media pressure has brought us back together again. Our marriage started to fall apart when we moved to Meath in 1994 because I was engrossed in my horses and he was into gambling. A lot of our problems were caused by the lack of space in the house. When John would show up, all my friends would be staying so we had no time to ourselves. In '95 we called it a day because I had more time for my horses than I did for him. The separation agreement was that he would finish the construction of the centre. It was an unorthodox split up because we remained friends.'

Then, in a direct reference to Gilligan's relationship with Rooney, she said: 'John and I are separated, he is free to do his own thing.'

The interview lasted for three hours during which time a helicopter hovered above the centre carrying a film crew. Finally she avowed that she had never been a bad person. 'I want to see Veronica's Guerin's killers caught. I watched her husband on *The Late Late Show* and felt the same as everyone else. I know he doesn't want to hear that but it's the truth. I so believe that John had nothing to do with it. The papers have made him out to be a killer. The reason why I'm giving this interview is because papers are printing stories about me and John which are not true. I don't have to prove anything to anyone. The media don't know me so how can they write about me? The future holds nothing. I don't think anyone wants to see me get justice. It's as simple as that.'

The Criminal Assets Bureau attracted a great deal of controversy due to the anarchic laws empowered in it. Fachtna Murphy was acutely aware of this and refrained from prosecuting cases where there was little or no hard evidence to link cash to drug trafficking. But the powers invested in CAB still caused genuine concern among civil rights activists and people like Ó Siodhacháin, who was still in regular contact with Geraldine. He didn't like CAB for ideological reasons more than anything else. In one of his many meetings with Geraldine, he advised her to speak with Michael Grimes in Cork. He was a man who would help, he told her, smiling.

Grimes was a spindly little man who revelled in trouble. He introduced himself as a tax expert – at other times he was a liquidator. 'It depends on what day of the week you get me,' he says.

Without having any formal legal qualifications, he is revered for his highly tuned legal mind, which has struck the fear of God into those who have crossed swords with him. Geraldine, out of desperation, said she wanted to meet him. A week later, she did.

They met in his office. Grimes studied her case paperwork. He looked Ó Siodhacháin straight in the eye and said, 'I can see the way their minds work.'

Grimes later said, 'I reached the conclusion that she might have a claim for half the property, but in my view she didn't because the money she used was his. On the face of it, she seemed hard done by, because she said she was separated from her beloved, though at that time she didn't quite use the word beloved.'

Geraldine didn't know what to make of the eccentric Cork man but, left with no other choice, asked him to help. 'Then she asked if I would look after John's representation and my viewpoint on that was it was an English case, it dealt with English law, it was highly specialised and there was no point in involving Irish lawyers of any kind. She then asked me if I would go see him.'

She left the meeting content and dined with O'Siodhacháin that evening, before catching the 6.30 p.m. train home. She didn't know what to think of Grimes. 'I don't know if he's mad or what,' she said. Meanwhile Grimes went to see Gilligan in prison.

'Belmarsh gave us our own room. You presume everything is bugged, so we wrote little notes to each other. His was, "I don't fucking care if this room is bugged."'

They discussed Gilligan's case strategy, the CAB raid on Jessbrook and the murder. 'As far as he was concerned, he was going to be out in three weeks, it was a terrible mistake,' said Grimes. 'I was quite blunt with him. I realised that even if I wanted to defend him, I wouldn't last 20 minutes because nobody who disagreed with him got anywhere. He knew exactly what he was going to do, because he was totally innocent of everything and he never heard of people like Paddy Holland or Brian Meehan. Now when he tells you straight to your face that he never heard of these guys, well you know what you're up against.'

Grimes subscribed to the belief that in court people should never ask questions they don't know the answers to. Gilligan struck Grimes as a dogged and determined person. 'John had a habit of deciding something, which was totally unreal. The real problem with him and Geraldine is facts don't influence anything. Once they decide something is true, well that's the end of it. The fact that the facts scream to high heaven to the opposite is neither here nor there. John would say that it was really her property and it was her decision. And she would say you'd have to ask the boss. So between the two of them, you never got an answer to anything. Not that he would give you an answer to anything.'

Grimes, who speaks with an alarming bluntness, later concluded that Geraldine was the person he should talk to. 'She was the cleverer of the two. John was plain stupid. John's only answer to everything was, "I'll bump him off."' Grimes set about devising a method to halt the CAB in its tracks.

Gilligan was in the act of fighting a losing battle at Belmarsh Magistrates Court. Customs and Excise were pressing ahead in conjunction with the Gardaí. The murder inquiry arranged for Dunne to be flown to London to testify for Customs in a move also aimed at frightening the rest of the gang who were operating from the shadows. When Gilligan heard that one of his own was going to give evidence, he was dumbstruck. He didn't really believe it was going to happen until Dunne took the stand. Gilligan watched from the dock in disbelief while Dunne told the judge that he never knew he was importing drugs. 'I was not told what was in the containers. I was not told what was the weight of them. There was no discussion.' It was comical. 'There was something not quite right,' he said with a degree of smugness.

Gilligan's lawyer, Clare Montgomery, saw through this and tore the witness to shreds, prising apart his evidence.

The case lasted for three days. The media had arrived *en masse*. Many of the journalists assembled were startled to discover that Gilligan was a small man. He took no notice. He sat back smiling. Sometimes he fiddled with his glasses while generally surveying all about him. At other times, he stared up at the ceiling, leaning back on his bench to rest his arms behind his head. He was outwardly jovial.

On the third day, the chief prosecutor told the court that Dermot Cambridge, a van driver innocently duped into the conspiracy by Dunne, was refusing to travel to England to give evidence because he had received a number of threatening phone calls and was 'frightened for his life'. Cambridge said anonymous callers were threatening to kill him, his girlfriend and his child.

GANGSTER

Gilligan was remanded in custody until 20 February.

The *Sunday Times* announced to the world that Grimes planned to reopen Jessbrook a week after the committal hearing had ended. Grimes, by a miraculous stroke of coincidence, said he had been hired by Joseph Saouma to retrieve a £4 million loan given to Gilligan. Grimes had also without anyone's knowledge been appointed by the British High Court as receiver to Gilligan's assets, including Jessbrook and two houses in Dublin. 'It is my intention to reopen the equestrian centre. It is the finest in Europe, it holds 2,800 people in an indoor arena,' he said, adding that he never worked for Gilligan. The CAB didn't know what to make of it all.

The Gilligans in the meantime were waging an all-out legal battle to stop the CAB. Immediately after the raid on Jessbrook, Geraldine sought a High Court injunction preventing the bureau from selling off her property. The CAB contested the injunction but lost. It was a temporary setback. Seven days later, on 12 February, lawyers acting for Gilligan failed to prevent the State from appointing a receiver over his properties. It was another blow to the cartel. But Gilligan was granted permission to challenge the constitutionality of the Proceeds of Crime Act 1996.

The tide turned six days later when Geraldine initiated an appeal against the seizure of her property. Her case centred on her claim that she was not liable for Gilligan's taxes. 'If I was taxable, then every separated wife in the country would be taxable for their ex-husbands. It made no sense to me.' Her lawyers argued that she was a married woman and that she and Gilligan were living as husband and wife at the time of the tax assessment. Because neither had opted for a separate tax assessment, it was her husband who was chargeable under the tax laws.

The CAB reaffirmed that she was a chargeable person, claiming that in the period of assessment, she had bank accounts with substantial sums in her own name. This was income in her own hands. The judge reserved judgement. The news came on 23 February that Geraldine had won her case in the High Court, which ruled that she was not liable for the massive tax bill of £1.6 million. She could not believe her ears. Mr Justice Morris, in delivering his judgement, said it was clear that significant consequences might flow from his determination of the issues but it was no part of his function to consider any such consequences.

In the meantime, Gilligan was sent forward for trial in Woolwich on 17 March, St Patrick's Day. David Cooper, the stipendiary magistrate, outlined the case against the gangster during a 20 minute written submission to the court. Gilligan, he said, did have a case to answer before a jury but the prosecution had not established a case beyond reasonable doubt.

On 20 February, at 1 p.m., there were crowds everywhere on Upper Street in Islington, allowing Detective Constable Patrick McElhatton to blend in easily. He was undercover, following a target with a covert operations team drawn from the South Regional Crime Squad. The target walked briskly, which caused his followers to do likewise. He headed into the public entrance of Angel Street tube station.

McElhatton watched as his subject and his girlfriend moved towards the south side of the entrance. Then there were three of them – the young couple and a much older male.

'The younger male was six foot tall, 30 to 35 years old, medium to heavy build, wearing spectacles. He was wearing a light brown suede jacket,' McElhatton noted. Bowden was looking smart for a fugitive on the run. He had just been released from Mountjoy Prison and skipped bail, taking Juliet Bacon with him.

McElhatton didn't know the identity of the man they were meeting but noticed he had a distinctive misshaped nose and was carrying a newspaper in his right hand. He moved in closer to hear their conversation. 'Don't say fuck all about me, I'm telling you, I've me alibi sorted.' The older man spoke loudly. There followed another conversation, which the policeman couldn't hear. The group walked off.

Holland decided to face the music and return home. He called the incident room and said he'd present himself at Lucan Garda Station with his solicitor. On the morning of 9 April, Garda Marion Cusack, a streetwise member of the Drugs Unit at Store Street Station, was monitoring passengers arriving at Dun Laoghaire ferryport. The night before, Holland had telephoned the incident room to say he would be arriving on the ferry. Cusack saw a red Volkswagen Polo car alighting from the ferry driven by a woman with a male passenger in the front seat and a boy in the back seat. She went to the passenger and asked his name.

Holland revealed his identity. He was immediately arrested under Section 30 of the Offences Against the State Act, on suspicion of having a firearm, and was taken to Lucan where he was interviewed at length. By chance a Garda searching through his belongings found what appeared to be a walkman among his possessions. Out of curiosity, he put the headphones on and heard what sounded like his colleagues interviewing Holland. He rushed into the interview room. The suspect was searched. Nothing was found. Later, his shoes were torn apart. Inside the police found two tiny transmitters. He had tried to record the interview.

Bowden was arrested and agreed to return home voluntarily. O'Mahony and Hanley flew to London City airport to collect him on the night of 11 April. He was sorry and told the police he'd testify in court.

.

CHAPTER 16

Fighting Back

'I'll send someone to kill you and
everybody around you if he goes Turk.'
BRIAN MEEHAN THREATENING CHARLES BOWDEN'S GIRLFRIEND, JULIET BACON

John Gilligan had been remanded to the maximum-security wing in Belmarsh Prison on the outskirts of London. Belmarsh Prison is built near the site of the wartime arsenal at Woolwich. It was opened in 1991 and is used as a dispersal prison. It accommodates 901 inmates. Houseblock No. 4 is where the maximum-security prisoners are held. Life there is a harsh regime where prisoners like Gilligan are confined for longer periods in their cells. With no way of escaping and locked up for most of the day, he resolved to fight the prosecution every step of the way. His strategy took two forms, both aimed at bringing about the same conclusion. His first stratagem was to denounce the prosecution every step of the way. From this starting point, he instructed his lawyers to appeal every decision pertinent to his extradition. The instructions were based on his own interpretations of extradition and constitutional law which he formulated through reading law books, massive manuals on extradition, criminal law and constitutional issues. The second, but far more effective, method of hindering the prosecution case, was the threat of extreme violence against anyone who considered testifying against him. Meehan saw to this.

The first of many hearings got underway on 17 March 1997, the feast of St Patrick, when Gilligan's lawyers sought a judicial review of his committal. It was supposed to be a routine hearing – and it was, until the prosecution announced that a further 54 Irish witnesses were available to give evidence.

The figure startled Gilligan. Even if most of the new witnesses were Gardaí, the news signalled certain trouble.

But he wasn't just fighting the British authorities. Back in Dublin he was mounting a legal challenge against the constitutionality of the Proceeds of Crime Act 1996. This complex legal case commenced on 18 March. It ran for three days. The powers invested in the bureau were described as 'the creation of a police state'. The CAB defence however was simple: the State had a right to confiscate the proceeds of crime. Judgment was reserved.

Gilligan, who with inspirational zeal was fast learning the mechanisms of criminal and constitutional law, was briefed on the developments. He believed there was real hope. After all, Geraldine had won her case against the bureau notwithstanding the odds.

But what Gilligan could not see was how Geraldine's life had changed irrevocably since Veronica's murder. The woman he gave everything to was no longer the lady of the country manor. What few friends she ever had no longer took her calls or enquired about her wellbeing. There were no more extravagant parties at Jessbrook. But Geraldine was a survivor. She took everything in her stride: Nothing fazed her. Least of all the Garda raids, court actions or pressure from the media.

Her daughter was the same. Darren, however, was different. He did not possess the same inner strengths as his mother or sister. The pressure of the Garda investigation into his father's criminal empire secretly impacted on him. He turned to heroin to escape. He became an addict. None of the family realised this until he was charged at a special late sitting of Dublin District Court on 2 April with a number of crimes, including burglary. He had committed the crimes while high.

Prison was supposed to neutralise Gilligan but it did no such thing. The Gardaí hoped Gilligan's arrest would strike fear into the gang, forcing them to go their separate ways. It was an idle hope, wishful thinking on the police's part. The gangster's arrest had the opposite effect. Meehan and Holland, more than the others, allegedly resolved to dispatch those planning to testify against them. Holland, intelligence reports alleged, sincerely regretted not killing Bowden when he had the chance in London. It was now too late. Bowden was in Arbour Hill Prison, under 24-hour armed guard for his own protection. Warren was just as safe. Gilligan had no idea he was helping the police. Warren met his handlers at clandestine locations. It was a dangerous game but one he played carefully. Dunne was also protected. His home in Cork lay surrounded by an impenetrable cordon of armed police. The threat against them was still very real.

Thomas Coyle, Gilligan's loyal friend, was desperately trying to find an assassin inside Arbour Hill willing to kill Bowden. He suggested mixing crushed glass or poisons in his meals. His preferred method of assassination, though, was a knife in the back while he showered. The reward he offered was £2 million. Coyle approached former IRA men to no avail. In one confidential memorandum, which Todd O'Loughlin, a senior officer on the case, wrote to Hickey, he outlined his fears for the safety of all concerned. It was headed 'Security of Witnesses in the Veronica Guerin murder investigation:'

> It is the consensus of opinion at the incident room at Lucan that the security of witnesses discussed hereafter should be given urgent consideration. Reports from a number of confidential sources indicate that the principals in this murder who are still at large, namely Brian Meehan, Peter Mitchell and Patrick Eugene Holland have come to the conclusion that the only way to stop the witnesses testifying against them, and to re-establish their control over these people, is to kill one or more of the witnesses. Their primary target at the moment is Charlie Bowden: statements attached.
>
> The gang are particularly annoyed at Charlie Bowden and profoundly regret not having killed him when he recently absconded to Britain. Attempts are now being made to find somebody who can kill him in prison. He is presently in Arbour Hill Prison as his security could not be assured in Mountjoy Prison. There is also grave concern for the safety of Juliet Bacon, who is Bowden's common-law wife, and is not in custody at the moment.
>
> In the case of Russell Warren, the threat is not imminent as his evidence has not yet been served and the Gilligan gang is not aware of the extent of it. Immediate consideration would need to be given to the position of Julie Bacon and [another criminal informant] who seem to be the most vulnerable at the moment.'

Hickey needed no convincing. If any of the witnesses came to harm, it would be a disaster. Not only would the others be too afraid to testify, there would be a knock-on effect. With the absence of any formal protection operation for state witnesses, the realisation that Gilligan's gang was perhaps even more dangerous than ever entered his thoughts. There was no other solution – the situation required the creation of a witness protection programme. The assistant commissioner sent a letter, with the word 'confidential' stamped on top, to C Branch, the force's intelligence section, on 4 April 1997. 'It is significant that intelligence indicates that the main players think that the absence of a witness protection programme in this country is to their advantage. There is no doubt but that they will resort to murder to prevent witnesses giving damaging evidence in court. I agree with inspector T. O'Loughlin's assessment that Julie Bacon and [another criminal informant] are most vulnerable at the moment and should be provided with protection in the short term. I think that we should review the situation following consultation with the DP. and if necessary set up a witness protection programme, as all the vital witnesses will be under severe threat if statements are served, and under prolonged threat if, and when, they give evidence.'

His analysis was correct. As he was writing, the gang was quickly coming to the conclusion that Bowden was now a sworn enemy. Their worst suspicions were partly confirmed when they discovered that Bowden was no longer being held in Mountjoy Prison but had been transferred to Arbour Hill. This suggested that Bowden was either in solitary confinement or, more likely, had turned supergrass.

Gilligan was losing his patience. He couldn't distinguish the lies from the truth in the coded messages relayed to him over the phone. Meehan and the others were equally confused. All they could do was wait for Charlie to make contact.

At 4 p.m. on 11 April 1997 Juliet Bacon walked into the Hole in the Wall pub on Blackhorse Avenue. She was accompanied by five armed Gardaí. One attached a recording device to the public phone in the pub. She made a few calls. The first was to a wrong number. The second reached a business contact of Gilligan's. She asked this man to call Meehan and tell him to get in touch. She hung up. Five minutes later, the phone rang. She got straight to the point. 'Charlie is going fucking mad, he wants to know what the fucking story is.'

She enquired about Holland's arrest at Dun Laoghaire. Meehan told her it was of no concern to Bowden. Trying to compromise him further, she continued: 'He said they nicked him . . . He got told that someone ratted that he was coming on the boat or else they said they had surveillance on the boats.'

'He has nothing to do with what Charlie got done for.'

'I know, he's just wondering, just worried what the story is, that's all,' she said.

'But it's got nothing to do with the murder and it's nothing. He's clear on the murder, he is, because they didn't do him with it, cause they've no evidence, right.'

Bacon enquired further, asking Meehan out straight about Holland's court appearance on drugs charges. She referred to this as 'the drugs thing'.

Meehan didn't need anyone to tell him that she was up to no good. Now he got straight to the point. 'Now listen to me and I'll tell you, cause I want to get things straight, cause things are looking very fucking fishy to me, right, and I'll tell you what. I'm after being good to everybody but I'm taking off my gloves now. If Charlie's going belly up, if Charlie is going gammy, he better fucking think very strongly about what will happen.'

'Are you threatening me, Brian?'

'Threatening, Julie? You'll have no idea what I'm going to fucking do if he goes Turk. Now, I'm telling you, I'm his friend still, I'm helping you every way I can, but I'm fucking starting to worry and worry and worry, cause I'll tell you who goes to Arbour Hill – fucking rapists and rats. I've done everything I fucking can to help him, everything. He has no worries against why Holland is home, unless he made a statement against him. Do you understand?'

'Charlie is going ballistic.'

She need not have bothered acting. Meehan knew she was lying. He exploded with rage. 'I'll send someone to fucking kill you this fucking day, do you understand what I'm saying?'

'What did you say?

'You are fucking hearing me. I'll send someone to kill you and everybody around you if he goes Turk. Now tell him I said that, right, and tell him I said I'm fucking considering doing him anyway, so he better not fucking think of going rat, right. That's the message now, right,' he roared.

'You're a fucking knacker, that's all, you're a knacker.'

'Charlie is a rat and if he rats on me, I'll fucking kill you,' he shouted.

'I don't fucking blame him if he does, you prick, you.'

'Yeah, you fucking scumbag.'

She screamed back: 'You're a scumbag. Fuck off.'

The next day, Bowden's semi-detached home in the Paddocks in Castleknock was petrol-bombed. There was no one at home. Bacon was in protective custody. The intimidation didn't stop there. Brendan 'Speedy' Feegan, the gang's representative in Northern Ireland, arrived in Dublin driving a red convertible BMW. He went searching for Bowden's children. If burning Bowden's home down didn't work, kidnapping and torturing his children might. Feegan aborted the plan on finding Bowden's family under armed guard. He was later arrested and told the police he never intended harming the children. He said he just wanted to take pictures of them. These would be sent to Bowden to force him to withdraw his statements.

The endless court appearances involving Gilligan continued. The Crown Prosecution Service sought permission for up to 50 witnesses to give evidence from Dublin, possibly before an Irish court. Permission was granted, prompting the gangster to seek a judicial review against this decision. Gilligan told his counsel there was no need for these security measures. He said he had no desire to prevent any witness from giving evidence. But there was a surprise in store. When his judicial review case was heard on 21 May 1997, Nigel Peters, the prosecuting barrister, said he wished to reintroduce two charges that had been struck out on the basis of statements made by one Charles Bowden.

Hickey's team took their time in preparing the murder case against Gilligan, until it became clear that Bowden would be required to travel to London to give evidence. The consensus was that Bowden would not stand up to a rigorous cross-examination before a London court, mainly because it was obvious that he was centrally involved in the assassination. Bowden could not account for his whereabouts on the day of the murder. His claim that when he loaded the Magnum he sincerely believed that Veronica would only be intimidated was so outlandish that not even the true believers in the Gardaí could have faith in his words.

Left with no other alternative, the Gardaí moved to extradite

Gilligan. There was a flurry of meetings with barristers, the murder investigation team and officials from the Department of Justice. Hickey argued that Bowden would not testify unless given immunity. This was granted on 4 July 1997. Barry Donoghue, a legal assistant in the DPP's office, wrote to Hickey confirming the news. 'I refer to recent consultations regarding the ongoing investigation into the murder of Veronica Guerin. The Director has taken the following decision. It is unconditional and irrevocable. He will not prosecute Charles Bowden for the murder of Veronica Guerin on the basis of (a) any statement, made orally or in writing by Charles Bowden up to today's date; (b) any further statement made orally or in writing which Charles Bowden may in the future make to a member of the Garda Síochána in the course of their investigation into the possible involvement of other persons in that murder; (c) any evidence which Charles Bowden may give in criminal proceedings against any other person.'

Warren's solicitor received similar notification on 17 August 1997. By this time, he was living under the protection of the Gardaí.

With the informants in place, Hickey flew to London and lodged 18 warrants with Scotland Yard seeking Gilligan's extradition. The gangster only learned of this on the day his trial on drugs trafficking was due to begin, 8 September. The warrants Hickey lodged included the charge of murdering Veronica Guerin, drug trafficking and gun running. British Customs set aside their charges allowing the murder extradition proceedings to take priority.

The day was one of extraordinary complexities. For a brief moment, Gilligan was released from custody outside Belmarsh Court. Seconds later, he was rearrested by the Metropolitan Police. Under heavy armed guard, he was transported to Plumstead police station where he was formally served with his extradition warrants. Once he accepted the papers, he was returned to Belmarsh Magistrates Court.

The extradition hearing began at 3.15 p.m. Clare Montgomery QC immediately issued a warning to the court that she would be seeking an adjournment for an abuse of process. She pointed to a bundle of legal papers, which she said she had just been served. 'This,' she said without hesitation was 'not acceptable'. She then made a prophetic announcement. She said Gilligan would pursue every line of appeal to the High Court or the House of Lords.

The media were everywhere. Reporters scribbled contemporaneous notes of the proceedings, what Gilligan looked like and his facial expressions. For the extradition to be valid, the court required a Garda to formally identify Gilligan. Detective Inspector Jerry O'Connell was nominated. He took the stand and pointed at Gilligan. 'That's John Joseph Gilligan,' he said. The judge was satisfied. Gilligan was remanded yet again.

On 8 October 1997, Bowden was sentenced to six years in prison by Judge Cyril Kelly in the Dublin Circuit Criminal Court. He sat in the dock next to two armed detectives who watched attentively, almost waiting for someone to produce a gun. The Gardaí were taking no risks. Bowden wore a bullet-proof vest under his shirt, which exaggerated his stature. He expressed no emotion as the sentence was delivered. He looked as if he couldn't care less.

Judge Kelly said Bowden would never be able to live a normal life again and may have to disappear. His judgment, he said, was centred on the many factors he had to take into consideration. These included Bowden's guilty plea, the likelihood of him re-offending and the savings to the State by avoiding a lengthy trial. He imposed seven sentences of six years each, and two sentences of three years, all to run concurrently from 11 March, the date when Bowden first went into custody. Bowden left the court a happy man.

Four days later, Meehan and Traynor were arrested in Amsterdam by an élite unit of the Dutch police. There was a young girl in their company. When Meehan saw the commandos approach, he panicked, losing control of his bowels and defecating in his trousers. Traynor was decidedly more relaxed. He raised his hands in the air, in a gesture that suggested he was waiting for the police to pounce. All three were taken in for questioning. Hours later, Traynor was released without charge along with the girl. The Gardaí did not seek his extradition. The official story leaked to the media was that they had not expected to find him in Amsterdam. Few familiar with the case believed it.

Gilligan received the news in prison. He was devastated. Meehan was his surrogate son, the one man he could trust above anyone else. Without Meehan, his hands were tied. The legal challenges took on a new importance and sense of urgency.

The British courts heard his extradition case on 22 October. It did not go very far because legal arguments broke out, forcing the judge to adjourn the case, but only after he had cited Gilligan for contempt. Gilligan had refused to recognise the court. Instead he sat down, crossed his legs and read a book. 'I'm not sure if he recognises this court,' said the prosecuting counsel, prompting the magistrate to proclaim that he considered the accused's actions to be a contempt of court. 'I'll deal with you at the end of these proceedings,' he said.

The same court ruled he should be extradited on 28 October 1997. He appealed the decision at once. The nightmare of extradition was slowly unfolding. With the passing of each week, he received more bad news. On 10 November 1997, Warren had pleaded guilty to money laundering charges in the Dublin Circuit Criminal Court. Like Bowden, he was treated leniently. He was given a five-year sentence. The news was relayed to Gilligan who interpreted the sentence as a clear signal that Warren intended giving evidence against him. The story Warren gave, though, was unbelievable because he was living in a state of self-denial. Everything he said distanced himself from the murder. He told the Gardaí that he never knew Veronica was going to be shot, that he had vomited after watching her death. His whole story was full of inconsistencies. He said he'd driven to Naas on the fatal morning in his van, which because of its small engine size could not keep up with Guerin's car. But none of the witnesses saw such a vehicle. Warren's statements were littered with so many inconsistencies that no matter which way anyone viewed them, they couldn't be explained. He was trying to distance himself from the murder. It was all lies.

Just when Gilligan believed things couldn't get any worse, more critical news arrived. On 28 November 1997, Holland was convicted in the Special Criminal Court for drug trafficking. He was sentenced to 20 years on the strength of Bowden's evidence. The trial itself was overshadowed by a short piece of testimony given by Marion Cusack, the officer who arrested Holland at Dun Laoghaire ferry terminal. When asked by counsel why she arrested the accused, she said it was because she believed he was the man who had shot Veronica Guerin on the Naas Road. That the court accepted Bowden's evidence was a solemn signal for Gilligan.

Bowden had never wanted to testify in court but had cut a deal. His co-operation with the inquiry was not based on any feelings of remorse but on the idea that he would somehow avoid serving any significant period in jail. This was clear to anyone who knew him or heard his evidence. In truth and behind the scenes, the Gardaí were fighting a battle trying to keep Bowden contented. From the outset he complained about prison. He despised jail. With no cocaine, money, women or debauchery to entertain him, he was overcome by resentment. Like Gilligan, he set out to secure his freedom, or at worst more privileges. He wrote vexatious complaints to the Department of Justice and communicated his grievances to the Gardaí. Much of this was relayed to O'Loughlin. The informer was convincing in his sincerity. The detective inspector wrote to Garda headquarters four days after Holland's conviction, highlighting his concerns about Bowden's wellbeing and the workings of the witness security programme. 'Witness Protection in this country is a completely new phenomenon as indeed is large scale organised crime. As it is likely to be with us in the future, standards of treatment of such witnesses must be agreed,' he wrote.

He outlined what be perceived to be the situation. 'In the case of Charles Bowden I wish to say that the evidence which he gave in the trial of Patrick Eugene Holland was invaluable. Holland was given a 20-year sentence on 28 November 1997. Equally his evidence against Brian Meehan and John Gilligan is of vital importance. He is in a unique position in the Irish prison system and cannot be associated with other prisoners with the exception of Russell Warren, who is in a similar position. His unique position in the prison also means that he is in solitary lock-up for longer periods than other prisoners. In effect his co-operation in this ongoing investigation is leaving him in a most awkward position without privileges.

He continued: 'Juliet Bacon, his common-law wife, is also seriously confined under Garda protection. She has been completely removed from her former life and is being kept at a secret location, completely removed from all her family and friends.

'Juliet Bacon visits Charles Bowden at Arbour Hill on a daily basis. Prior to Bowden giving evidence for the State against Patrick Eugene Holland, Bowden had special visiting times to facilitate the special security arrangements in place on himself and Juliet Bacon. Unfortunately the prison authorities have now removed the privilege of special visiting times for Bowden. This is most unfortunate from a security point of view and it is unhelpful in relation to our efforts in securing his continued assistance in the prosecution of the main figures in the Gilligan gang.

'I ask that the prison authorities be requested to restore these special visiting times as a matter of urgency. Russell Warren and his wife Debbie are in a similar position and have had the special visits privilege withdrawn. It is accepted that Warren has not yet given evidence but it is his intention to do so in the main trial of John Gilligan. I would ask that the special visiting times be restored to him also. Russell Warren's wife is expecting a baby in late December and because of the unique position that she and her husband are in they have both requested that Russell Warren be permitted to have temporary release for the birth. This temporary release would be under the supervision of the witness protection Gardaí assigned to Debbie Warren.

'Due to the similar unique position of Charles Bowden and Juliet Bacon, Bowden also requests a two-day temporary release over the Christmas period. Again this will be under the supervision of the witness protection Gardaí.

'Charles Bowden and Russell Warren are both serving relatively short sentences and have been given unconditional and irrevocable immunity in relation to the Veronica Guerin murder. We are depending on the goodwill and sense of moral duty of these two men to give evidence against the leaders of the Gilligan crime organisation. It is imperative that these men receive fair treatment while they are incarcerated, bearing in mind their unique position. It would be most unfortunate if they failed to make good their undertaking to testify because of some perceived harshness in their incarceration.

'I would ask that the matters I have raised be addressed as a matter of urgency with the Department of Justice so that efforts of the Gardaí and the prison service be co-ordinated to achieve the desired result in the matter.'

On Monday, 7 December, Hickey attended a meeting at the Department of Justice. Those present included Patrick Dunne, the Governor of Arbour Hill, Chief Superintendent John McGroarty from Garda headquarters and O'Loughlin. Dunne set out the position in relation to the supergrass prisoners pointing out that there was no special category into which they fitted. Therefore he could not grant them special privileges. It would invariably have a knock-on effect with other inmates. There was nothing he could do.

Four days later, on 11 December, Hickey drafted a seven-page report recommending a series of measures to keep the witnesses content. This memorandum was marked confidential. In the correspondence, he stated that Bowden and Warren were unique in the prison system and that their commitment to giving evidence should not be taken for granted. 'If Bowden or Warren were to decide not to give evidence against Meehan and Gilligan, these cases would almost certainly collapse. The other members of this gang are fully aware of the danger that testimony from these two men can do to them. We are aware that there is a very serious threat to Warren and Bowden and to their immediate families.'

He recommended the following proposals. These, he wrote, should, alleviate the problem.

> (1) That Bowden and Warren be permitted additional weekly visits by their families which would help to counter-balance their isolated positions. (2) The concerns and worries which these prisoners have about their families' isolation under Garda Witness Protection scheme would also be allayed by such extra visits. (3) The fears that the family members have in relation to visiting hours are impacting upon the prisoners. The family members are very apprehensive about meeting up with the families of other criminals who are present in numbers during normal visiting hours. Special visiting times would be necessary to overcome this problem.
>
> Due to the unique position of these prisoners inside the prison and the restricted movements of their families under Garda protection outside, I recommend that urgent consideration be given to their temporary release for a period of Christmas 1997. This temporary release might be conditional to them spending that period at the location where their families are under Garda protection.
>
> . . . I believe however that we must address the problems which have arisen immediately and this may involve creating a new category of prisoner. I would ask that these matters be examined immediately as the trial of Paul Ward is listed for early January 1998 and the extraditions of Brian Meehan and John Gilligan are imminent. I believe that a reversal of Bowden's and Warren's decision to testify in these cases would be severely embarrassing and damaging to the administration

of justice in this State. It would almost certainly cause the cases against John Gilligan and Brian Meehan to collapse. Every effort should be made to ensure that Bowden and Warren adhere to their commitment to testify and are not tempted to take the easier route of silence. I believe that the measures recommended herein will balance the scales in the correct direction.

Warren and Bowden enjoyed Christmas and the New Year. They were granted temporary release. They spent time with their families and children.

Gilligan vowed to continue the fight but it was all doomed to failure. Back home the family kept their spirits up. Darren underwent a miraculous recovery from his addiction in the Coolmine Therapeutic Centre, a drugs rehab situated on the outskirts of Dublin. He was released home for the Christmas break conditional on Geraldine banning any alcohol from the house. She covered the bar pumps in her mini-bar and threw out her supply of alcohol in preparation for her son's return home. The younger members of the family missed Gilligan, particularly his grandchildren. When Tracy's daughter Shannon asked about her grandfather, Geraldine would reassure the child by saying, 'He's driving the buses in England.'

The New Year brought more bad news. In January, Lord Justice May and Justice Astell rejected Gilligan's application for a writ of habeas corpus in the London High Court. His extradition was upheld. Clare Montgomery QC argued that there had been an abuse of process. 'The extradition process,' she said, 'has been deliberately manipulated.' Gilligan vowed to challenge the judgment.

Back in Ireland, Grimes was toiling away. When the CAB lost its case against Geraldine, the bureau decided to try to cut a deal. The negotiations took weeks to finalise and were carried out in strict secrecy. The draft agreement offered to her was £12,500 immediately, £100,000 at a later date and a £500,000 waiver of taxes. In return, she would leave and sign a statement admitting Jessbrook was financed with the proceeds of crime. The deal was strictly confidential.

She gave the CAB offer much thought. She looked at properties for sale in Kildare and found a small cottage which she could afford and liked. In her own mind, she had decided to accept the offer but made the mistake of showing it to Grimes, who took pleasure in announcing its existence to the press. The *Sunday Times* published the story on 19 January. 'I have seen an agreement between an unspecified arm of the state and Geraldine Gilligan,' said Grimes. 'Part of the agreement was that she was to confirm that Jessbrook [represented] the proceeds of crime, which would mean that my principal, Joseph Saouma was engaged in crime, which is not true.'

The article sparked off debate. Jim Higgins, the Fine Gael spokesman on justice, asked O'Donoghue to comment in the Dáil. He refused. The bureau's defence was that the offer was legitimate because it gave Geraldine an amount that she was legitimately entitled to. Geraldine couldn't comprehend what had happened. Afterwards she said of Grimes, 'I think he's fucking mad.'

Although Gilligan didn't know it, Bowden was deeply unhappy in prison. He exchanged correspondence with the Department of Justice to no avail. He wanted freedom. This was the essence of the problem. Warren wanted the same. They formulated a plan aimed at pressurising the State into conceding to their demands.

On Tuesday, 11 August, Hickey received a message from one of Debbie Warren's bodyguards asking him to make contact. He called her directly and was told Warren wished to meet him as soon as possible. There was urgency in her voice.

Three days later, accompanied by Detective Sergeant John O'Driscoll, one of the Gardaí whom the informants trusted, Hickey arrived at Arbour Hill Prison where Andy O'Riordan, the chief prison officer, greeted him. He said Warren and Bowden were waiting. He took them to a private visiting-room.

The prisoners were brought into the room. Bowden declared he was speaking with Warren's authority. Warren indicated to Hickey that this was the case. Bowden spoke with the sincerity of a liar. He said he wanted to make it clear that both he and Warren were utterly committed to giving evidence in forthcoming trials. This, he said, would not change. But there were certain issues he wanted clarified. He asked Hickey to meet with Chris Houricane, who would discuss these matters. This conduit would protect all involved against any accusations of impropriety.

A week later, Hickey and O'Driscoll met Houricane at the Skylon Hotel in Drumcondra. The solicitor thanked the Gardaí for their assistance then came straight to the point. His clients wanted answers to the following series of questions, which Hickey later wrote in yet another confidential memo. (1) What is the Witness Protection Programme? (2) Were his clients and their families assimilated into the Witness Protection Programme? (3) Who is organising the Witness Protection Programme and who is in charge of it? (4) Could his clients be informed of their probable release date on termination of their custodial sentences? (5) Could a more humane prison regime be introduced for his clients, as the present regime was almost consistent with solitary confinement in that it offered no association within the prison with anyone other than each other. (6) Are the visits being monitored electronically? (7) Would the Witness Protection Programme consider some type of custody under the auspices of An Garda Síochána as no secure environment existed within the prison system, e.g. special secure units? (8) What would the position be in relation to Temporary Release and the granting of it and could some formal mechanism for their release be put in place? Mr Houricane stated that temporary release into Garda custody would not cause any difficulty whatsoever. (9) Mr Houricane asked what was envisaged on completion of his clients' custodial sentences. Would they be given the full protection of the State, relocated, or was any strategy in place for this eventuality?

Houricane said Bowden and Warren were of the opinion that Gilligan would use every legal avenue to delay his extradition and ultimately his trial. Regardless, they promised to give evidence against him, even after the termination of their custodial sentences. He then said the informers were considering a habeas corpus application to secure their freedom. This drastic course of action was against his advice but Warren and Bowden were, in his opinion, not thinking rationally. He attributed this to the nature of their confinement and a degree of pressure from their families. He said he had been instructed to look at English case law with relevance to similar confinement. Hickey promised that he would give these concerns immediate priority. The informers were given more privileges.

Meehan was flown home on 4 September 1998, having taken every legal route to block his extradition in a battle that lasted ten months. His fate had been sealed on 15 July when the Dutch Justice Minister, Winner Sorgdrager, ordered his deportation.

He was handed over to O'Loughlin at 1.15 p.m. on a runway at Eindhoven military base, a military installation that lies on the outskirts of Amsterdam. He was flown to Casement Aerodrome in Baldonnel in County Kildare on board a military aircraft. The flight touched down at 4 p.m. He was formally arrested when he stepped off the plane onto Irish soil. He never said a word. Later that night, he was brought before the Special Criminal Court. The hearing lasted no more than 20 minutes. He was remanded to Portlaoise where Ward and Holland were serving their sentences.

It was now imperative that Bowden and Warren kept their promise. Hickey had pressed for the Department of Justice to create a special category of prisoner for his two witnesses, not because he liked them but because they were essential to securing convictions. It was a case of the worse of two evils. On Monday, 21 September 1998, together with Detective Chief Superintendent John McGroarty, Hickey met officials from the prison section of the Department of Justice. The officials understood the wishes of the Gardaí. They offered to recommend a mechanism for perhaps monthly temporary release. But O'Donoghue had concerns in case regular temporary release suggested preferential treatment. If highlighted in court, he said, this would reflect unfavourably on the State. In the end, Bowden and Warren were granted more concessions.

Bowden, as promised, testified against Ward when his trial started in the Special Criminal Court on 7 October. Months of legal arguments over the release of statements made by some 20 criminal informants to Ward's legal team had delayed the prosecution. When Bowden took the stand it was the end of the illusion for Gilligan. For the first time since Veronica's murder, the realisation that his organisation was now shattered struck him.

This view was compounded by Hippo's decision to admit he was a drugs dealer in the absurd belief it would help his defence. He reckoned that the prosecution could link him to distributing cannabis so there was no point denying it. In any case, Hippo blamed Bowden for implicating him in the murder. Bowden, he said, partly told the truth and partly told lies. 'I am a victim of being accused of this. Mr Bowden is the main man, the main person who has me here. I know the guards have to do their job. I am not making myself out to be a saint, far from it. I don't blame the guards, I blame Mr

Bowden for the lies he said about me and he is after convincing the guards. He is putting poison in the guards' minds saying that I was involved in that woman's murder. I wasn't.'

Hippo spoke with absolute candour, portraying himself as a worthless heroin addict, a mere pawn used by Gilligan. He denied emphatically that he disposed of the gun and motorcycle used in the killing. But the court accepted Bowden's word, although the judges could see the latter's motive for testifying. After six weeks of evidence and complex legal arguments, Hippo was convicted on Friday, 27 November. He remained stone-faced as the court sentenced him to life.

But it was a tainted victory for the Gardaí. In its 40-page ruling, the Special Criminal Court criticised the police handling of the case. It described Bowden as a liar and expressed dissatisfaction with the admissions Hippo made about the murder.

Predictably, the judgment was greeted with controversy. Pat Byrne was coerced into ordering an internal inquiry, which drew further scorn on the investigation team. This generated much indignation, which Hickey took personally.

Many journalists made reference to Ward's heroin addiction, speculating that Gilligan would never have trusted an addict with disposing of the murder weapon or the bike. There was even speculation that Hippo might be innocent. Of course, the irony was that Ward had corroborated much of the prosecution's case through his admissions of drug trafficking, his lavish lifestyle and ultimately his friendship with Gilligan.

For his part, Gilligan didn't care much. It was a case of every man for himself. His only concern was fighting extradition.

CHAPTER 17

Retribution

'I'll come back, if they give me a jury.'
JOHN GILLIGAN

Gilligan's fight against extradition continued. But the arrival of the year 1999 did not herald any good news. The passing of the New Year brought personal troubles. Sarah, his ageing mother, was taken ill with pneumonia during the holiday period. She died from a heart attack on 12 January. Gilligan, a son she adored, never had the chance to say goodbye or attend the funeral. The death affected him deeply, unlike his father's when he died approximately one year before. Gilligan became more aggressive, if not openly hostile towards the prison authorities and the courts. He craved freedom.

In part to satisfy his own personal need to assign responsibility onto someone else, he sacked his legal team and hired new lawyers. He threatened prison staff and doubled his efforts to target the gang members co-operating with Hickey's team.

His worsening attitude towards the British courts could be gauged from the contents of a letter read out at a remand hearing on 18 January by Tomas O' Maoileoin, his new counsel. The letter was written in Gilligan's own hand. In it, the gangster pleaded with the court to extend his custody time limits, pending his challenge to the House of Lords, which in turn was busy hearing a case concerning the Chilean dictator General Augusto Pinochet.

Gilligan wrote that his continued detention in Britain was at 'enormous cost to the taxpayer'. Sustained by an inner rage, he offered to plead guilty to the British charges if extradition to Ireland was ruled out. His trial judge, James Rucker, sympathised with his predicament, but did not sway. Gilligan was remanded to Belmarsh once more.

Gilligan did not even try interpreting his situation rationally. He possessed a remarkable ability to convince himself that he was innocent. It was of course a delusion, but one which gave him the strength to continue with his legal fight.

He decided to write directly to Warren from his cell. His cronies were unable to penetrate the security shield guarding his former associates. Gilligan began by acknowledging Warren's plight, who by this stage was in a deep depression over the fact that his parents were charged with money laundering offences. They must be 'going through hell', he wrote.

The letters came as a complete surprise for Warren who interpreted them as threats because if the gangster was to be convicted, it would be on his evidence. In the letter, Gilligan claimed that there never was any threat against Warren and told him to ignore the lies in the newspapers. 'The press are talking shit,' he wrote. He then referred to Bowden and Dunne, but not by name. 'Please tell your friends to stop taking notice of all the shit in the newspapers.'

In typical form, he compared his legal fight with Warren's, insisting that he was an innocent victim. He ended the letter: 'Believe me, I wish I could help your families – your friend John Gilligan.'

He wrote another letter several days later, trying to reassure Warren that he did not need to avail himself of the witness protection programme. The purpose of this letter was to dupe Warren into withdrawing his evidence in the full knowledge that any withdrawal of evidence could be used against the other witnesses, or at worst collapse the case. 'You don't need to leave your country over me, say what you like in court,' he wrote. 'You have a home and family now and your new child may well want to come back to where he was born.' The reference to Warren's child was meant to be a threat. Gilligan was engaging in reverse psychology. 'You have my word on it. No one is after you. The papers are mad. They'll do anything to sell them.' He ended this letter with the words: 'God bless and take care and I wish you all the luck in the world, your friend, John G.'

The police interpreted the letters as a signal that he believed time was running out. Aware that they too should keep up the pressure, they continued searching for new witnesses. Carol Rooney had fled to Australia weeks after the murder and refused to return home. On April Fools' Day, in the misguided belief that life had somehow moved on, she flew into Dublin Airport. She made her way to Palmerstown to visit her parents, a respectable and hard-working couple, who were deeply disappointed in their daughter. When news of her visit reached Lucan Garda Station, she was arrested and taken in for questioning.

The press reports were sketchy. Some journalists announced that she would testify at his trial. This, of course, was not true, but Gilligan didn't know it. And he had no way of finding out. A sense of panic intensified because he knew that she had heard him discussing Guerin's murder with Warren on his mobile phone minutes after the killing.

If she agreed to co-operate, she could cause irreparable damage. She could corroborate Warren's evidence, which he considered most damaging. It would also turn Geraldine against him for once and for all.

What he did not know was that his young lover had already told the investigation team all they needed to know. But she was no Bowden and refused to testify. Gilligan, she said, had beaten her, savagely assaulted her and warned her that he would kill her parents if she ever betrayed him. No matter what they said, she would not put her parents through the nightmare of witness protection. She begged the Gardaí to understand her predicament. Left with no other choice, they released her and she returned to Australia.

Whether it was her arrest or simply a yearning for liberty, at his next court appearance on 26 April, Gilligan launched a passionate attack on the British legal system when he appeared at Woolwich Crown Court. He protested his innocence, declaring that he was '100 per cent innocent of all the charges' yet he had been unjustly detained without trial for 31 months. He said the only way the English drugs charges could be left on file was with his consent, and this he would never give. The Crown's decision not to allow his trial to go ahead was an abuse of process: 'A manipulation of my legal rights,' he declared, speaking with a counterfeit legal expertise. In no uncertain language, he warned Judge Rucker that the situation in Ireland was brought about 'by not showing impartiality, independence, dignity and one of the other great tenets of the legal system: that all are equal before the law'. He pleaded with the judge to end his 'purgatory'. 'You have not got the power this year, had not got the power last year and will not have the power next year to leave this on file,' he said with the grace of a lawyer. Rucker listened to his outburst, sympathised with him, but remanded him once more.

The failure of any hired assassin to get close to the State witnesses dominated Gilligan and Meehan's everyday thinking. Although their efforts to reach either Bowden or Warren had failed, they did not yield in trying to organise intimidation. Meehan, in particular, was convinced that anything was possible given time. This certainty compelled him to keep fighting. Working in absolute secrecy from his cell in Portlaoise Prison, he conspired with Gilligan to silence those who could put him away. Meehan viewed Gilligan's talk of putting a £2 million contract on Bowden and Warren's head as an idle hope. He wanted action.

This gave rise to the question of whom to attack. He chose Julian Clohessy, one of the witnesses that planned to testify in his trial. Meehan, lost in a blizzard of cocaine one night, had told Clohessy that he was a killer. After months of trying to locate Clohessy, he found an address and smuggled it to an associate who assured him that Jules would be seen to at once. The plan was to threaten him into silence.

Like their paymaster, the gunmen he sent were not intelligent men. They called to the wrong address and hammered down the door of a house where a member of the Provisional IRA lived. This man answered the door to be confronted by a masked man wielding a handgun. 'This is a message from Brian Meehan. You better keep your fucking mouth shut,' he shouted. 'This is your last warning.' The republican said nothing, which seemed a wonder to anyone who knew him. But the next day, he reported the incident to the IRA's Officer Commanding in Dublin.

Meehan, in the meantime, went on trial for Veronica's murder at the Special Criminal Court. There was solid evidence stacked against him. The three supergrass witnesses recounted their evidence, which Gilligan monitored through the dozens of press clippings sent to him by friends on the outside. Warren and Bowden gave yet more differing accounts of their involvement in the murder.

Back on the streets of Dublin, the IRA had lost no time in tracking down the gunman who delivered the threat. The Dublin O/C sent a secret message to Kevin Walsh, the IRA's commander in Portlaoise Prison. Walsh, a formidable republican, promised he would give the matter his urgent attention. He went straight to Meehan, cornering him in the prison laundry. Walsh, a man who speaks with a soft Limerick accent, barely raised his voice while he told Meehan to back off. The IRA, he said, wasn't scared of anyone, never mind a drug pusher called The Tosser, a nickname given to Meehan after he was convicted for masturbating in police custody in front of a female Garda. The blood drained from Meehan's face and he signalled that he understood. Walsh was emphatic. His threats would not be tolerated. Neither Meehan nor anyone of his ilk should try to intimidate the republican movement. Meehan would soon discover why.

Kevin Meehan, Brian's father, had stood by his son. He too was facing money laundering charges in connection with the gang. Each day he would travel from his home on Stanaway Road in Crumlin to watch the evidence unfold. His wife Frances often accompanied him, as did his daughter Vanessa. On the night of Monday, 20 July, he was preparing to go to bed when he heard the doorbell ring. This was a complete surprise because they were not expecting visitors. Kevin Meehan answered the door to a man who said he was lost. This seemed strange because his home lies on a road where the neighbours know each other on first name terms; in other words, few people get lost. By the time Meehan realised something was wrong, the caller had produced a gun and fired two bullets. The first ricocheted off a wall; the second hit its target in the shoulder, knocking him to the ground. Meehan collapsed in a pool of blood while the gunman made good his escape.

Brian Meehan learned of the attack the next morning on his way to Dublin from Portlaoise. When he returned to the prison that night, he went straight to Walsh and pleaded for mercy. He said he was sorry. It was all a terrible mistake. Walsh said nothing as Meehan continued to demonstrate his desperation. When he finished begging, he then asked if the IRA would be able to get to any of the witnesses, in return for a cash donation. When he asked the question, The Tosser immediately knew he had overstepped the mark. He apologised once again.

The following week, on 29 July, he was convicted for Veronica's murder and sentenced to life in prison. This time, the court ruled that Bowden's testimony couldn't be believed. Instead, it accepted Warren's evidence that Meehan inspected the motorcycle, directed repairs and renovations to be carried out, later road tested the motorcycle and returned to collect the motorcycle on the morning of 26 June 1996.

'The court is satisfied that this evidence leads to only one conclusion, namely that the accused was a fundamental part of the conspiracy or plot to murder Veronica Guerin, that he participated fully in the event,' the judge added. But the court discarded the evidence given by Bowden and his common-lawwife Juliet in relation to the murder, although it accepted their evidence concerning Meehan's role in the drugs and firearms.

Of Bowden, Justice Freddie Morris, the presiding judge, noted: 'In cross examination Meehan's defence counsel suggested to Charles Bowden that he was deliberately bolstering the evidence which he was giving so as to be the witness who implicated the accused in the crime and thereby make himself a more 'saleable commodity' if he sold his story to the newspapers or wrote a book.

'Charles Bowden denied in positive terms that he ever considered such a thing. He did so in explicit terms. Subsequently defence counsel produced and established to the court's satisfaction that Charles Bowden had in fact contacted a journalist with a view to collaborating with him in the publication of his involvement in this matter. Charles Bowden acknowledged to the court that he had lied to the court.'

These were but some examples of the way the court found his evidence unsatisfactory. 'The court rejects this witness's evidence as unreliable in relation to count number one.' Justice Morris declared that the court treated the evidence of Juliet Bowden on the same basis as that of an accomplice. She had lied on a number of occasions to the court.

Dealing with the drugs offences, the judge said the court approached Bowden's evidence on the drugs and firearms offences with extreme caution. He noted that Bowden was prepared to lie under oath and had been found to do so in this trial. But he was satisfied that while carrying out his function as a drugs distributor, Bowden acted under the direct control of Meehan.

With each gang member's conviction, Gilligan grew more desperate. He was thrown into bouts of depression because no matter how much he tried he could find no mechanism to secure his freedom. He knew what lay ahead but couldn't accept it. His worst-case scenario was realised on 5 October when the House of Lords paved the way for the extradition.

In one of his more novel appeals, Gilligan had asked the Lords to rule that extradition was unlawful because the offences contained in the Irish warrants did not correspond to English offences. The appeal lasted two days but Lord Browne Wilkinson and four other law lords unanimously rejected his claim in less than 15 minutes. Although his appeal did not succeed, Gilligan refused to give in. He went back to his cell and consulted his reference books on extradition and with great bravado submitted a writ of habeas corpus, written in his own hand, to the Divisional Court in London. The writ declared that he was being illegally held in Britain. If extradited, he declared, he would be tried for Veronica's murder in the Special Criminal Court. In his opinion, this was fundamentally wrong because trial without jury does not occur in England and Wales.

It worked. His application pre-empted the publication of the written judgment by the Law Lords and further delayed his extradition because he was entitled to address the court. It was a smart move, for on 13 December he was granted bail for the British charges but still held in custody for extradition.

The truth of the matter was that the British courts were deeply uneasy about holding him for much longer. Therefore, it came as no surprise to anyone when the Crown Prosecution Service was ordered to make its position clear the following week as to whether it would proceed with the English trial or drop the charges altogether. Gilligan felt elated. Things were finally going his way, it seemed.

Christmas came but didn't pass without incident. Gilligan wrote directly to Bowden's and Warren's families from Highdown Prison in Surrey. He was transferred to this prison after he attacked a prison officer. Once again, he set off alarm bells. The letters were enquiring into the recipients' health. But there were secret messages in the new letters. In one letter, he offered an olive branch to Bowden. He wrote that he believed the Gardaí had forced him to make a statement. The message was simple: all would be forgiven if he retracted his evidence. The ruse did not work

Gilligan reached the end of the road on 3 February when the High Court in London dismissed his habeas corpus application. Lord

Justice Brown, sitting with Justice Klevan, threw out his application. It was not merely misconceived, they said, but was an abuse of process. Gilligan was half expecting as much and was not present at the 20-minute hearing in London. He was preparing to fly home. As soon as the judgment was delivered, the gangster was brought from Highdown Prison to the RAF base at Northolt. He was peculiarly silent and said not a single word during the trip. He arrived there at 2.30 p.m. when Detective Sergeant John Warren of Scotland Yard handed him over to O'Loughlin. His prisoner was overcome by sickness, brought about by the drama. He was flown home in an Air Corps CASA jet which arrived at Baldonnel's Casement Aerodrome at 4.35 p.m.

The media were everywhere. Photographers and television camera crews jostled for the best positions. It was a circus. When Gilligan finally descended from the aircraft, O'Loughlin arrested him. Hickey, never a man to court publicity, made a point of staying away.

Gilligan, the big, bad bogeyman of the Irish underworld, was seen in his true colours. He wore a green and yellow prison uniform with a prison insignia stamped on the back. He cowered, covering his face with his hands to shield off the cameras. Old habits die hard.

A convoy of military and police vehicles brought him to the Special Criminal Court on Green Street. A helicopter hovered above the court building. Sniffer dogs and armed soldiers were everywhere. The convoy drove straight past the photographers and camera crews and into a yard adjacent to the Special Criminal Court building. The doors slammed behind the vehicle as Gilligan stepped out of the van and was taken into the court. For the accused, the prospect of having to face the court was too much. He had spent years fighting extradition in the beleaguered hope that the case would somehow fall apart, that Bowden would be exposed as a liar, that Warren would refuse to testify out of fear and that any evidence from Dunne could be proved unreliable. In pursuit of these objectives he had done all he could. Now the game was over.

He stood in the dock. He answered 'yes' when asked by the court registrar if he was John Gilligan. Justice Johnson, the presiding judge, asked if he was legally represented and he replied: 'No, your honour, I am representing myself.' The hearing lasted no longer than 25 minutes. When it concluded, Gilligan, in one of the more surreal moments, asked: 'Bail would be out of the question, wouldn't it?'

Gilligan adopted the same policy of fighting the Gardaí every step of the way from his cell in Portlaoise. If the prosecution thought Gilligan would stop making legal challenges, they were wrong. And so started another series of legal manoeuvres aimed at stopping his trial from going ahead.

He made a series of pre-trial submissions in April. Because he was not legally represented, he was asked to stand at the bench normally used by junior defence barristers. Gilligan, in bold fashion, made his way from the dock to the lawyers' bench, where in gruff language he denied making threats against people prepared to give evidence against him. He had not put a 'price' on their heads. 'The only thing I ordered was a cappuccino,' he said.

He spoke for 50 minutes and applied to have the charge of murder dealt with separately from other drugs and firearms charges. It was a clever move designed to break down the credibility of the supergrass. Speaking without the grace of a barrister, he told the three judges that he was objecting to the court because it was not independent or impartial and he submitted documents from a United Nations Human Rights Commission hearing. But after doing so well, at the end of the submissions, he thought aloud: 'I don't do this every day. I am not too sure of myself. I thought I'd be able to handle this case. I certainly can't handle it. I'd like to apply for legal aid. I haven't a penny.'

The IRA meanwhile were under pressure to move against the dealers – largely because the dealers were importing military weapons into Dublin, and these were being sold to loyalist terrorists and dissident republicans. Various people in the republican organisation were charged with investigating this trade. Within a short space of time, the trail led back to the Netherlands and Spain. John Cunningham, an old friend of Gilligan's, was funnelling a steady stream of weapons to Ireland from the Hague. But the inquiry implicated Traynor, who they found living between holiday apartments on the Costa del Sol. A team of republicans travelled to the area at once and started monitoring Traynor's activities. Then by chance, they stumbled upon Geraldine and Tracy Gilligan who were travelling to a holiday villa in Alicante. They followed them everywhere, photographed them and logged their movements. They even watched and photographed Geraldine sunbathing by the pool. Traynor's every move was watched. When he went into bars, those drinking beside him were IRA intelligence officers monitoring him. Peter Mitchell was also monitored. Then, after much debate, they decided to execute Traynor on the strict condition the shooting would not be claimed. 'Its purpose was to send a message to drug dealers that they could run but they couldn't hide,' said one of the team involved.

The plan was to shoot Traynor dead in the hope the media would attribute his murder to a rival criminal gang. A trained assassin was flown to Spain and through another contact a suitable weapon was acquired for the hit. Like all IRA operations, there would be other republicans in the vicinity to assist the killer escape and dispose of the weapon.

Everything was going according to plan when Traynor failed to show at a prearranged meeting. They waited and, fearing that one of their number might be stopped by the police, they got rid of the weapon. Traynor eventually did resurface but it was too late. He had escaped within an inch of his life and didn't even know it.

Back home, the judge dismissed Gilligan's application and remanded him to Portlaoise until 22 May. It was in Portlaoise that he met the man he would hire as his solicitor, Joe Rice. The Belfast solicitor was working for Sean 'Bap' Hughes, an INLA terrorist facing charges for murdering a Garda. Every Sunday like clockwork, he would drive from Belfast to Portlaoise to discuss the pending trial with Hughes. This was of great interest to Gilligan who was struck by his dedication. One morning, while Rice was briefing Hughes, Gilligan interrupted the meeting.

'Jesus, lads, you're very committed.'

Rice, an amicable man, said he'd do the same for any client.

Using this remark as a starting point to introduce himself, Gilligan asked if Rice would be interested in reading his book of evidence. The next week, Gilligan asked him to take his case.

The solicitor said no problem, but on one condition: 'John, it must be on legal aid.' He formally came on board on 22 May when this was granted.

On 26 June, on the third anniversary of Veronica's death, he was told his legal attempts to have the murder charge dealt with separately from drugs and firearm charges had failed. But he did get access to transcripts of the Ward and Meehan trials.

Gilligan's trial was scheduled to begin on 3 October, but as with everything in his life, there had to be a challenge. In July, he succeeded in having two of the three judges removed from case. Justice Kevin O'Higgins of the High Court and Judge Matthew Deery of the Circuit Court discharged themselves, leaving William Hamill of the District Court.

The month of September brought more challenges. The opening of the trial on 3 October brought even more when Gilligan sacked his counsel, forcing the adjournment of the trial for a week. Justice Diarmuid O'Donovan, who was appointed to hear the case, warned him that he should not dismiss any more counsel as it would not be tolerated.

The week's adjournment was given only to allow Eugene Grant QC and Dr Michael Forde SC, his new lawyers, time to prepare a proper defence. Further application was refused because the trial date had been fixed since February. The judge also noted that Gilligan's solicitor and his junior counsel, Peter Irvine, had been with the case since an early stage. A week later, Rice read letters to the court from Grant and Irvine stating that the barristers could not properly prepare a defence in the time allotted by the court. Left with no other option, the court adjourned the trial to 21 November.

Gilligan thought this was a great accomplishment. He was fighting various cases and had taken a challenge to the Supreme Court appealing another decision by the High Court's refusing him a right to trial by jury. The Supreme Court reserved judgement. In this whirlwind of legal challenges, on 20 October he took yet another step seeking secret Garda reports into a series of telephone conversations in 1996 between a Garda detective and the Attorney General, Michael McDowell. When this proved a futile exercise, conscious that Bowden and the others were most likely worried about testifying, Gilligan decided to resort to his old tactics. He granted an interview to the *Sunday Business Post*. 'We will find the truth through the families – wives, mothers, fathers, brothers and sisters. They will all be called to give evidence,' he declared. When the interview was published, his senior counsel withdrew their services at once. Matters of professional privilege had forced their hand.

When news of the resignations was communicated to the court, it was the last straw. Since Gilligan was charged, he had lost some of the most gifted counsel in the State. The judges saw through his decision to talk to the press and proclaimed the trial would still go ahead on 21 November. But it didn't and was adjourned for the third time to 4 December. Rice's solid legal advice bought Gilligan the extra time. The solicitor told the court that he had approached 33 senior counsel but none were available to begin the trial.

'My client has instructed me that he would like the case to start as soon as possible. He is frustrated,' Rice said.

Justice O'Donovan heard him loud and clear but warned in no uncertain terms that this would be the last adjournment. 'No excuses whatsoever will be entertained by the court for an adjournment of this trial. If counsel decide to opt out, this case will still go on and Mr Gilligan may well have to defend himself,' he said.

Gilligan's trial was an anti-climax of giant proportions. After nearly four years of legal manoeuvres to stop it from going ahead, when it did finally commence at 11.35 a.m. on 4 December 2000 the public gallery was barely occupied. Only a handful of journalists showed up. There was no packed gallery, no sightseers seeking a glimpse of the great gangster of the Irish underworld. There were just the police, the solicitors, their barristers and the prison officers.

After the court clerk read out the charges, Gilligan sat down, crossed his legs, leaned back and looked above his head, smiling, gnawing at his jaw, as if he was chewing gum.

The dock where the accused sits is raised about five feet above the ground. From this position, Gilligan could look down into the courtroom itself where those with a professional interest in the case took their seats. Sitting directly opposite to him, across the room on what looks like a small balcony, sat his three trial judges – Joseph Mathews, Diarmuid O'Donovan and William Hamill. Judge Mathews was noticeably younger looking than his colleagues and spoke, when he did, with an authoritative voice. Judge O'Donovan was slightly smaller in stature. He smiled constantly and often leaned back into his chair to ponder, if not to avoid the harsh spotlight that illuminated his seated position. Judge Hamill wore no wig, only a gown, which gave him a more casual appearance than that of his colleagues.

The opposing legal teams were seated below, facing in the direction of the three judges. To Gilligan's right sat the prosecution team headed by Peter Charleton. On his feet, he stood over six feet tall, but he leaned slightly to one side when he addressed the court. His height coupled with his voice allowed him to assert his authority without having to raise his voice. Beside him sat Eamonn Leahy, a giant of a man whose robust stature almost filled two spaces on the narrow wooden bench. Alongside him sat Tom O'Connell, another barrister.

Gilligan's defence contingent sat to the right on the same wooden bench. Michael O'Higgins headed the defence. He was a barrister who had his feet planted firmly on the ground, having worked as a journalist writing on justice and social issues before deciding to study law. Of his many articles, his interviews with Martin Cahill stood out as the best. It was said that Cahill had given him great insight into the underworld because O'Higgins showed no airs, graces or pomposity. Although middle aged, he possessed a youthful expression that belied a razor sharp wit. When he spoke, his face became animated.

To his left sat Terence McDonald, a rather stern-looking barrister who practised at the Belfast bar. Always mindful to look sombre in court, in truth, he smiled and exchanged courtesies with just about everyone. Peter Irvine, a barrister, sat beside him. Rice sat on a wooden bench immediately behind the defence team. Tony Hickey, who arrived in full uniform, sat on the same bench, but at the opposite end.

And so the trial of John Gilligan began.

No sooner had Charleton started delivering his opening submission than O'Higgins jumped to his feet, objecting to any possibility that Bowden, Warren and Dunne take the stand. Charleton threw his eyes to heaven. O'Higgins proclaimed that the witness protection programme was tainted. The court, he said, had a duty to ensure its own process was not damaged. This, he said, was an essential part of justice, as in the moisture that hangs in the air.

And with that began another legal argument that effectively delayed the trial for two days. Bowden, O'Higgins asserted, was so impugned that he couldn't give any credible evidence because he was a proven liar. The barrister, with one foot placed on the wooden bench, read from the verdict delivered in Meehan's case. This found that Bowden had lied. 'Does it follow that he'll lie again?' asked Judge O'Donovan. O'Higgins suggested he would. They retired till the next day when the court discounted the submission.

Charleton was back on his feet outlining the State's case against Gilligan, whom he said controlled the minds of those who carried out the shooting. 'Anyone who spoke out against him was subjected to threats and terror,' he said. Gilligan, content in the knowledge that he would hear a lot more of this, never looked down. He assumed a more comfortable position, sitting with legs crossed, smiling. He never moved for the rest of Charleton's speech, which seemed to encapsulate his entrance into the murky world of drug dealing, his meetings with Guerin, her murder and the destruction of his organisation – effectively chronicling the creation and fall of his drugs empire.

The trial got under way. Garda witnesses were called and cross-examined. Much of what they had to say was not controversial; it was simply evidence which had to be read into the court records for legal requirements.

Aware that he had everything to play for, Gilligan listened attentively to the evidence, for he knew he would pay dearly for any lack of concentration. Rather than allow his lawyers to run the case without contributions from him, he scribbled down notes. The prison officers handed these to his solicitor. It was all a desperate act. As the weeks passed by Gilligan became noticeably more worried looking. He stopped smiling, sat up straight and gazed forlornly as more damning evidence was given. When the court rose for the Christmas break, he looked somewhat relieved.

The trial resumed hearing on 12 January. It started in much the same way with O'Higgins and Charleton tussling over obscure legal points of law. The strategy chosen by the gangster's lawyers centred on discrediting any evidence from the supergrass witnesses, which wasn't particularly difficult to do. Bowden had told so many variations of what happened on 26 June 1996 that he was relatively easy to demolish. He represented no great threat.

O'Higgins zoned in on the fact that few of the people named by Bowden had been charged, as indeed had the supergrass himself with all the offences he'd admitted to. This question was asked of Detective Inspector John O'Mahony. O'Higgins made it clear that he would continue asking the same questions until he got a satisfactory answer. O'Mahony responded by saying the file was sent to the Director of Public Prosecutions, prompting O'Higgins to ask, 'Do I hear the sound of a buck being passed?' This line of questioning continued for several days. O'Higgins demanded to know why others named by Bowden had not been charged with the other offences he admitted to. He also made much of the fact that no member of Bowden's family had been charged with any offence. Then he dissected Bowden's statements with the skill of a pathologist. He read dozens of selected quotes, asking O'Mahony to confirm they were lies, which he did. It was a thorough cross-examination and one which Gilligan appeared to enjoy.

John Dunne became the first supergrass witness to take the stand at 3.25 p.m. on 23 January when he stepped into the witness box. He didn't make eye contact with Gilligan who eyeballed him up and down.

Dunne looked a hardened criminal. His head was shaven and he looked lean but oddly pale. His skin pigmentation was off colour from never being allowed outdoors.

His evidence appeared straightforward at first. He recounted the story of how he met Gilligan, how he joined Sea Bridge and got involved in the drugs business. O'Higgins listened attentively as Dunne told the court he had surrendered the money he made to the Gardaí. 'I decided to be truthful,' he said without a hint of ambivalence.

'Well, then, why did you tell them that you only earned £30,000 to £40,000?' asked O'Higgins, who pointed out there were 96 consignments in all between 1994 and 1996 and that Dunne had said he was paid on average £1,000 for each consignment. Dunne could think of nothing to say.

Anyone listening to Dunne was struck by his knowledge of the law. He appeared more than capable of answering O'Higgins' questions about the witness protection programme. O'Higgins himself was struck by his apparent expert knowledge of the scheme that seemed a mystery to anyone other than the Gardaí.

When the barrister asked Dunne if he thought the three-year sentence imposed on him for drug trafficking was fair, Dunne, speaking with the brazenness of a lawyer, said he thought it was. 'There's no point in me bitching about a sentence,' he said before quoting case law to the lawyer, who seemed taken aback. The witness went further, detailing how he, Bowden and Warren, tried to secure temporary release by waging a war of attrition with the Department of Justice.

O'Higgins pressed him to talk about his future.

'I will only get what I am entitled to, if you know what I mean. I'm happy with my deal.'

Gilligan certainly wasn't.

Russell Warren was the next to take the stand.

McDonald handled his cross-examination. If his client was to beat the murder charge, it was critical that his evidence be admonished and this is exactly what happened. McDonald chose a simple strategy of asking Warren simple questions, which often caused some of the assembled spectators to throw their eyes up to heaven because there appeared to be no purpose in them. But there was. McDonald had fought and won supergrass trials in Northern Ireland.

Warren answered each question, but because he was still in a state of self-denial about his own role in the killing, he tried to distance himself from the murder. Warren maintained that he never knew Veronica was going to be murdered. He said Gilligan or Meehan had told him to go to Naas and look for a red sports car parked near the courthouse, which he did. He stuck rigidly to his story that he drove to Naas that morning in his blue van, a Toyota Liteace. When he arrived in Naas, he said he initially got lost. It got better. Speaking like a true liar, he said he parked his van outside another building, which he mistook for the court. He said he was walking into this building when he looked behind and saw a traffic warden walking towards his van. Warren said he turned back and ran to the warden shouting, 'I'll move it.' According to his version of events, he moved his van to another location nearer the court. When the van was parked, he said he walked into a newsagent's and bought a packet of crisps, a Club Orange and the *Star* newspaper.

He gave two different accounts of what happened next. In the first, he said he'd sat back into his van when he noticed Veronica's car in traffic. According to his second version of the truth, he saw Veronica's car at a distance while walking away from the court. This evidence was the invention of his imagination working in tandem with his conscience.

His most blatant lie came when he said he recognised Veronica's car because of the spoiler on its rear. He described to Judge Mathews what the spoiler looked like, gesturing with his hands to show how large it was.

McDonald said nothing, then asked him if he was sure. Warren affirmed his version of the events again. The barrister handed him a photograph of Veronica's car. This showed there was no spoiler. Warren looked shocked.

The prosecution case continued to fall apart.

McDonald put it to the star witness that everything he said was 'a complete fabrication, a total lie and out-and-out lies'. Warren, at one point, agreed he was a perjurer.

As the days passed, he rambled through more of his evidence, giving more contradicting testimony. He said he'd followed Veronica's car in the slow lane. Then after the killing had been executed, he said he drove his van from the fast lane of the Naas Road, through the slow lane to escape via a slip road.

McDonald pointed out to him that none of the other witnesses saw a van near the scene. The slow lane was also blocked. But they did see a blue Volvo car driving away at breakneck speed. Warren said he didn't notice it, leaving many observers to conclude that he was the driver and Bowden was a passenger. A theory developed that Bowden had watched Veronica Guerin from the roof of the Naas District Court. Warren's story about talking to a traffic warden was also shown to be no more than a figment of his imagination. The traffic warden gave evidence of having no such conversation. Gilligan's defence team compromised his entire testimony but most importantly of all discredited his version of the conversation that took place between the witness and Gilligan immediately after the murder.

Warren said he rang Gilligan a couple of minutes after witnessing the murder and told him that 'somebody's after being shot'. 'He said, "Are they dead?" and I said, "I suppose so, they were shot five times." He said, "Did they get away?" I said, "Yes, they drove off." He said, "Tell your friend that the same thing will happen to him if anyone says anything about the bike."'

The phone records produced to the court showed that this conversation, if true, lasted ten seconds.

He kept lying. He proclaimed that Gilligan had told him to go to Naas on the day of the murder.

McDonald asked him why he didn't mention this detail in his statement made to Gardaí three months after the murder. The statement, Warren said without a hint of irony, contained some lies. He continued to exaggerate, saying he was in constant mobile phone contact with Gilligan after he travelled to Naas and spotted Veronica's car.

McDonald suggested that Gilligan had not told him to go to Naas. Warren replied: 'I know he told me to go to Naas. It was the morning or the evening over the phone. He said, "Do what Brian Meehan wants you to do, go to Naas." It was the evening before or the morning before the murder. Those were my instructions.'

McDonald said nothing about this piece of evidence. He pressed him further, causing the criminal to break down saying, 'I only drove the woman to her death. I only sent the woman to her death.'

The court adjourned for five minutes to allow him to compose himself. When he returned, he told the three judges: 'I am very sorry about that.'

Bowden's evidence was of the same calibre. He claimed that although he'd loaded the gun, he never realised she was going to be shot. 'I thought myself that there would be an attempt to warn her off or an attempt to shoot her to warn her off,' he proclaimed with a degree of smugness. He couldn't account for his movements on the day of the murder. This reinforced the opinion that he was present at the scene of the killing and had participated in Veronica Guerin's murder.

The defence proceeded to question everything. Garda witnesses conceded they had returned money which had been seized to Dunne, Warren and Bowden. McDonald cross-examined Detective Bernie Hanley in this regard. Hanley said in evidence that he gave Warren £1,920 before Christmas 1996 and another £1,000 in April 1997. This was Warren's own money, from his industrial cleaning business, and he was returning it to him after it had been seized by Gardaí. 'There was no question of payment for information,' Detective Hanley said. If he had wanted to pay Warren for information, Garda procedures existed, which he could have followed.

Baltus had agreed to give evidence, linking Gilligan to dozens of arms imports but suddenly refused to travel to Dublin. He claimed someone had tried to kidnap his daughter. He would not risk her life by testifying. The truth was that he didn't want to give evidence. There was no kidnapping attempt reported to the Dutch police because there *was* no kidnapping attempt.

And so after 43 days of evidence from 200 witnesses, including the three supergrass witnesses, it was over. Eamonn Leahy delivered the final closing submission. He said it was not the prosecution contention that Gilligan was present at the Naas Road when Veronica was shot dead by the pillion passenger on a motorbike who fired six bullets from a .357 Magnum into her body. But it was the prosecution's contention that Gilligan played a leading part in a pre-arranged plan to shoot Guerin and was therefore complicit in the murder and guilty in law.

O'Higgins delivered the closing submissions, which lasted four days. He said he would not use the description 'supergrasses' or 'protected witnesses', but he thought a fair description was 'compromised witnesses'. The relationship that existed between these witnesses and the State was such that the witnesses were 'utterly compromised'. 'It threatens to compromise the entire criminal justice system as we understand it,' he added. Bowden's evidence, he said, did not 'pass muster'. The court should 'effectively disregard everything he said.'

When he finished, Justice Diarmuid O'Donovan, said the court would have to take some time to consider every aspect of the case. Gilligan stood up and said, 'Thank you very much' before being led from the dock.

Epilogue

15 March 2001

Gilligan was welcomed to the Special Criminal Court with a much greater reception than even he could ever have predicted. The media were everywhere. There were vans with giant satellite dishes pointing at the heavens, ready to relay the court verdict to the world when it was delivered. Radio journalists spoke into microphones attached to complex devices. Newspaper reporters hustled together in small gangs, engaging in idle chat, some offering bets on what sentence Gilligan would get. They had all gathered for one thing – to see Gilligan's ultimate demise.

Outside the court building Joe Rice and Peter Irvine stood and watched the circus. But the lawyers remained quietly confident of winning the case although just about everyone else was assured of Gilligan's guilt. Minutes before 11 a.m. they walked inside to find a courtroom packed full to capacity. O'Higgins was already sitting down but on his own. Illness had caught McDonald. When every seat was occupied in the gallery, a bell rang to signal that the judges were about to enter and deliver the verdict.

At that moment, Gilligan's head appeared from an underground tunnel, which leads from the court cells to the dock. He looked relaxed and smiled at the judges, at the same time trying not to show any fear or even recognise the crowd that had turned out to hear his future. Gilligan's world was about to change, although at that moment in time he had no idea how.

Judge O'Donovan addressed the court. His colleagues Judge Mathews and Judge Hamill remained silent, never uttering a word as a strange subterranean silence enveloped the court. The learned judge outlined the prosecution's case against Gilligan, then the defence adopted by the accused.

Gilligan looked as if he had prepared for the worst, trying not to allow the judge's scathing remarks about Warren, Bowden and Dunne lift his spirits. 'The Court recognises the danger of convicting an accused person on the uncorroborated evidence of an accomplice and that principle has been to the forefront of the mind of the Court when considering the evidence tendered by Messrs Dunne, Ward and Warren,' he read.

Gilligan hadn't anticipated that his case would be assisted by the strict application of the law. But as Judge O'Donovan continued to read the verdict, the unbearable realisation that nothing was going according to plan began to dawn on the police. As the judge continued to read, the gaping holes that were the hallmarks of the prosecution's case were exposed. The judges criticised the return of cash seized from the supergrass witnesses. Bowden and Warren, the star witnesses who had milked the Gardaí for what they could get, became liabilities. The court described them both as liars.

Then in a kind of apocalyptic message from the court, Gilligan was found guilty on the drug-related charges because Dunne's evidence had been corroborated.

By now Gilligan was staring at a fake skylight affixed to the ceiling in an act of defiance against the verdict which Judge O'Donovan continued to read aloud. Then he heard he was acquitted of importing weapons. He looked around to see if his mind was playing tricks. It wasn't; he had beaten the weapons charge because the Gardaí had not documented evidence found in Unit 1B when they first raided it. If Baltus had testified, this outcome too may have been different.

Now he waited to hear whether he was a murderer, which just about everyone listening presumed he was.

The judge continued to read the verdict, which continued to highlight the glaring disparities in Warren's evidence. In reality, Gilligan knew he was already going to jail once the verdict was delivered, but beating the charge was personal. The drama continued to unfold.

The judges correctly proclaimed that the finger of suspicion could easily be pointed at Traynor. 'The only evidence which could possibly implicate John Gilligan in the murder of the late Veronica Guerin was that of Russell Warren,' the judge said. Then the judge announced that this evidence was simply unreliable: 'He contradicted evidence which he had previously given at the trial of Brian Meehan. In the light of the foregoing, bearing in mind that at all stages during a criminal trial an accused person has, at law, the presumption of innocence and remains at all times throughout an innocent person unless and until that presumption is displaced at the end of the trial by a finding based on evidence which is either reliable testimony, circumstantial evidence or a reasonable inference drawn from established facts that that person is, indeed, guilty as charged beyond any reasonable doubt; while this Court has grave suspicions that John Gilligan was complicit in the murder of the late Veronica Guerin, the Court has not been persuaded beyond all reasonable doubt by the evidence which has been adduced by the prosecution that that is so and, therefore, the Court is required by law to acquit the accused on that charge.'

No sooner had Judge O'Donovan finished delivering his verdict than the entire court turned and looked directly at Gilligan, waiting for him to say something. Nobody could tell if he was upset or elated. Perhaps for the first time in his life, he could think of nothing to say.

The prison guards brought him back to his senses when they asked him to walk back down to his cell for ten minutes, while the court adjourned to deliver an appropriate sentence.

By the time he returned, he had grasped the importance of decision. He now addressed the court as a drug dealer and not a convicted murderer or, as he dreaded, Veronica Guerin's murderer. And he had Russell Warren to thank for it. What neither Gilligan nor anyone else could have foreseen was that Warren, one of Gilligan's collaborators, would secure his acquittal because he lived in a state of self-delusion. By trying to convince the court that he didn't know Veronica was going to be murdered, he invariably lied and further implicated himself, while distancing Gilligan from the conspiracy. In the end, it boiled down to his version of what Gilligan had said when he called immediately after Veronica's murder. Its contents had not been corroborated. If Rooney had taken the stand, maybe the outcome would have been different.

Judge O'Donovan spoke in a much sterner voice when he returned. He looked Gilligan directly in the eye, saying he had 'grave suspicions' that he was involved in Veronica's murder. The observers in the court went much further, proclaiming within earshot of the accused that he in fact had just got away with murder.

Gilligan, however, took no notice as the judge attacked him for causing a haemorrhage of harm, saying he had shown insatiable greed and no remorse. 'Never in the history of the State has one person been responsible for so much wretchedness to so many,' the judge declared.

Gilligan himself looked chuffed. He turned to me, winked and then smiled. Seconds later he was momentarily taken aback when the judge imposed a 28-year sentence, but he soon regained his composure and was led away.

There is no happy ending to this story. Gilligan is now appealing against his sentence and will probably succeed in having it reduced. If he behaves himself and the Court of Criminal Appeal rules in his favour he could be released much earlier than anyone expects. John Traynor, Shay Ward and Peter Mitchell are still on the run. The latest reports suggest they are running a drugs distribution business in Spain, somewhere on the Costa del Sol. Brian Meehan and Paul Ward are appealing their cases. Patrick Eugene Holland vehemently denies carrying out Veronica's assassination. His 20-year sentence was reduced to 12 years by the Court of Criminal Appeal. He too is continuing to seek his freedom.

The three supergrass witnesses are due for release and will be resettled, most likely in Canada, the United States or Australia. Geraldine Gilligan is still living in Jessbrook.

The drug dealers Gilligan's cartel supplied are still out there, pushing drugs. Few were charged and even fewer convicted.

The whereabouts of Gilligan's millions is a mystery. In truth the police have no idea where the money lies. As Michael Grimes put it: 'I'd say John has about £50 million, but funnily enough I think he's the only one who knows where it is.'

Thursday, March 15, 2001

THE SPECIAL CRIMINAL COURT

Bill No. SF0021198

THE PEOPLE AT THE SUIT OF THE
DIRECTOR OF PUBLIC PROSECUTIONS

-v-

JOHN GILLIGAN

The accused man in this case, John Gilligan, comes before the Court to answer 16 counts on an indictment preferred against him which include the murder of an investigative journalist by the name of Veronica Guerin on the 26th day of June, 1996 at Naas Road, Clondalkin in the County of the City of Dublin, five offences of unlawful importation of a controlled drug; to wit, cannabis resin, between the 1st day of July, 1994 and the 6th day of October, 1996 contrary to Section 2 1(2) and Section 27 of the Misuse of Drugs Act 1997, as amended by Section 6 of the Misuse of Drugs Act 1984, five offences of possession of a controlled drug; to wit, cannabis resin, within the state between the 1st day of July, 1994 and the 1st day of October, 1996, for the purpose of selling or otherwise supplying it to another in contravention of the Misuse of Drugs Regulations 1988 and 1993 made under Section 5 of the Misuse of Drugs Act 1977 and contrary to Sections 15 and 27 of the Misuse of Drugs Act 1977, as amended by Section 6 of the Misuse of Drugs Act 1984, one offence of possession of a controlled drug; to wit, cannabis resin on or about the 3rd day of October, 1996 at Unit 1B, Greenmount Industrial Estate, Harold's Cross in the City of Dublin for the purpose of selling or otherwise supplying it to another in contravention of the Misuse of Drugs Regulations 1983 and 1993, made under Section 5 of the Misuse of drugs Act 1977 and contrary to Section 15 and Section 27 of the Misuse of Drugs Act 1977, as amended by Section 6 of the Misuse of Drugs Act 1984, one offence of possession or control of firearms with intent to endanger life at Old Court Road, Tallaght in the County of Dublin between the 10th day of November

238

1995 and the 3rd day of October 1996 contrary to Section 15(a) of The Firearms Acts 1925/1971, as amended by Section 21 of the Criminal Law Jurisdiction Act 1976 and Section 14 of the Criminal Justice Act 1984 and Section 4 of the Firearms and Offensive Weapons Act 1990, one offence of possession or control of ammunition with intent to endanger life at Old Court Road, Tallaght in the County of Dublin between the 11th day of November, 1995 and the 3rd day of October 1996 contrary to Section 15(a) of the Firearms Acts 1925/1971, as amended by Section 21 of the Criminal Law (Jurisdiction) Act 1976 and Section 14 of the Criminal Justice Act 1984 one offence of possession or control of firearms at Old Court Road, Tallaght in the County of Dublin between the 10th day of November, 1995 and the 3rd day of October, 1996 with intent to enable another person by means thereof to endanger life, contrary to Section 15(b) of the Firearms Act 1925/1911, as amended by Section 21 of the Criminal Law (Jurisdiction) Act 1976 and Section 14 of the Criminal Justice Act 1984.

When opening the case to the Court, Counsel for the prosecution, Mr Peter Charlton S.C., while conceding that, on the date of the late Ms Guerin's untimely death, the accused was actually outside of the Republic of Ireland having travelled to the city of Amsterdam in the country of Holland on the previous day, submitted that the evidence would establish that Ms Guerin's murder was orchestrated and committed by a group of people acting under the control and command of the accused so that, at law, he was as responsible therefore as an accessory before the fact to her murder as if he had actually killed her himself. Moreover, Mr Charlton submitted that the evidence would also establish that the accused was the spiritus rector of each and every act which comprised the several offences with which he is charged and that he threatened anyone who spoke out against him, including the deceased, Veronica Guerin. In this regard, Mr Charlton asserted that the evidence would establish that the accused controlled an organisation which had been developed and promoted by him for the purpose of perpetrating crime; an organisation which had characteristics of secrecy and terror and an organisation which was responsible for the importation into the Republic of hundreds of kilos of cannabis resin and consignments of firearms and ammunition.

In the course of his opening address to the Court, Mr Charlton also adverted to the fact that the evidence which would be led by the prosecution to establish the offences with which the accused is charged would include evidence from persons who could be considered to have been accomplices of the accused and that, while some of the accomplices' evidence is corroborated by other evidence, much of it is not and accordingly the Court recognises that, while there is no rule of law that a Court may not convict an accused person on the uncorroborated evidence of an accomplice, it is accepted by the Court that it is extremely dangerous to do so and perhaps even more so in this case, given that a number of the persons, who would be considered to have been accomplices of the accused and who gave uncorroborated evidence against him, are also persons who are the subject of a witness protection scheme initiated by the State to safeguard those persons and their families following the termination of these proceedings. Accordingly, the Court recognises and acknowledges that, insofar as it is uncorroborated, the testimony of persons, who would be deemed to be accomplices of the accused, must be subjected to absolute scrutiny before it is deemed to be worthy of acceptance.

In the light of the evidence which we heard, there is no doubt in the mind of the Court that, on the 26th day of June, 1996, the late Veronica Guerin was brutally murdered as she sat in her car waiting for the traffic lights to change at the junction of the Naas Road with Boot Road, near Clondalkin in the City of Dublin. While there was considerable controversy with regard to detail in the sense that several witnesses, who purported to be eye witnesses to the occurrence, gave conflicting evidence when describing the perpetrators of the crime and, in particular, their apparel, the type of vehicle on which they were travelling and its dimensions and colour and the number of shots which were discharged in the direction of the deceased, the Court has no doubt but that, at the material time, a motorcycle, on which there was a rider and a pillion passenger, drew alongside the car in which the late Veronica Guerin was travelling as it was stationary at traffic lights, that the pillion passenger broke the window in the driver's door of Ms Guerin's car and then fired a number of bullets at point blank range into the car. In the light of the evidence of Professor John Harbison, the State Pathologist, who conducted a post-mortem examination of the deceased, we are satisfied that she was struck by six bullets as a result of which she suffered injuries which gave rise to her almost instantaneous death.

With regard to foregoing, Detective Sergeant Patrick Ennis gave evidence about which we have no doubt at all, that he took possession of the bullets which had been taken by Professor Harbison from the remains of the late Veronica Guerin and that he also took possession of bullets which he found in Ms Guerin's car. He described these bullets as .357 Magnum calibre of lead composition and of the semi-wadd cutter type; in other words they were of a semi-conical shape with a flat nose. Sergeant Ennis said that this type of bullet was principally used in game shooting or target shooting and that it was a reloaded bullet rather than a factory-loaded bullet. He said that the bullets taken from the deceased and from her car were consistent with having been discharged from the same revolver and that that revolver would have been of the same calibre as the bullets.

GANGSTER

While the accused is charged with Ms Guerin's murder, as has already been indicated, it is no part of the prosecution's case that he was either the gunman, or the cyclist of the motorcycle on which the gunman was travelling, or even that he was present at the scene of the crime. On the contrary, the prosecution believe that Mr Gilligan was in Holland at the material time. Nevertheless, the prosecution believe that it was the accused who determined that Ms Guerin was to die and that it was he who was principally responsible for planning the circumstances under which she was to meet her end. Furthermore, it was contended that the perpetrators of the crime were acting under the accused's control and command at the time that Veronica Guerin was assassinated. In this regard, on the authority of a Judgment of the Supreme Court given in the case of *Ellis* -v- *O'Dea* (1991 JLRM at page 346) the Court accepts that, where two or more persons are engaged in a joint venture constituting a criminal offence, each is responsible for the acts of the others. Accordingly, any one of the persons so engaged is amenable to trial by the Courts of this country if one of his accomplices does an act in furtherance of that crime within this country. Therefore, if the Court concludes that those who were directly responsible for Veronica Guerin's death were, at the material time, either acting under the accused's control and/or command, or as a result of a preconceived plan which was devised between them and the accused, then the Court is satisfied that the accused is as guilty of the offence of murder as if he, himself had squeezed the trigger of the gun which was responsible for Ms Guerin's death.

Before reviewing the evidence which the prosecution maintain establishes the complicity of the accused in the murder of the late Veronica Guerin, it is, in the view of the Court, appropriate that it should first consider other matters, the determination of which will have a significant impact on the outcome of this trial.

Three witnesses were called to give evidence on behalf of the prosecution; evidence which, depending upon whether or not it found favour with the Court, would largely determine the guilt or innocence of the accused with regard to the offences with which he is charged. These witnesses were John Dunne, Charles Bowden and Russell Warren and, in the event that certain aspects of their evidence were accepted by the Court, it is clear that, to a greater or lesser extent, each one of them was an accomplice of the accused. In that regard, as has already being acknowledged by the Court, the Court recognises the danger of convicting an accused person on the uncorroborated evidence of an accomplice and that principle has been to the forefront of the mind of the Court when considering the evidence tendered by Messrs Dunne, Ward and Warren. However, whatever infirmities there may be in the evidence of these three men arising from the fact that they are accomplices of the accused, their reliability as witnesses and their general credibility is challenged by the defence on a variety of other grounds.

In particular, insofar as all three of them are concerned, it was suggested that their evidence was coloured by the fact that, when each of them pleaded guilty in Court to a variety of offences; including, in particular, drug-related offences, allegedly committed in association with the accused, each of them was, comparatively speaking, treated extremely leniently by the Courts; presumably, in the wake of representations by the DPP that they had cooperated with the prosecution and were expected to render further assistance to the authorities in connection with their investigations into related offences allegedly committed by other persons. Moreover, it was suggested that the evidence of these three men was suspect because each one of them and members of their families are participants in a witness protection programme organised by the State as a result of which each one of them and members of each of their families are, to a greater or lesser extent, currently financially dependent on the State and, when they have completed the sentences of imprisonment which each of them are presently serving, they and the members of their families will, for the foreseeable future, have to depend on the good offices of the State for their wellbeing and day to day living.

Accordingly, it is suggested that each of these three men has tailored his evidence to please the authorities, thereby securing a better future for themselves and for their families. Furthermore, insofar as the witnesses, Charles Bowden and Russell Warren are concerned, it is suggested that, in the circumstance that these two men have been granted immunity from prosecution in respect of the murder of the late Veronica Guerin; although, arguably, there is evidence available upon which each of them might be convicted of that offence, that favour was granted in consideration of their agreeing to give evidence favourable to the prosecution at the trial of these proceedings and other related proceedings.

In the view of the Court, insofar as it is suggested that the honesty of John Dunne, Charles Bowden and Russell Warren is open to question arising from the fact that, after they had agreed to give evidence on behalf of the prosecution in this and related trials, they were treated leniently by the Courts and, indeed, probably faced less serious charges than those which might have been preferred against them, had they not agreed to give such evidence, that would all now appear to the Court to be 'water under the bridge' in the sense that the DPP cannot, as it were, turn back the clock and arrange to have these men's cases reopened before the Courts with a view to having more severe penalties imposed upon them and neither, at this remove, can the DPP prefer more serious charges against them. Accordingly, it seems to the Court that, what has been done cannot be undone and, therefore, that Messrs Dunne, Bowden and Warren have nothing further to gain by giving perjured evidence on behalf of the prosecution and that begs the question 'why would they bother telling lies if there was no benefit from so doing?'. In the view of the Court there is no good reason why they should do so. The same considerations would appear to apply to the immunity from prosecution for the offence of murder which has been granted to Charles Bowden and Russell Warren because, in the letter granting that immunity, it is expressly stated that the favour is 'unconditional and irrevocable'. Accordingly, no matter what evidence these two men gave at whatever trials they chose to give evidence on behalf of the prosecution, including this trial, they can never be prosecuted for the murder of Veronica Guerin and, therefore, is there sense or logic in their giving perjured evidence? The Court thinks not.

Different considerations from those mentioned above arise when the credibility of these three men is called into question on the grounds of their participation in the witness protection programme; the essential difference being that, whether or not it is true, one or more of them could be apprehensive that, in the event that they did not give evidence which measured up to the expectations of the authorities, either they, or members of their families, would suffer on that account by being less well protected, or less well provided for in the future. On the face of it, that would not appear to be an unreasonable fear and, therefore, there would appear to be some basis for doubting the honesty of the evidence given by one or more of these men. However, although the Court accepts that, during the initial stages of the witness protection programme, each of these three men was less than enchanted with the information which they were then receiving about the realities of the programme, insofar as it was going to affect them and their families in the future and each of them was expressing reservations on that account, the Court is satisfied that, eventually, a situation of some trust developed between the men and those who were responsible for organising the witness protection programme and it appears to the Court that each man is now more sanguine about his future and that of his family.

Moreover, apart from the question of trust, it appears to the Court that the capacity of the Garda Síochána to combat organised crime is every increasingly dependant upon the cooperation of criminals which, in turn, necessitates the existence of a witness protection programme and, in the event that the authorities did not honour their obligations under that programme, there is little doubt but that those, who might otherwise have been persuaded to cooperate with the Garda Síochána would be dissuaded by such dishonour from so doing with the result that irreparable damage would be likely to be caused to the capacity of the Garda Síochána to combat organised crime. Accordingly, reneging on their obligations under the witness protection programme does not appear to the Court to be either a real or a sensible option for the authorities and that is a fact which should be so obvious to participants in the programme and, in particular, to Messrs Dunne, Bowden and Warren that there is no incentive to them to tell lies to the Court.

In that regard the Court was referred to the decision of The House of Lords in a case of *R -v- Hester* (1973 AC) by which it was decided that, if a witness is not creditworthy, his or her evidence must be rejected and the question of corroboration does not arise because corroboration is not for the purpose of giving validity or credence to evidence which is deficient or suspect of credibility but is only relevant to confirm and to support that which, as evidence, is sufficient and satisfactory and credible. In other words, the question of corroboration does not arise unless the Court is satisfied that the evidence of a witness in respect of whose evidence corroboration is sought is, itself, credible although not necessarily believed by the Court. While the Court is not aware that the decision in *R -v- Hester* has ever been considered by any Court in this jurisdiction it has been noted with approval by a number of Courts in the United Kingdom and, accordingly, the Court is persuaded that it is a decision which is sound in principle.

Apart from the foregoing and, in particular, apart from the suggested implications with regard to the credibility of the witnesses Dunne, Bowden and Warren arising from their participation in the witness protection programme, it was suggested on behalf of the defence that, viewing the matter globally, the methodology adopted by the Garda Síochána for harvesting evidence from these three men coupled with the relationship which developed and existed between them and the State was such that they are utterly compromised; so much so that their evidence was without any value whatsoever.

Indeed, Mr O'Higgins, on behalf of the accused, went so far as to suggest that the manner in which these three men were brought forward to give evidence threatens to compromise the entire criminal process system, as it is understood in this country. Referring to the decision of the Court given in the case of *The People (Trimbole) -v- The Governor of Mountjoy Prison* (1985 IR at page 550), he said that there was a positive duty on the Court to ensure that its own processes were protected and that it was not just simply a question of the Court admitting or rejecting the evidence of these three men because, if the processes of the Court were damaged in the course of harvesting their evidence, confidence in the judicial system would be threatened.

In that regard, Mr O'Higgins made specific reference to what he described as policy decisions which, apparently had been taken by senior members of the Garda Síochána, supported by the Minister for Justice and approved of by the Director of Public Prosecutions, whereby, in the course of the investigation into the events which gave to rise to the charges against this accused and, indeed, similar charges against other persons, a regime was embarked upon and put into place which was quite different from any such regime in other criminal prosecutions.

In particular, that regime lacked transparency and accountability, in that: (a) for the first time ever, it included a witness protection programme for witnesses, whose evidence was vital to a successful prosecution of a number of accused persons and, yet, the implications of that programme with regard to the benefits which participants were to obtain from it was clouded in secrecy although it was clear that those participants would receive financial support to a greater or lesser extent, (b) immunity from prosecution was granted to vital prosecution witnesses in circumstances which were never explained, (c) those vital witnesses and, indeed, a number of other persons, were never charged with a variety of serious offences in respect of which there was evidence to suggest that a conviction might have been obtained and no explanation for this omission was forthcoming, (d) vital prosecution witnesses were frequently interviewed and interrogated by the Garda Síochána without any record being kept of the content of those interviews, (e) payments were made by the Garda Síochána to those self same vital witnesses which purported to be monies belonging to them but which, in reality, is more likely to have been the proceeds of crime and (f) those self same witnesses received concessions in the course of serving prison sentences which were different from that received by other prisoners and there were indications that they would never be required to serve the full sentences of the Court imposed upon them.

Having regard to that regime, it was submitted that those vital witnesses, and in particular the witnesses Warren and Bowden, themselves had a perception, which they acknowledged in evidence, of intimidation and blackmail by the State and a belief that, despite contrary indications in correspondence, they would never be considered for early release unless and until they gave evidence on behalf of the prosecution and, generally speaking, that they believed that their situation was performance related in the sense that, unless the evidence which they gave at whatever trial they were required to give evidence was deemed to be satisfactory, they would be less well off. Indeed, the Court was referred to certain portions of the evidence given by Charles Bowden from which a clear inference can be drawn that he perceived that the purpose of the evidence which he gave at this trial and, indeed, at other trials, was to secure the conviction of the accused. In all those circumstances, it was submitted that, irrespective of whether or not the authorities had behaved with propriety, the effect of the regime which they followed was such as to create a perception in the minds of the witnesses Dunne, Bowden and Warren and especially that of Messrs Warren and Bowden which may well have affected their capacity to give unprejudiced evidence and that, therefore, their evidence should be rejected out of hand on the grounds that it would be impossible to conclude beyond any reasonable doubt that they were telling the truth, even though there might appear to be corroboration for certain aspects of their evidence.

In the light of the foregoing, the Court accepts that the regime which was put in place in the course of investigating the events which gave rise to the charges which have been preferred against this accused and, indeed, the investigation of similar charges against other persons, did include the several aspects referred to by counsel for the defence. In that regard, it would appear that this was the first occasion since the foundation of the State upon which a witness protection programme was put in place by the authorities and, as it is manifest that such a programme is essential for preserving the wellbeing of persons who have engaged in organised crime and are yet prepared to give evidence against their partners in crime, the Court has no doubt but that the authorities were well entitled to operate such a programme and not only to operate it but to cloak its details (including details of the benefits accruing to participants) in complete confidentiality because, if the public at large had access to those details, it is the view of the Court that the whole purpose of the programme would be defeated. Furthermore, the Court has no doubt but that the DPP has no obligation whatsoever to explain why immunity from prosecution is granted to any person or why any persons are not charged with offences in respect of which there may appear to be evidence to sustain such charges and that it is not necessarily in the interests of justice that such explanations are forthcoming. The Court is, however, concerned that Detective Garda James B. Hanley, who, despite his own protestations, was established in the eyes of the Court to have been a significant member of the team, who was involved in the investigation of the events which gave rise to the charges against this accused, amongst others, conceded in evidence that he kept no record whatsoever of several meetings which he had, in the course of his investigations, with the witnesses Charles Bowden and Russell Warren and this omission is all the more to be regretted because of suggestions by the defence that certain aspects of formal statements made by Messrs Bowden and Warren which varied previous statements made by them had been provoked or induced by Detective Garda Hanley in the course of such meetings.

The Court was also satisfied that there was no reasonable ground upon which the Garda Síochána could have believed that either Charles Bowden or Russell Warren had a legitimate claim to any portion of the monies which had been seized by the Garda Síochána in the course of their investigation and, therefore, those monies should not have been returned to those men and, in particular, monies should not have been returned to Russell Warren in instalments, as it was. Apart from any other considerations, the evidence of Mr Horan, Mr Warren's accountant, to the effect that Mr Warren's profit from his industrial cleaning business for the year ending December, 1995 was only £7,386 and Mr Horan said that there was no evidence that he had received any earnings from his business since the 5th March, 1996. In those circumstances, the Court cannot understand how the Garda authorities concluded that any of the monies found when they searched Mr Warren's residence and that of his parents in September, 1996 were not the proceeds of crime but rather legitimate profits from his cleaning business and, therefore, money which he was entitled to have returned to him. As has already been indicated, it is the view of the Court that there was no justification whatsoever for that view. While the Court accepts that, in a situation of dire need, it would not be inappropriate for the Garda authorities to advance monies to a potential witness, it does not appear to the Court that either Charles Bowden or Russell Warren were in such need when the decision was taken to return those monies to them. In this regard, while the Court is prepared to accept the bona fides of the members of the Garda Síochána concerned when the decision to return those monies was taken; albeit that, in the view of the Court, that decision was very wrong, the Court is concerned that the fact that when those monies were returned to Messrs Bowden and Warren it could have created a perception in their minds that the payments were being made in consideration of their incriminating their partners in crime.

Having regard to the foregoing, the conclusion of the Court is that any perceived benefits to the witnesses John Dunne, Charles Bowden and Russell Warren from giving evidence on behalf of the prosecution at this trial is more imagined than it is real and, accordingly, the Court is not persuaded that any one of those men gave perjured evidence in consideration of those perceived benefits. Neither, indeed, was the Court persuaded that it should doubt the honesty of either one of those men merely arising from the fact that each of them was told in correspondence that it was unlikely that he would be required to serve his full sentence, for the simple reason that the Court was told that virtually any prisoner, who sought early release, was given that assurance. However, the Court is concerned that both Charles Bowden and Russell Warren made formal statements to the Garda Síochána in which the accused, John Gilligan, is implicated in one or more of the charges which have been preferred against him after they had had those unrecorded meetings with Detective Garda Hanley and after monies had been returned to them by the Garda Síochána because it is the view of the Court that, in those circumstances their evidence is compromised. It does not follow, however, that the Court views the evidence of these two men as being incapable of belief in any or every respect. However, given that the Court is of the view that Charles Bowden and Russell Warren are compromised witnesses, that each one of them is an accomplice and that his evidence must be viewed in that light and that, apart altogether from those considerations, their evidence was ridiculed by the defence, who invited the Court to disregard it on the grounds that it was so riddled with inconsistencies and contradictions and so lacking in corroboration that its credibility was fatally flawed; particularly, as both men were exposed in the witness box as perjurers and self-serving liars, the Court acknowledges that it should have grave reservations about the truthfulness of any piece of evidence which either of these men gave in the witness box and the fact of the matter is that the Court has approached their evidence in that light. Nevertheless, however unreliable their evidence may have been, the Court cannot accept that there was no vestige of truth contained in the evidence given by either Charles Bowden or Russell Warren. In the view of the Court, there were certain aspects of the evidence of each one of them which was creditworthy and capable of belief and, while the Court was not prepared to act upon any piece of evidence given by either of those two men which stood by itself; notwithstanding that the Court may have believed that piece of evidence to be true, in the event that the Court was satisfied that there was significant corroboration for it, the Court was prepared to act on it.

Insofar as the evidence of the witness, John Dunne, is concerned, Mr Dunne's honesty, apart from his purported identification of the accused, does not appear to have been seriously challenged by the defence. Moreover, it does not appear to the Court that he is affected by the matters which, in the view of the Court, compromises the evidence of Charles Bowden and Russell Warren. Nevertheless, he is an accomplice and, while the Court would be entitled to act on his evidence without some corroboration, in the circumstance that it recognises the dangers of so doing, it is not disposed to do so.

While, as indicated above, the Court is of the view that certain aspects of the procedures followed by the Garda Síochána in the course of investigating the events which gave rise to these proceedings and, in particular, the manner in which Charles Bowden and Russell Warren were dealt with, has compromised the evidence of those two witnesses, the Court rejects, without reservation, the suggestion on behalf of the defence that the methodology adopted by the Garda Síochána for harvesting evidence in this case was so inappropriate that the entire criminal process system in the country was compromised. Certainly it is the view of the Court that it was improper to interview Messrs Bowden and Warren without keeping a record of what transpired at those interviews and it was unfitting to return monies to them while they were still assisting the Garda Síochána in their inquiries; given that there were no reasonable grounds to suppose that they had a legitimate claim to those monies. However, while those shortcomings are to be regretted and, in the view of the Court compromised the evidence of those two witnesses, the Court is not persuaded that the entire criminal process system in the country was thereby threatened. The Court accepts that it has a duty to protect its own processes and it is for that reason that the Court is critical of certain aspects of the manner in which Messrs Bowden and Warren were dealt with by the Garda authorities. However, in the view of the Court, it is a leap too far to suggest that the irregularities to which the Court has referred threatened the entire criminal process system.

Among the offences with which the accused is charged is that of unlawful importation into the State of a controlled drug; to wit cannabis resin, between the 1st July, 1994 and the 6th October, 1996. In that regard, one of the first matters to be determined by the Court is, irrespective of John Gilligan's alleged involvement, whether or not the prosecution has established that there was, in fact, an unlawful importation of cannabis resin into the country between those dates.

Ms Jennifer Fitzpatrick and Mr John O'Sullivan who, at the material time, were respectively the Operations Manager and an employee of a freight company known as Teca Shipping Services which had depots in both Cork and Holland, Mr Vivian O'Brien who, at the material time, was General Manager of a freight company known as Shipping Transport Cork Limited and Messrs Dermot Murphy and Michael Cashman who, at the material time, were respectively a Director and an office clerk of Seabridge Limited of Sitecast Industrial Estate, Little Island, County Cork, gave evidence which was not challenged and the combined effect of which was that between the months of April 1994 and October 1996, inclusive, Teca Shipping Services were instrumental in shipping goods designated as 'spare parts' from Holland to Cork; goods which were contained in sealed cartons, initially of timber construction and, laterally, of cardboard construction and which were transported in containers. No one of these four witnesses ever saw the contents of these cartons and, accordingly, had no reason to believe that they contained anything other than their designated contents. The combined evidence of these four witnesses also established that the named consignees of the said cartons were mostly, either a firm known as Alcan Casings Limited or a firm known as McCarthy Commercials Limited, although the fact of the matter was that neither such company ever existed. In fact, the reality was that, at the behest of Mr John Dunne, who, at the material time, was Operations Manager of Seabridge Limited, those consignments of cartons were either collected from the terminal building to which they were brought on arrival in this country by Mr Dunne, personally, or by a representative from Seabridge Limited. Alternatively, they were delivered to the offices of Seabridge Limited. Moreover, although there appears to have been a general assumption that it was Seabridge Limited who paid the freight charges in respect of those consignments, Mr Cashman gave evidence, which was not challenged and which we have no reason to doubt, that Mr Dunne, personally, paid the invoices in respect of freight charges for those consignments with a bank draft. In the course of their evidence, these four witnesses referred to documentation kept in the ordinary course of business by Teca Shipping Services, by Shipping Transport Cork Limited and by Seabridge Limited which satisfied the Court beyond any doubt that, during the period April 1994 to October 1996 inclusive, John Dunne, under the umbrella of Seabridge Limited, was responsible for the importation into the State of over 100 consignments purporting to be 'spare parts', the total weight of which, including the weight of the cartons in which they were transported, being in excess of 20,000 kilos.

In this regard, Mr John Dunne, himself, gave evidence which, inmost of its aspects and its implications, was similar to and supportive of the evidence given by Ms Fitzpatrick and by Messrs O'Sullivan, O'Brien, Murphy and Cashman with regard to the importation into the State of those consignments of cartons and he identified box types, labels and the binding of boxes which were subsequently found by the Gardai at a lock up garage at Emmet Road, Inchicore, and at Unit lB at the Greenmount Industrial Estate, Harold's Cross in the City of Dublin as being similar in kind to the box types, labels and binding used in the said consignments of cartons. Furthermore, Mr Dunne gave evidence that, initially, when those consignments of cartons carried by Teca Shipping Services arrived at Cork docks, they were either collected by himself, personally, or by someone on his behalf, who would bring them to him and he would then transport them to the Ambassador Hotel, Naas, where he would hand them over to two men; one of whom was called Joe but was subsequently identified by Mr Dunne as a man named Brian Meehan and the other who was never identified by name by Mr Dunne. However, Mr Dunne said that, when he was on holidays, the services of a man named Dermot Cambridge, who was then an independent courier operating in the City of Cork and its environs, were engaged to transport the said consignments of cartons from the Cork docks to the Ambassador Hotel in Naas and Mr Cambridge, himself, gave evidence which corroborated that of Mr Dunne in that regard.

Indeed, following Mr Dunne's return from holidays, he continued to avail of the services of Mr Cambridge to transport consignments of cartons from Cork docks to the Ambassador Hotel in Nass. Moreover, Mr Cambridge gave evidence that, when he arrived at the Ambassador Hotel, Naas, with a consignment of cartons, he handed them over to two men; one of whom he identified as a man named Charles Bowden and the other of whom he said he knew by the name Shane but subsequently identified as the man in photograph No. 1 of exhibit 88 produced by the prosecution, who was identified to the Court as Mr Shay Ward. Mr Cambridge gave four other pieces of evidence which, in the view of the Court, were of some significance. In the first place, he said that, on each occasion on which he delivered a consignment of cartons to the Ambassador Hotel, in Naas, he was given a closed envelope, which varied in bulk, for transmission to Mr Dunne. (Mr Dunne said that he was paid £1,000.00 for each consignment). Secondly, he said that Mr Charles Bowden drove a blue Opel Kadett van into which was generally transferred the consignments of cartons which he brought to the hotel but that there were occasions on which he arrived with such a large consignment that it could not be accommodated in Mr Bowden's van and, on such occasions, Mr Bowden would take Mr Cambridge's van and, some time later, would return it without its load. (Mr Bowden gave similar evidence). Thirdly, Mr Cambridge gave evidence that, when he first brought consignments to the Ambassador Hotel they would have been in wooden boxes but that, laterally, they changed to cardboard boxes and he also said that, at the request of Mr Dunne, he used to pickup boxes at the Kent Railway Station in Cork which were addressed to Seabridge Limited and he would bring them to Mr Dunne.

The most significant aspect of Mr John Dunne's evidence, insofar as these proceedings are concerned, was, of course, his allegation that it was the accused, John Gilligan, who had requested him to make appropriate arrangements for the importation of the said consignments of cartons into this country. In this regard, given that it is corroborated in virtually every respect by the combined evidence of Ms Jennifer Fitzpatrick and of Messrs John O'Sullivan, Vivian O'Brien, Dermot Murphy, Michael Cashman and Dermot Cambridge, the Court has no doubt whatsoever but that John Dunne was responsible for the importation of those consignments of cartons into the country and that he disposed of them; either by himself bringing them to the Ambassador Hotel, in Naas or by arranging for Mr Cambridge to do so. However, insofar as Mr Dunne alleges that it was at the accused's request that he arranged for the importation of those consignments into the State and arranged that they would be transported to the Ambassador Hotel in Naas, there is no corroboration of that assertion; an assertion which is challenged, essentially on the grounds that, if such requests were made of Mr Dunne (which was not admitted), they were not made by the accused, but by some other person, and that Mr Dunne is mistaken when he identifies the accused as the person concerned. In that regard, Mr Dunne gave evidence that he met man who made those requests of him and who he has identified as the accused face to face on six or seven occasions; one of which lasted upwards of 20 minutes and, accordingly, it seems to the Court that if Mr Dunne is considered to be a credible witness, then his identification of Mr Gilligan is beyond doubt. In the view of the Court, given that there is independent evidence which supports the evidence of Mr Dunne to a considerable degree, there is every reason to believe that Mr Dunne is, indeed, a credible witness and that, therefore, there is no good reason to doubt the accuracy of his identification of the accused. Incidentally, the Court considered Mr Dunne's identification of the accused; not so much as a dock identification but more as a recognition of someone who he had known previously. In this regard, the Court has taken into account; firstly, that, when asked to describe the man who requested him to arrange for the importation of the said consignments Mr Dunne said that he was a 'small, low sized, stocky man with basically black hair who was then 40/45 years of age'. While Mr Gilligan is certainly a small man, a stocky man and might easily have been considered to have been about 40/45 years of age when Mr Dunne says that he first met him some six years ago, he certainly does not now have black hair. However, from photographs which the Court has seen during the course of the trial, it is clear that, at one stage of his life, the accused had black hair and, accordingly, the Court is satisfied that it could well be that, some six years ago, his hair could reasonably have been described as 'basically black'.

Secondly, the Court has taken into account the fact that, if the accused is convicted of the several offences of unlawful importation of controlled drugs with which he is charged, then John Dunne would be an accomplice of his and, accordingly, the Court has scrutinised his evidence with that in mind, but, yet, accepts his identification of the accused. Reference has already been made to boxes which were found by the Gardai at a lock-up garage at Emmet Road, Inchicore and at Unit 1B at the Greenmount Industrial Estate, Harolds Cross. In that regard, we heard evidence from a Mr Derek Behan, who said the that he looked after a lockup garage at the rear of No. 90, Emmet Road, Inchicore, which belonged to a lady called Catherine Osbourne. He said that, in the month of October 1994, that lock-up was rented by Ms Osbourne to a man who gave his name as Andrew Bowden from whom he (Mr Behan) obtained a deposit of £40.00. He said that, during the period that the man named Andrew Bowden occupied the said lock-up, he (Derek Behan) had visited the premises and saw inside wooden boxes stacked up to the ceiling which were lined with polystyrene and spray foam. He said that quite an amount of those boxes and packaging was left behind when the man named Andrew Bowden left the premises and that he (Mr Behan) had pointed out those boxes to the Gardai. He also said that the man who called himself Andrew Bowden was one and the same person as a man shown at photograph No. 8 in exhibit 76 who, in fact, is Charles Bowden. As Mr Behan's evidence was not challenged, the Court saw no reason to doubt it and neither did it doubt the evidence of Ms Lucy Divine and Mr Paul Byrne, who said that, in the month of December 1994, Unit 3E at the Kylemore Industrial Estate was rented to a man, who gave his name as Paul Conroy, but who both witnesses gave a description of; a description which satisfied the Court that, in fact, that man was Charles Bowden. Mr Byrne was unable to say when the man who called himself Paul Conroy vacated those premises because he left them without warning and Mr Byrne had to break into them. On doing so, he found that the premises were empty save for the presence of some empty boxes which had, as Mr Byrne said, 'Styrofoam' packaging which he cleaned out; not thinking that they were of any significance. Furthermore, the Court heard evidence from Mr Thomas Harrington, the owner of the said premises at Unit 1B at the Greenmount Industrial Estate that, on 10th November, 1995, he leased that unit to a man, who gave his name as Paul Conroy of 3 J.F. Kennedy Industrial Estate, who agreed to pay a deposit of £500.00 and £500.00 a month in rent and who gave Mr Harrington £1,000 in cash on 10th November, 1995 to cover the deposit and one month's rent in advance. In addition, the man who called himself Paul Conroy, signed a caretaker's agreement in respect of the said premises. Mr Harrington was subsequently shown an album of photographs in which he identified the man who called himself Paul Conroy as being Charles Bowden.

On 6th October, 1996, Inspector Jeremiah O'Connell of the Garda Síochána obtained a search warrant in respect of the said premises at the Greenmount Industrial Estate and, on being searched, the premises and their contents presented as appears in photographs one to twenty inclusive in an album of photographs (exhibit No. 59) produced by the prosecution. The contents included boxes or cartons, both constructed of timber and of cardboard, which were strewn around the premises; one of which cardboard boxes was lined with foam and contained nine ounce bars of cannabis resin. In this regard, Detective Sergeant Patrick Ennis, a forensic ballistics expert, gave evidence that there were twenty-six such boxes on the premises, each of which had an inside compartment surrounded by polystyrene sheeting and compressed aerosol foam. Detective Sergeant Ennis calculated that each box could accommodate approximately 150 slabs of cannabis resin; each weighing approximately 250 grams; in other words, a total of approximately 975 kilograms of cannabis resin.

These 26 boxes were examined by Dr Daniel O'Driscoll, a forensic scientist, and Dr O'Driscoll said that he found debris in 25 of the cardboard boxes and that the debris from 22 of those 25 boxes contained traces of cannabis resin. In addition to those boxes, some bags were found on the premises which also contained bars of cannabis resin and, furthermore, Detective Sergeant Ennis gave evidence that there was also found on the premises two camouflage pouches designed to hold a machine pistol and a silencer and he said that these pouches were similar to pouches found in a Jewish cemetery on the Old Court Road. On the 19th March, 1997 Inspector Jeremiah O'Connell aforesaid obtained another search warrant in respect of the said lock-up garage at Emmet Road and, on being searched, the Gardai found a number of broken up cardboard boxes with foam attached to the inside which were identified to them by Mr Derek Behan as the boxes already described by him. The significance of this evidence is that Charles Bowden, who was identified as the lessee of the lock-up garage at Enunet Road, Unit 3B at the Kylemore Industrial Estate and unit 1B at the Greenmount Industrial Estate successively from the month of October 1994, gave evidence that the boxes (both wooden and cardboard), which had been found on those premises by the Garda Síochána and described by Paul Byrne had been included in consignments which he had collected at the Ambassador Hotel, Naas, from either Mr John Dunne, or Mr Dermot Cambridge. He said that all of those boxes had contained quantities of cannabis resin and that, on occasions, they also contained quantities of cocaine and weapons and ammunition including pouches for those weapons. Mr Bowden gave evidence that, after he collected these consignments from the Ambassador Hotel, it was his responsibility to open the boxes, to section orders for drugs which would have been given to him by a man named Brian Meehan and that he would then deliver those drugs. Moreover, when the consignments contained weapons, it was his responsibility to have them cleaned and oiled and, having done so, he arranged to have them secreted in a grave in the Jewish graveyard on the Old Court Road.

In this regard, virtually every aspect of Mr Bowden's evidence was challenged by the defence on the grounds that he was an inveterate liar who was incapable of speaking the truth. However, given that there was independent evidence that it was Mr Bowden who had leased the said premises at Emmet Road, at the Kylemore Industrial Estate and at the

Greenmount Industrial Estate, that the boxes found in those units by the Garda Síochána were identified by Mr Michael Cashman, by Mr Dermot Cambridge and by Mr John Dunne as similair to those included in the consignments of what were described as spare parts imported into this country by Teca Shipping Services, that Mr Dermot Cambridge identified Mr Bowden as one of the persons to whom he delivered those consignments at the Ambassador Hotel, Naas, and that quantities of cannabis resin were found in at least one of those boxes and debris of cannabis resin in 22 of the boxes when the Garda Síochána raided the Greenmount Industrial Estate on 6th October, 1996, the Court is satisfied that the evidence of Charles Bowden insofar as he asserts that, when he opened those cartons having collected them from the Ambassador Hotel in Naas, they contained quantities of drugs was truthful. Moreover, given that, on 8th October, 1997, Mr Bowden pleaded guilty in the Circuit Court to offences of possession of cannabis for the purpose of sale, the Court has little doubt but that Mr Bowden's description of what he did with the drugs when he opened those boxes is also true.

In the light of the foregoing, the Court has concluded that a link was established between the request which the accused made of Mr John Dunne to arrange for the importation of consignments of cartons into this country and the cannabis resin which was ultimately found in those cartons; both in the form of slabs and included among debris which was found therein. In other words, the Court is satisfied beyond reasonable doubt that the consignments of cartons which, at the request of the accused, Mr John Dunne arranged to have imported into this country contained cannabis resin and given that the Court is satisfied that John Gilligan agreed to and did, in fact, pay John Dunne the sum of £1,000 in respect of the importation of each of the said consignments; a sum of money which, on any view, is grossly in excess of what would be a normal charge for such a service, the Court has no doubt whatsoever that John Gilligan was aware of the fact that those consignments of boxes contained quantities of cannabis resin.

In arriving at the foregoing conclusions, the Court has not overlooked the fact that Mr John Dunne never stated in evidence that it was drugs that he was importing at the behest of John Gilligan. He did say that he believed that it was contraband that was involved and he conceded that, as a result of that importation, he had pleaded guilty to ten counts of importing cannabis resin into the State. In the view of the Court, those two factors (Mr Dunne's concession that he believed that he was importing contraband and his plea of guilty) are persuasive evidence of Mr Dunne's guilty knowledge. Neither is the Court unmindful of submissions on behalf of the defence; (a) that, even were it true that the accused had requested Mr Dunne to arrange for the importation of cannabis resin into the State on his behalf early in the year 1994, there was no evidence of the accused's continued involvement in that activity after that date and (b) that, in the light of the evidence of Russell Warren, it was open to the Court to conclude that the contents of the consignments of cartons which it is alleged that the accused requested Mr Dunne to import into the State on his behalf was tobacco, rather than cannabis resin. In fact, the Court considered and rejected both of those submissions, firstly on the grounds that, accepting that the accused requested Mr Dunne to arrange for the importation of the said consignments of cartons into the State early in the year 1994, the Court is satisfied that the pattern of importations between that time and the month of October 1996 is consistent only with accused's continued involvement therewith.

Secondly, in the light of the contents of the documentation referred to by the witnesses Jennifer Fitzpatrick, John O'Sullivan, Vivian O'Brien, Dermot Murphy and Michael Cashman insofar as it purported to indicate the weight of the several consignments of cartons imported into the State as aforesaid, when compared with the evidence of Dr O'Driscoll following tests carried out by him, which suggested that one of those cartons full of cannabis resin would weigh three and a half times of a similar carton full of tobacco, the Court had no difficulty in concluding beyond any doubt that those cartons did not contain tobacco.

While, for the reasons outlined above, the Court is satisfied that the accused, John Gilligan, was the prime mover in the importation of cannabis resin into this country through the medium of Teca Shipping services from early in the year 1994 until the Garda Síochána raided Unit lB at the Greenmount Industrial Estate on 6th October, 1996 and, in arriving at that conclusion, was influenced by the evidence of Charles Bowden to the extent indicated above, it does not follow that the Court was satisfied that, insofar as other aspects of his evidence were concerned, Charles Bowden was a truthful witness.

In that regard, it is the view of the Court that, under cross-examination, he was exposed as a self serving liar in a variety of different ways; so much so that the Court was compelled to conclude that, in the interests of justice, it would be unsafe to rely on any evidence which Charles Bowden gave unless it was supported by circumstantial evidence, or independent testimony. In that regard, the accused is also charged with offences of possession of cannabis resin for the purpose of sale or supply in contravention of relevant misuse of drugs legislation and, to some extent, the case for the prosecution in support of those charges is dependant upon the evidence of Charles Bowden.

GANGSTER

In that regard, the essentials of Mr Bowden's evidence was that, after he had collected cartons containing quantities of cannabis resin at the Ambassador Hotel, Naas, he would bring them to whatever lock-up was then being used by him and by his associates as a base for the distribution of those drugs. In that regard, as has already been indicated, the Court has accepted that, when Charles Bowden opened those cartons, having collected them from the Ambassador Hotel in Naas, he found that they contained quantities of drugs and, given that there is independent evidence that, from the month of October 1994, Charles Bowden successively leased three lock-up premises (the garage at Emmet Road and the units at Kylemore Industrial Estate and the Greenmount Industrial Estate), the Court has no difficulty in accepting that Mr Bowden used those lock-ups as a base for his drug trafficking activities.

In this regard, Mr Bowden said that there was a group of five, who were to the forefront of the sale and distribution of the cannabis resin which had been imported into the State. These were himself; a man named Peter Mitchell, Messrs Brian Meehan and Shay Ward, to whom reference has already been made and Mr Shay Ward's brother, Paul Ward. Mr Bowden said that those five had an equal interest in the drug trafficking business in which they were engaged in the sense that they divided everything in excess of £2,000 per kilo which they received in respect of cannabis resin sold by them.

Although the fact of the matter is that, in the course of his evidence, Mr Bowden said that the first £2,000 per kilo for which the cannabis resin was sold went to the accused, John Gilligan, he conceded he was not aware of that fact of his own knowledge but had heard that it was so. Accordingly, that evidence is based on hearsay which the Court must and does ignore.

However, while the Court only has Mr Bowden's word for how and between whom the profits derived from the drug trafficking activities in which he was engaged were divided, there was considerable independent evidence of association; one with the other, between the five persons, who Mr Bowden named as those who shared all monies in excess of £2,000 for which the cannabis resin with which they were dealing was sold and some independent evidence of association between one or more of those individuals and the accused, John Gilligan. It is unnecessary, we feel, to review in detail all the independent evidence which we heard, which we had no reason to doubt, and which pointed to the fact that Charles Bowden, Paul Ward, Brian Meehan, Shay Ward, Peter Mitchell and the accused, John Gilligan, were all well known to each another and were accustomed to fraternising one with the other for whatever reason.

In that regard, Garda Michael Moran gave evidence that, on the 1st October, 1996, he saw Charles Bowden, Shay Ward, Peter Mitchell and Brian

Meehan lunching together at the Hotpot Restaurant in the Sundrive Shopping Centre during which they were laughing and joking among one another. Moreover, Garda Moran gave evidence that, after they left the restaurant, Charles Bowden and Shay Ward went into a haberdashery shop next door which was named Traceys where they purchased a red yard brush, which was hanging on a rack outside and some rolls of black refuse sacks. Then, we had video evidence of a wedding in St Lucia in the month of March 1996 which was attended (inter alia) by John Gilligan, Brian Meehan, Paul Ward and Peter Mitchell. In the month of August 1994, the Gardai stopped a car driven by Brian Meehan in which Peter Mitchell was a passenger and in which the Gardai found a sum of money in excess of £46,000 which John Gilligan subsequently claimed belonged to him and that he had given it to his 'trusted friend', Brian Meehan. There being no other claimant for that money, it was returned to Mr Gilligan by the District Court. In May 1995, the Gardai again found Peter Mitchell and Brian Meehan together in possession of high powered motorcycles; this time at the rear of Paul Ward's residence in Walkinstown.

On 26th June, 1996 Gardai saw Brian Meehan get out of a car driven by Seamus Ward at the junction of Aungier Street and Stephen's Street in the city of Dublin with a mobile phone in his hand. In October, 1996 Gardai found Brian Meehan travelling as a passenger in a car driven by Paul Ward and Dermot Cambridge gave evidence that he met Charles Bowden in the company of Shay Ward. There was an abundance of evidence of records of telephone calls passing to and fro between mobile telephones belonging to or under the control of Charles Bowden, Brian Meehan, and John Gilligan and while, of course, the Court has no direct evidence as to who actually made those telephone calls, their multiplicity was such that, in the view of the Court it would defy the laws of logic and coincidence were it a fact that the majority of those telephone calls had not been exchanged by the actual owners of those mobile telephones, or the persons who, according to the evidence, habitually had control over them. In all these circumstances, the Court had no difficulty in coming to the conclusion that the association between Charles Bowden, Paul Ward, Brian Meehan, Shay Ward, Peter Mitchell and the accused, John Gilligan, was such that it was reasonable for the prosecution to describe them as 'a gang'.

However, was it a gang whose principal activities involved drug trafficking? Charles Bowden said so, but then, as has already been pointed out, the Court has grave reservations about Mr Bowden's truthfulness. Nevertheless, because there is independent evidence to support it, the Court has no doubt but that Mr Bowden was speaking the truth when he indicated that there was a relationship between the six men, whom the prosecution choose to refer to as the 'gang' and, if that relationship was not for the purpose of engaging in drug trafficking activities, for what purpose did these men associate with one another; apparently, on a fairly regular basis? No alternative purpose to that of drug trafficking was ever suggested to the Court but, apart from that omission, there is, in the view of the Court, persuasive evidence which associates this 'gang' with drug trafficking activities.

In the first place, the findings of the Garda Síochána, when they raided Unit 1B at the Greenmount Industrial Estate on 6th October, 1996 provides convincing evidence to corroborate the evidence of Charles Bowden that that unit was used as a base for his drug trafficking activities. That evidence principally comprised the slabs of cannabis resin which were found in the unit, the traces of cannabis resin found in the debris in the boxes which were found in the unit, the cutting equipment and the weighing scales which were found and which would be consistent with the activity of portioning and weighing quantities of cannabis resin and the lists of initials with weights after their names which were found in the unit confirming Mr Bowden's evidence that lists of customers were kept.

Moreover, Mr Brian Meehan's fingerprints were found on some of those lists and a similar list was found by the Gardai when they searched Brian Meehan's house in September 1996. There was the evidence that a brush was found at the Greenmount unit which was identified as the self same brush that Charles Bowden and Shay Ward had purchased at Traceys General Store beside the Hotpot Restaurant on 1st October, 1996 and, furthermore, when Paul Ward was stopped and searched by the Gardai in October 1996, a slip of paper was found on him which contained entries which were very similar to entries on the lists found in that unit.

In addition, there was the evidence of Russell Warren which, when considered in the context of the other matters to which reference has been made, led the Court to the inexorable conclusion that the accused John Gilligan, did, indeed, either directly or vicariously, engage in the sale and supply of cannabis resin at the material time. This begs the question, was John Gilligan, as the prosecution assert, the leader of this gang? Certainly the Court has no doubt but that he was the prime mover insofar as the importation of cannabis resin into this country was concerned.

Moreover, without relying on any evidence that might be considered to be hearsay, it seems to the Court that a reasonable inference to be drawn from such evidence as has been available to the Court with regard to the distribution of the proceeds of the sale of cannabis resin which Mr Gilligan was responsible for importing into this State is that he was the largest beneficiary. That would suggest that he was the supreme authority among the members of the gang but, in the view of the Court, the evidence falls short of establishing that Mr Gilligan played an active role in the day-to-day activities of the gang. Reference has been made to the evidence of Russell Warren whose honesty, truthfulness and general credibility was disparaged and ridiculed by the defence for a multiplicity of what appeared to be very valid reasons. In this regard, Mr Warren was a self-confessed perjurer, a proven self-serving liar (under cross-examination, he specifically conceded that telling lies did not worry him; as he said, 'if you can get away with lies, you would') and a person who, apparently, did not care who he hurt, if by doing so there was some benefit to himself. In that context, he conceded that he had given information to the Garda Síochána implicating his parents with criminal activity, he had cheated on his wife and his best friend and, indeed, had exploited his younger sister.

Moreover, in the course of giving evidence to this Court, he was noticeably evasive in his answering and, generally speaking, his evidence was riddled with inconsistencies and contradictions; not only insofar as the evidence which he gave to this Court was concerned but when compared with the evidence which he gave at the trial of Brian Meehan in the month of June 1999.

Furthermore, of course, Mr Warren's evidence had to be viewed in the light of the fact that, if the accused was convicted of the several offences of drug trafficking with which he is charged, Mr Warren would be an accomplice of his. In all those circumstances, it has to be stated that the Court viewed Mr Russell Warren's evidence with scepticism. Indeed, it was not disposed to act on any evidence which he gave unless it was strongly supported by independent testimony or circumstantial evidence. That begs the question as to how the Court can justify the assertion that it was influenced by the evidence of Russell Warren when arriving at the conclusion that the accused had been engaged in the sale and supply of drugs.

In that regard, Mr Warren gave evidence of collecting, counting and laundering money on behalf of John Gilligan from early in the year 1996 until his arrest on 30th September, 1996. In the course of that evidence, he described, how, from time to time, he would telephone John Gilligan to advise him as to the amount of money which he had collected and how he made frequent trips to the continent of Europe and, in particular, to the City of Amsterdam, carrying large sums of money in punts and in sterling (more often that not, sums in excess of £100,000 at a time) and, there, at the express directions of Mr Gilligan he would convert that money into Dutch guilders.

He said that, in the course of such activity, apart from the many telephone conversations which he had with Mr Gilligan, he would meet him face to face on many many occasions and, indeed, apart from collecting and laundering money for him, he said that he provided other services for Mr

Gilligan; such as driving him to the bookies. Mr Warren said that telephonic communications between himself and Mr Gilligan were carried out by mobile phone; that the mobile phone which he used was in the name of his father and had the number 087/455571 and that the number of the mobile phone used by John Gilligan was 087/440106.

Mr Warren's evidence was corroborated in a number of different respects. First and foremost there was the evidence of the letters which Mr Gilligan wrote to him while he (Mr Warren) was a prisoner at Arbour Hill prison and, in the course of which, Mr Gilligan sometimes addressed him as 'Russell my friend'. Moreover, in the course of that correspondence, in addition to writing on his own behalf, Mr Gilligan purports to be writing on behalf of Brian Meehan and Paul Ward which, of course, is another indication of his association with the group who the prosecution choose to describe as 'the gang'. Then there was the myriad of records of telephone calls passing between the mobile telephones used by Mr Warren and by Mr Gilligan during the material time and there was video evidence of John Gilligan strolling down Main Street in Lucan in the company of Russell Warren.

In the view of the Court, those three factors provide eloquent evidence of close association between John Gilligan and Russell Warren. What was the basis for that relationship? Was it family? Was it social? Was it legitimate business? The Court has never been told and while, of course, the Court recognises that the accused is under no obligation to explain anything, it is the view of the Court that, in the absence of an explanation for that association or, indeed, any rational hypothesis upon which the basis for the association can be understood, the Court is entitled to look to other evidence for elucidation with regard to the question of why John Gilligan and Russell Warren were associates.

The only testimony that the Court has in that regard is that of Russell Warren, himself, although it is arguable that some of the testimony given by Charles Bowden pointed in that direction. However, the evidence of Charles Bowden is subject to the same infirmities as that of Mr Warren. Mr Warren said that the £63,000 odd which was found by the Garda Síochána when they searched his parents' house on 30th September, 1996, was money which he had collected on behalf of John Gilligan.

Neither he nor his parents laid any claim of ownership to that money nor, indeed, did anyone else and, accordingly, it was forfeited to the State by order of the Dublin Circuit Criminal Court made on 10th November, 1997; the same date upon which Russell Warren affirmed a plea of guilty to handling the said money knowing or believing it to represent another person's proceeds of drug trafficking. In the light of Russell Warren's proven association with John Gilligan, his account of the reasons for that association and his account for the source of the money found by the Garda Síochána on 30th September, 1996, and in the absence of any other evidence; either to account for that money or otherwise account for the association between Mr Warren and Mr Gilligan, the Court is quite satisfied to accept Mr Warren's evidence in that regard; notwithstanding its view that, generally speaking Mr Warren is a person in respect of whose evidence little reliance can usually be placed. John Gilligan is also charged with the possession or control of firearms and ammunition with intent to endanger life and the possession or control of firearms and ammunition with intent to enable another person, by means thereof, to endanger life. It is manifest that those charges stand or fail on the testimony of Charles Bowden.

In this regard, Mr Bowden gave evidence that on a couple of occasions, in addition to containing quantities of cannabis resin, the cartons which were imported into the State by Teca Shipping Services and which have already been referred to, also contained quantities of weapons and ammunition. He said that, when that occurred, it was his responsibility to clean and oil the weapons; which he did, and they were then taken and secreted in a grave belonging to a lady named Miriam Norcot located in the Jewish cemetery at the Old Court Road.

Moreover, testimony from members of the Garda Síochána confirmed that, on being advised of that fact by Mr Bowden, they had visited the Jewish cemetery on the Old Court Road, and, when they pushed back the slab covering the grave of the late Miss Norcot, they found a quantity of weapons and ammunition, as Mr Bowden had said that they would. Furthermore, Mr Bowden gave evidence that, when weapons and ammunition were included in the cartons, he would advise Mr Gilligan of that fact on the telephone although he agreed that, on those occasions, he never actually mentioned weapons; merely telling Mr Gilligan 'there's something extra in the boxes'.

We only had Mr Bowden's word for it that quantities of weapons and ammunition were sometimes included with the consignments of cannabis resin and that, when that occurred, the weaponry and the ammunition ended up in the Jewish cemetery at the Old Court Road. It was suggested by the prosecution that Mr Bowden's testimony in that regard was corroborated by evidence that some of the cartons imported into the State through the medium of Teca Shipping Services were heavier than others and, indeed, it is a fact that there was such evidence.

However, it is the view of the Court that there are any number of reasons; other than that they contained weapons, why some of those consignments of cartons might be heavier than others; e.g. some might have contained more cannabis resin than others and, therefore, the Court is not persuaded that the difference in the weights of the consignments is corroborative of Mr Bowden's evidence that some of them contained weapons.

It is also suggested on behalf of the prosecution that Mr Bowden's evidence that he unloaded weapons and ammunition from cartons which also contained quantities of cannabis resin at Unit lB of the Greenmount Industrial Estate is corroborated by the fact that, when the Garda Síochána searched those premises on 6th and 7th October, 1996, they found a camouflage pouch for a pistol and a camouflage pouch for a silencer which were similar to like pouches found in the grave at the Jewish cemetery.

However, the Court has a problem with the evidence of certain members of the Garda Síochána with regard to the finding of the said pouches at the Greenmount Industrial Estate. In particular, the Court could not understand why, if, as members of the Garda Síochána concerned said in evidence, the said premises were subjected to a detailed search when visited by the Garda Síochána on Sunday, 6th of October, 1996, the said pouches were not found until the following day.

Apart from that curious fact, neither Detective Sergeant Ennis nor Detective Garda Howley, both of whom gave evidence with regard to the finding of those two pouches at the Greenmount Industrial Estate, had noted their find in their Garda notebooks, neither pouch was photographed 'in situ' although the vast majority of items which were considered to be of significance which had been found in the Greenmount Industrial Estate were photographed 'in situ'.

Indeed, the photograph of the box in which the two pouches were allegedly found was not included in the original album of photographs of the contents of Unit lB at the Greeenmount Industrial Estate which was produced to the Court but was only introduced after Detective Sergeant Ennis had commenced his evidence and, then, was introduced because Detective Sergeant Ennis said that a colleague of his had requested him to refer to it.

Another curious feature about these two pouches was that Detective Inspector O'Mahony said that, when the pouch for the pistol was produced to Mr Bowden for the purposes of identification, it had a sellotape wrapping in it; apparently, the type of wrapping that might be used for containing cannabis resin but, when the pouch was produced in Court, that wrapping was not in it and no explanation was forthcoming with regard to its absence. Furthermore, Mr Bowden had purported to identify the pouch produced to him; that is, the pouch which allegedly had been in found at the Greenmount Industrial Estate, because he had spilled oil on it while cleaning the weapon to which it belonged. However, there was no oil on the pouch which was produced in Court. Indeed, lest there was any doubt about whether or not there was any oil on that pouch, Dr Daniel O'Driscoll was asked whether or not it could be tested for traces of oil and he agreed that it would be possible to do so and that he could organise such a test.

However, the Court was never advised as to whether or not such a test was ever carried out and, if so, with what result. Finally, there was no mention of the finding of either of those pouches in the statement of evidence which was served on behalf of the Detective Garda Howley; the first intimation that he would be giving evidence in respect of the finding thereof being when he got into the witness box.

In all those circumstances, while it may well be that those two pouches were found by the Garda Síochána during the course of searching Unit 1B at the Greenmount Industrial Estate, the Court cannot but have a doubt in that regard and, accordingly, as the accused is, at law, entitled to the benefit of every doubt the Court is not persuaded that there is any evidence which is corroborative of the evidence of Charles Bowden with regard to the source of the guns and ammunition that were found in the Jewish cemetery on the old Court road. That being so and given that Mr Bowden is an accomplice of the accused and that, in any event, his evidence is suspect for the reasons detailed above, the Court is not satisfied that the prosecution has established a case beyond all reasonable doubt against the accused in respect of the several offences of possession of arms and ammunition which have been preferred against him. We now come to consider the evidence which the prosecution maintain establishes the complicity of the accused in the murder of the late Veronica Guerin. In this regard, the Court is persuaded beyond any doubt by the evidence of Mr Felix McEnroy SC that, on 15th September, 1995, in the course of a telephone call to her, which Mr McEnroy overheard, the accused, John Gilligan, threaten Miss Guerin that, if she wrote about him, he would kidnap her son and sexually abuse him and that he would shoot her.

In that regard, Mr McEnroy said that the actual words used by the accused were 'I will kidnap your fucking son and ride him. I will fucking shoot you. I will fucking kill you.' The Court has no doubt but that the accused used those actual words and, that if the Court had any reservations about the matter which, in fact, it does not, any such reservations would be allayed by the evidence of Ms Elizabeth Allen, which we also accept without question that, in an interview with the accused on 1st July, 1996, he admitted that he had threatened Veronica Guerin and that he had threatened members of her family; in particular that he had threatened to kidnap her son and to sexually abuse him albeit that, on that occasion, the accused also told Ms Allen that he had made those threats because he was angry, that he did not mean them and that he had nothing whatsoever to do with the death of Veronica Guerin.

While the Court accepts that, on the 25th June, 1996; the day before Veronica Guerin's murder, Detective Sergeant Keane and Detective Sergeant (now Inspector) Dominic Hayes met the accused outside Kilcock District Court and had a conversation with him, given that neither police officer made a contemporaneous note of that conversation and, indeed, neither of them appears to have recorded it in writing for some time afterwards and, having particular regard to the fact that Sergeant Keane's statement with regard to that conversation was not included in the book of evidence served on the accused although Sergeant Keane appears to have been one of the team involved in the investigation of Veronica Guerin's murder, the Court is not satisfied to entertain the evidence of these two Garda officers with regard to the details of that conversation. On the other hand, the Court notes the threats which were implicit in the letters which the accused wrote to Russell Warren while he was a prisoner in Arbour Hill Prison; not only the threats implicit in the contents of those letters but the threat which was implicit in the fact that Mr Gilligan was able to insure that Mr Warren received one of those letters although it was not posted through usual channels. The Court also notes that, before her death, the late Veronica Guerin had made a complaint to the Garda Síochána as a result of which a prosecution for assault was initiated against the accused; a prosecution which, of course, was frustrated by Veronica Guerin's murder. The suggested implications of that fact, insofar as the allegation of murder against the accused is concerned, are noted by the Court.

While evidence that the late Veronica Guerin's life was threatened by the accused and evidence that the accused had also threatened a man (Russell Warren) who he perceived as someone who was a threat to him and evidence that the accused was prosecuted by Veronica Guerin, who was subsequently murdered, all gives rise to the suspicion that the accused had some hand, act or part in that murder, in the view of the Court, that evidence amounts to no more than suspicion and suspicion is not a ground upon which a man may be convicted of any criminal offence; much less a murder. Given that there was evidence that a Mr John Traynor had initiated proceedings against the late Veronica Guerin and the Court were informed that, in the course of those proceedings, Mr Traynor had made what were described as 'vile' accusations against Ms Guerin and given that the Court heard evidence which indicated that the said Mr Traynor had associations with the gang of whom the accused was one, it could equally be said that a finger of suspicion of complicity in the death of the late Ms Guerin could also be pointed at Mr Traynor. In fact, it is the view of the Court that the only evidence which it heard which could possibly implicate John Gilligan in the murder of the late Veronica Guerin was that of Russell Warren.

In the course of the trial, there was some suggestion that the testimony of Charles Bowden might also implicate the accused in the murder but the Court does not accept that that is so. In that regard, Mr Bowden gave evidence that, at the request of Brian Meehan, he loaded the gun which, apparently, was the weapon which was used to murder Veronica Guerin and that he did so in the presence of Brian Meehan, Shay Ward and Peter Mitchell; each one of whom (including Charles Bowden, himself) were shown to have been associates of the accused at one time or another.

Accordingly, the Court was invited to draw the inference that, although he was not present at the time, John Gilligan, because he had a history of associating with all of these men at one time or another, must be deemed to be a party to the plan to kill Veronica Guerin. In the view of the Court, that would be guilt by association and that alone, which is not a concept recognised in our criminal jurisprudence.

Having regard to the foregoing, the Court is satisfied that the only evidence on which John Gilligan might be convicted of the murder of Veronica Guerin is that of Russell Warren. However, as it has been established to the satisfaction of the Court; not only that Russell Warren is an accomplice of the accused so that his evidence must be viewed in that light, but also that his evidence is so suspect for a variety of other reasons that the interests of justice demands that it ought not to be relied upon except insofar as it is corroborated by persuasive independent evidence. In summary, the picture of complicity in the murder of the late Veronica Guerin which Russell Warren painted insofar as John Gilligan is concerned was that he (Russell Warren) stole a motorcycle and, when he told Mr Gilligan that he had done so, Mr Gilligan told him to 'hang on to the bike. I might need it'. Mr Warren then recounted how, at Mr Gilligan's request, he had kept the motorcycle, that Mr Gilligan had arranged to have it test driven by Brian Meehan after which he (Russell Warren), again at the request of Mr Gilligan and with the help of a friend, Steven McGrath, made the motorcycle roadworthy.

Mr Warren then described the events which he said occurred on the day of Veronica Guerin's murder. He says that, at the request of Mr Gilligan and Mr Meehan, he had gone to Naas to look out for Veronica Guerin's car which he was told would be in the vicinity of the Courthouse so that he might advise Messrs Gihigan and Meehan of the direction in which the car travelled after it left the Courthouse. He said that, throughout the morning, he was in regular telephonic contact with both John Gilligan and Brian Meehan, that, eventually, he spotted Veronica Guerin's car, advised both Messrs Gilligan and Meehan of that fact and that the car was travelling in the direction of Dublin, that, at Mr Meehan's request, he pursued the car; keeping in regular telephonic communication with Messrs Gilligan and Meehan for the purpose of advising them as to its progress and that, ultimately, at the traffic lights at the junction of the Naas Road with the Boot Road, he saw the pillion passenger on a motorcycle being driven by Brian Meehan shoot the occupant of that car several times and that, within minutes of that event, he had telephoned John Gilligan to advise him of what happened only to be met with the response, 'Are they gone? Did they get away?' And when Mr Warren said yes, Mr Gilligan retorted with, 'Are they dead?' to which Mr Warren replied, 'Well they shot somebody five times; what is going to happen?' And, according to Mr Warren, Mr Gilligan's response was, 'The same thing will happen to you and your mate if you say anything about it. I will contact you later.' Furthermore, Mr Warren said that the motorcycle which was being driven by Brian Meehan at the time of Veronica Guerin's murder was the self same motorcycle that he had stolen some time previously and the one which, at the request of John Gilligan, he had helped to make roadworthy.

If the foregoing events, as recounted by Russell Warren, are true, then the Court has no doubt but that John Gilligan played a pivotal role in the murder of Veronica Guerin and ought to be punished on that account. However, each and every aspect of Mr Warren's evidence with regard to the events which he said occurred on the days preceding Veronica Guerin's murder and with regard to the events which he maintains had occurred on that day itself were challenged by the defence on the grounds that they were a tissue of lies or, perhaps, it would be more accurate to say, a figment of his deceitful imagination. Moreover, apart from pointing to the absence of corroboration for Mr Warren's account of events and the fact that he had been proven to be a self serving liar who conceded that it was easy to tell lies and better to do so if there was some benefit to be gained from so-doing, the defence pointed out that, although Mr Warren purported to give the Garda Síochána an accurate account of his activities and movements-around the time of Veronica Guerin's murder in a statement which he made within a few weeks of the event, and supplemented that statement from time to time thereafter, it was not until nearly a year after Veronica Guerin's death that he told the Garda Síochána for the first time that he had actually witnessed it and, in no one of these statements which he made to the Garda Síochána did Russell Warren ever suggest that it was John Gilligan who requested him to go to Naas.

Moreover, it was suggested by the defence that that admission was made in or about the time that Mr Warren had received a payment of money from Detective Garda Hanley one of the team involved in the investigation of the murder of Veronica Guerin. Apart from the fact that a Mr Ian Keith comfirmed that a motorcycle, which had been identified by Mr Warren as the motorcycle which he had stolen, was his (Mr Keith's) motorcycle and that it was taken from him without his consent, it appears to the Court that there is, in fact, no corroboration whatsoever of Mr Warren's evidence with regard to Mr Gilligan's complicity in the death of the late Veronica Guerin. There is only Mr Warren's word for it that Mr Gilligan told him to hang on to that motorcycle, when he learned that Mr Warren had stolen it, that Mr Gilligan arranged to have the motorcycle test driven by Brian Meehan and then requested Mr Warren to make it roadworthy, that Mr Gilligan told Mr Warren to go to Naas to look out for Veronica Guerin's car, that he went to Naas, located the car, advised Mr Gilligan of that fact, followed the car, witnessed the murder and then telephoned Mr Gilligan to tell him all about it; provoking the response which he says that he got from Mr Gilligan.

Not only is there no corroboration of any of Mr Warren's testimony in that regard, but a number of witnesses gave evidence which would appear to cast a doubt on what Mr Warren said. For example, Mr Warren said that Mr Brian Meehan, who he maintained was riding the motorcycle from which Veronica Guerin was shot, was wearing a silver-grey helmet and that he did not notice any visor on it; a variety of other eye witnesses variously described the driver of that motorcycle as wearing a black helmet with no visor, a black helmet with a full visor and a white helmet, no witness said that he was wearing a silver-grey helmet. Moreover, although Mr Warren said that, after the pillion passenger had shot Veronica Guerin, he put the gun into the waistline of his trousers, no other eye witness confirmed that fact and, indeed, the pillion passenger was variously described as puffing the gun inside his jacket or into his hip pocket after he had shot the deceased.

In addition, although Mr Warren said that, after he had witnessed the shooting, he moved the blue Liteace van which he was then driving which was then located in the fast lane through the slow lane into a slip lane leading to the Boot Road, in the light of the evidence of several eye witnesses that the slow lane was fully occupied at that time, that would appear to have been highly unlikely. It is also curious that no other eye witness saw the blue Liteace van which Mr Warren says that he was driving at the time and Mr Warren, himself, did not see a blue Volvo car which, according to a number of eye witnesses, followed the motorcycle on which Ms Guerin's assassins were travelling through the traffic lights immediately after the killing. In addition, not one of the eye witnesses gave a description of the motorcycle on which Ms Guerin's assassins were travelling which corresponded with the description of the motorcycle which Mr Warren had said that he had stolen and which he said that Mr Meehan was driving at the time of the murder. Admittedly, two witnesses said that the motorcycle that Mr Keith identified as that which had been stolen from him and which Mr Warren identified as that which was being used by the killers was similar to the one that they saw at the scene but, if they did, two other witnesses specifically rejected the suggestion that Mr Keith's motorcycle might have been the one which was used by the killers.

In the light of those inconsistencies and given that Mr Warren did not first suggest that he had witnessed Ms Guerin's murder until nearly a year later, the Court was concerned that, perhaps, notwithstanding his evidence, Mr Warren had not been present and had not witnessed Veronica Guerin's murder. However, the Court had evidence of the records of telephone calls made by the deceased from her mobile telephone on the day that she was murdered and, in particular, evidence of a call which terminated at 12.54 p.m. on that date, together with a recording of what the late Ms Guerin had said in the course of that conversation. In the light of that evidence, the Court had no doubt but that Veronica Guerin met her death at 12.54 p.m. on 26th June, 1996. The Court also had evidence, which it did not doubt, that, at 12.57 p.m. on that date, i.e. some three minutes after Veronica Guerin's death, a telephone call was made from a mobile telephone habitually used by Russell Warren bearing number 087/455571 to a mobile telephone habitually used by John Gilligan, that is a telephone bearing the number 087/440106. The evidence of that call would appear to afford some confirmation of the evidence of Russell Warren that, immediately after witnessing Veronica Guerin's murder, he had telephoned John Gilligan, although, it does not, of course, corroborate the content of the alleged conversation which Mr Warren said took place. It would, however, suggest that, despite the inconsistencies in Mr Warren's account of the killing, he was, indeed, at the scene at the material time. If not, it might be considered to be an amazing and unlikely coincidence that he should telephone John Gilligan within three minutes of Veronica Guerin's death. Nevertheless, the fact of such a phone call, either by itself or even assuming that it followed immediately after Mr Warren had witnessed Veronica Guerin's murder, does not establish that Mr Gilligan had any hand, act or part in the killing. If Mr Gilligan is to be visited with complicity, the Court would also have to be convinced of the truth of Mr Warren's description of the events which preceded it; not only on the day itself, but on the preceding days. In other words, the Court would have to be satisfied that the motorcycle used by the killers was a motorcycle which Mr Gilligan had arranged to make roadworthy, that Mr Gilligan had instructed Mr Warren to locate Ms Guerin's car on the day of her murder and to keep him advised as to its movements and that Mr Warren had complied with those instructions.

In fact, as the Court has already adverted to, Mr Warren's evidence with regard to these matters was evasive and inconsistent and, not only did he contradict himself in the witness box but he contradicted evidence which he had previously given at the trial of Brian Meehan. Moreover, although the prosecution led evidence of records of telephone calls exchanged by mobile telephones controlled by Russell Warren, by John Gilligan and by Brian Meehan on the day of Veronica Guerin's murder, the Court is not persuaded that those records are fully corroborative of Mr Warren's evidence.

In this regard Mr Brian Price, Ms Guerin's solicitor and a Ms McCabe, gave testimony which the Court accepts without reservation was their honest belief that, after her case had been disposed of, the late Veronica Guerin left the Courthouse in Naas at approximately 12.40 p.m. on 26th June, 1996. However, given that she met her death at the junction of the Naas Road with the Boot Road at 12.54 p.m. on the same day; only fourteen minutes after it is suggested that she was leaving the Courthouse, in the light of the evidence of Mr B. Murphy, an engineer, which the Court had no reason to doubt, that that road junction is some 12.37 miles distance from the Courthouse in Naas, and given that the deceased would have had to negotiate a significant portion of the town of Naas before reaching the dual carriageway leading from the town of Naas to the city of Dublin, the Court considers that it is extremely unlikely that she would have traversed that 12.37 miles inside a time of fourteen minutes.

Accordingly, the Court is persuaded that, perhaps, the estimate of Mr Price and Ms McCabe that Ms Guerin left the Courthouse in Naas at 12.40 p.m. is not quite accurate and that it is more likely that she left the Courthouse some minutes before that. In this regard, Mr Warren gave evidence that, immediately after he had spotted Veronica Guerin's car leaving the Court Hotel in Naas, he advised Mr Gilhigan and Mr Meehan of that fact on the telephone but the telephone records which were produced to the Court suggest that Mr Warren did not telephone Mr Gilligan between 11.18 a.m. (when Ms Guerin was still in Court) and 12.57 p.m. (after Ms Guerin was dead), which would appear to give the lie to Mr Warren's evidence that he had telephoned Mr Gilligan after he allegedly saw Ms Guerin's car coming out of the Court Hotel. On the other hand, those telephone records indicate that Mr Gilligan telephoned Mr Warren at 12.36 p.m. which the Court accepts might well be in or about the time that the late Ms Guerin left the Court Hotel in her car and, and, therefore, it could well be that Mr Warren was mistaken when he said that it was he who telephoned Mr Glligan to advise him that he (Mr Warren) had seen Ms Guerin's car and that the fact of the matter is that it was Mr Gilligan, who rang Mr Warren, just as Ms Guerin was leaving the Court Hotel, only to be advised of that fact by Mr Warren. If that is so, however, the Court considers that it is an amazing coincidence that Mr Gilligan should have chosen to ring Mr Warren just at the time that Ms Guerin was leaving the Court Hotel. The telephone records introduced by the prosecution also establish that, at 12.33 p.m. and at 12.35 p.m. there were telephone calls from Mr Warren to Mr Meehan which might well confirm Mr Warren's testimony that he telephoned Mr Meehan immediately after he saw Ms Guerin's car coming out of the Court Hotel. The only other telephone call which appears to the Court to be of any relevance is a call from Mr Meehan to Mr Warren at 12.48 p.m., which was only six minutes before Veronica Guerin died.

Clearly, the Court cannot entertain the testimony which Mr Warren might have given with regard to the content of that phone call because it would be hearsay and, of course, the Court cannot speculate on its contents; no more than that the Court is not entitled to have regard for the fact that, in another Court, in different proceedings, Brian Meehan was convicted of murdering Veronica Guerin because, as a matter of law, that fact is not relevant to any issue which the Court has to decide in these proceedings. However, as there appears to have been only one telephone call before Ms Guerin's death passing between Mr Warren and Mr Meehan after 12.35 p.m. on that day, it seems to contradict Mr Warren's evidence that he was in constant telephonic communication with Mr Meehan after he alleges that he first saw Ms Guerin's car. In the foregoing circumstances, the Court is not convinced that the records of those telephone calls are sufficiently corroborative of Mr Warren's evidence and, indeed, they might be interpreted as disproving his testimony in certain respects.

Accordingly, as there was no evidence whatsoever to corroborate the events involving Mr Gilligan which Mr Warren said had occurred in the days preceding Ms Guerin's murder and no evidence to corroborate his testimony that he had been in Naas on the morning of that day, the Court could not but have a doubt about all of those matters.

In the light of the foregoing, bearing in mind that at all stages during a criminal trial an accused person has, at law, the presumption of innocence and remains at all times throughout an innocent person unless and until that presumption is displaced at the end of the trial by a finding based on evidence which is either reliable testimony, circumstantial evidence or a reasonable inference drawn from established facts that that person is, indeed, guilty as charged beyond any reasonable doubt; while this Court has grave suspicions that John Gilligan was complicit in the murder of the late Veronica Guerin, the Court has not been persuaded beyond all reasonable doubt by the evidence which has been adduced by the prosecution that that is so and, therefore, the Court is required by law to acquit the accused on that charge.